Well folks,

Always remember that
there is more beauty in the South's past
than we ever expect to know — but at
times, from a certain
distance

much more sense, at times, from a certain
distance

Hoping the South looks good
from a distant bay as it does from
a Northern clime

Gary '93

The Florida Negro

A Federal Writers' Project Legacy

EDITED, WITH AN INTRODUCTION, BY

GARY W. MCDONOGH

UNIVERSITY PRESS OF MISSISSIPPI

JACKSON AND LONDON

Introduction and Afterword Copyright © 1993 by
the University Press of Mississippi
All rights reserved
Manufactured in the United States of America

95 94 93 92 4 3 2 1

The paper in this book meets the guidelines for permanence and
durability of the Committee on Production Guidelines for Book
Longevity of the Council on Library Resources.

Library of Congress Cataloging-in-Publication Data

The Florida Negro : a Federal Writers' Project legacy / edited, with
  an introduction by Gary W. McDonogh.
      p.   cm.
  Includes bibliographical references and index.
  ISBN 0-87805-588-6
  1. Afro-Americans—Florida. I. McDonogh, Gary W. II. Federal Writers'
Project.
E185.93.F5F57   1992
975.9'00496073—dc20   92-28493
                                                             CIP

British Library Cataloging-in-Publication data available

Contents

Introduction

Many Americans know of the Works Progress Administration from the buildings, art, and public works of the 1930s that still adorn our national landscape. Some have explored the heritage of one of its programs, the Federal Writers' Project, through the general *American Guide* or through state guides that provided travel and historical compendia for American states of the era, as well as Alaska and Puerto Rico.[1] More avid readers may have encountered some of the hundreds of local and topical guides that were also assembled under the aegis of a collection of local units and various kinds of sponsorship. Meanwhile scholars use thematic collections that emerged from the project and perhaps transcended it: *These are Our Lives* (1939), the searing life narratives of people in North Carolina, Tennessee, and Georgia; *Drums and Shadows* (1940), an investigation of African and slave lore among blacks on the Georgia coast; *Copper Camp* (1943), stories from Butte, Montana, or *Gumbo Ya-Ya* (1945), a collection of Louisiana folklore. Investigators also have returned to these rich portraits and the archives that remain from state projects for specific uses of its assembled materials, as in B. A. Botkin's *Lay My Burden Down* (1945), Horace R. Cayton and St. Clair Drake's *Black Metropolis* (1945), Stetson Kennedy's *Palmetto Country* (1942), Roi Ottley's *New World a-Comin': Inside Black America* (1943), and Gilbert Osofsky's *Harlem: The Making of a Ghetto* (1965). Thus we continue to recognize that the work of the Federal Writers' Project, from its initial collection activities through the gradual appearance of publications in many states, provided a unique vision of American life in the 1930s and 1940s.

It is difficult today to realize the scope and the idealism of the undertaking represented by the Federal Writers' Project and its successor, the Writers' Project, during the eight years of their existence from 1935 to 1943. Program participant and historian Jerre Mangione cites a review of the early guides for the *New Republic* by urbanist Lewis Mumford that provides a glimpse of the contemporary reception: "Of all the good uses of adversity one of the best has been the conception and execution of a series of American guidebooks . . . the first attempt, on a comprehensive scale, to make the country itself worthily known to Americans. . . . Future historians will turn to these guidebooks as one who would know the classic world must still turn to Pausanias' ancient guidebook to Greece" (1972:216). Yet in the late 1930s and 1940s, as administrative opposition to WPA politics grew and as funding dried up in an America oriented toward war, many embryonic WPA projects were abandoned before publication. Some were lost; others have remained inaccessible. The archives of other projects have been lost or neglected. It is a rare event when we can add a new volume to the distinguished tradition of WPA writings or examine the processes through which these monumental, yet seemingly anonymous, collective texts took shape. *The Florida Negro* illustrates the WPA's complex vision of depression America, while also presenting questions regarding matters of process and editing that are of interest to historians, social scientists, and general readers.

A first reading of *The Florida Negro*, fifty years after its compilation, raises inevitable concerns about content, authorship, audience, and meanings. A reader may wonder at its selection of historical data, which provide only a fractured narrative of Florida life, valuing experience over chronology. Depictions of slavery, while incorporating instances of punishment and resistance, also present more moderate visions of good times, which could have appealed to the constructed nostalgia of a white southern audience. The explanations of hoodoo, conjure, and superstitions seem products of an outdated approach to folklore and tradition, even as they provide invaluable data. Sometimes emphasis is surprising: the manuscript devotes more time to *bolita*, a gambling game, as an aspect of everyday life, than to such classic and "positive" themes of black historiography and public presentation as the role of the church. While the amenities in black bourgeois life are referred to in discussions of amusements and leadership, the working lives and problems of other groups within the state are not passed over, again raising questions of how this might be read by either black or white audiences. Yet all these readings, which I have shared in the review of manuscripts and their multiple sources, also point beyond the text, demanding that we situate *The Florida Negro* as a moment in a process when black voices, though within limitations, became part of the Federal Writers' Project's vision of American diversity.

The authors of the general Florida state guide for the Writers' Project, in fact, underscored the state's diversity:

> Through more than four centuries, from Ponce de Leon in his caravels to the latest Pennsylvanian in his Buick, Florida has been invaded by seekers of gold or of sunshine; yet it has retained an identity and a character distinctive to itself. The result of all this is a material and immaterial pattern of infinite variety, replete with contrasts, paradoxes, confusions, and inconsistencies (*Florida* 1939:3).

Even these inconsistencies could be approached with critical irony: "Politically and socially, Florida has its own North and South, but its northern area is strictly southern and its southern area by definition northern. In summer the State is predominantly southern by birth and adoptions, and in winter it is northern by invasion" (*Florida* 1939:3).

Florida researchers and writers in Jacksonville, Miami, Pensacola, and Tampa developed many projects, including studies of such areas as St. Augustine and Key West and of Florida birds, Spanish missions, and the Seminoles. Songs and stories were collected around the state for folklore projects.[2] Meanwhile a black team assembled documents for a project on black history and experience in the state. Beginning with a host of now little-known authors including Martin Richardson, Alfred Farrell, Viola Muse, James Johnson, Rachel Austin and others, the project was later joined by well-known Florida author and folklorist Zora Neale Hurston. This Florida Negro unit, created in the early days of the Federal Writers' Project, indicated the interest of its director, Henry W. Alsberg, in preserving an Afro-American legacy within that project. According to the study of Gary Mormino (1988), Corita D. Corse, Florida Writers' Project state director, was directly encouraging interviews with former slaves by 1936. The project expanded along the lines suggested by the national editor of Negro affairs, Sterling Brown, who felt that "The Negro has too seldom been revealed as an integral part of American life" (Mangione 1972: 258). Over twenty-five hundred pages of information, including seventy-two interviews with ex-slaves and various drafts of reports, were collected. These materials are now stored in the archives of the Florida Historical Society, at the University of South Florida, and at the P. K. Yonge Library at the University of Florida in Gainesville by decision of Corse and Stetson Kennedy, folklore editor. Some duplicate and additional materials are preserved in the records of the U. S. Works Project Administration/ Federal Writers' Project, Library of Congress, Manuscript Division.[3]

Black researchers in Florida collected autobiographies from ex-slaves and materials on folklore, tasks undertaken by white researchers in some other states. A synthetic narrative picture of slave life and culture developed by Martin Richardson from these reminiscences is included in this volume.[4] Contemporary life, with its achievements and strengths, was examined as well. Thus a narration about the spread of gambling games such as bolita along the Atlantic coast would be balanced by proud descriptions of institutions and of leading figures among the state's black population. Portraits of Jacksonville-born author James Weldon Johnson and his brother, composer John Rosamond, appear alongside healing cures and spells. The files from the project never incorporated into the manuscripts are even more extensive, ranging from discussions of folk localities of hell to documents on Catholicism among Florida blacks.

But as the collection and preparation of potential manuscripts proceeded, the days of the WPA and the Federal Writers' Project were fading. The Harlem Renaissance was in the past and the nation increasingly turned away from social programs of the Depression and efforts to understand black life. Even Hurston seemed to have reached the apogee of her career, as the publication of *Their Eyes Were Watching God* (1937) was followed by the less successful *Tell My Horse* (1938) and *Moses, Man of the Mountain* (1939). A letter from Macmillan and Co. to Hurston on May 10, 1939, provided an epitaph to the early history of the manuscript now published here. The editors regretted that, although they had found *The Florida Negro* project interesting ("We appreciate the fact that the material is unusual and colorful"), nonetheless, "We have reluctantly been forced to the conclusion that there is no place where such a volume would fit in with our publishing schedule." In fact, it is apparent that they never looked at a manuscript, which evidently had no market. [5] The typescripts of several versions of the text, with handwritten comments, along with original interviews, reports, and correspondence were confined to archives and the attention of scattered scholars until this publication.[6]

This introduction situates *The Florida Negro* from my perspective as an anthropologist who has worked with black society and culture in the Southeast and as a student of FWP materials. The first section considers the Federal Writers' Project texts as visions of America, read for both general appreciation and serious academic investigation. The second section highlights certain facets of the manuscript itself and suggests future investigation concerning the

WPA heritage and the social sciences. Throughout, I have relied on documents and voices of the WPA to evoke the ambience and excitement of the project itself and its authors.

This introduction is followed by an annotated version of the completed manuscript of *The Florida Negro* now in possession of the Florida Historical Society, which has supported this publication with enthusiasm under the direction of Gary Mormino and Nicholas Wynne. The annotations relate elements of the text to the fragmentary files of original interviews and materials and clarify events, attitudes, and people, where possible. These suggest points for future reading as well as background in evaluating the data presented. An afterword by anthropologist Gertrude Fraser brings us back to the multi-vocalic readings of the text in contemporary America, fifty years after its completion.

Finally, appendixes supplementing this primary manuscript with other materials from the FHS, UF, and Library of Congress files are: (a) a report on a state prison visit included in the earliest manuscript but dropped in this version; (b) raw materials for alternate descriptions of Hurston's home community of Eatonville; and (c) a listing of authors and primary texts that I have examined. This presentation will be, I hope, both an introduction to the legacy of the Florida Negro project archives and a stimulation for future work in Florida and around the nation that the Federal Writers' Project once explored.[7]

America and the WPA

In complex and varied ways, the local, state, and national Writers' Projects reflected America "warts and all." It is possible to see in retrospect that the program lost focus because of the vast range of topics explored. Yet the works that reached publication were selected to accommodate the interests of lobbyists, local support groups, or national publishers. Final texts, both as an arrangement of raw materials and as a selection by outside publishers, provide only glimpses of what the WPA may yet tell us about specific groups in America or about the nation itself.

Writers' Projects' investigations of contemporary America nevertheless achieved significant goals still evident in their publications: compilations of local records, examinations of regional histories, production of state and local guides, and assembled notes on unexpected topics ranging from the history of cement to Nebraska dance calls (*The Story of Cement* [1943]; *Nebraska Folklore Pamphlets #23* [1940]). Alongside major projects, attention was paid to the use of lotteries to fund the Louisville Free Public Library, to major arteries, including U. S. One and the Farmington Canal, and to groups such as new citizens of San Francisco (*Libraries and Lotteries: A History of the Louisville Free Public Library* [1944]; *U.S. One: Maine to Florida* [1938]; *Boats Across New England* [1941]; *Almanac for Thirty-Niners* [1938]). As the guides rolled out, tourism, history, high culture, and folklife became intermingled, state by state.

States differed in their interests and project completion rates. While New York and Washington, D. C., produced many studies, Maryland turned out only a few and Missouri only its state guide. Kentucky was a rich source, as was Nebraska, which published *The Negroes in Nebraska* (1940). Alaska and Puerto Rico, although territories, produced their own volumes, while Hawaii, insofar as I can tell, did nothing. Topics and areas also varied, as did the organization and points of interest even within the guides.

Thus each volume and state and local production raises its own questions. In his preface to *The Italians of New York* from the New York Writers' Project, Edward Corsi celebrated his reading of his own Italian heritage:

> After reading the pages of this book I could not help but exult in the pageant of contributions and achievements of New York's Italians, for I too am Italian. I have come to know personally many of those mentioned in the book, having grown up with them in the city. Of the others, I have often heard or read with enormous pride which, I confess, springs from the fact that so many of them were merely hopeful immigrants who once passed through Ellis Island into the promised land as I did. Theirs, in another sense, is another chapter in the greater story of New York, so rightly called the door to a melting pot of the world (*The Italians of New York* 1939: vii).

This book, also published in Italian (*Gli Italiani di New York* 1939), was the first of the New York series planned by a WPA "racial" group.[8] New York authors developed the city's image as a melting pot in the popular *New York City Panorama* (1938), in which subjects included immigrants, language, music, labor, sports, the arts, and education. Their sense of the melting pot proved neither simplistic nor idealized:

> During the great migrations from Europe after 1880, it was predominantly these "men of different sects and nations" who erected physical New York— its streets, bridges, tunnels, railroads, wharves and buildings, creating with their own hands much of its material wealth, yet somehow finding leisure to leave to their city a considerable legacy in science and the arts, in social improvement and political leadership.
>   In the process the immigrant gave far more than he received. His rich agrarian culture he exchanged for the poverty-stricken culture of industrial

society. He traded his native string orchestras and folk tunes for commercial tumpety-tump; expressive group dances for cheap dancehalls; traditional historic or romantic rhymed narratives for machine-made fiction and the distortion of contemporary history in the news columns (*Panorama*, 1938: 82).

Nonetheless, even in this volume, American blacks were set apart. After devoting an analytic section to the history and life of Harlem, the authors concluded:

> The question of what will ultimately happen to the Negro in New York is bound up with the question of what will happen to the Negro in America. It has been said that the Negro embodies the "romance of American life"; if that is true, the romance is one whose glamor is overlaid with shadows of tragic premonition (*Panorama* 1938:151).

In histories of the project, in participants' recollections, and in some guides themselves, there is the evidence of the tension between those who sought to criticize depression America and those involved in local boosterism.[9] Though in general the volumes showed evidence of pride, adopting an upbeat and inviting tone, not all writers could be sanguine about their situations. In Puerto Rico, although the *Guide to the Island of Boriquén* declared that it was not "designed to add another to the volumes 'discussing the problem of Puerto Rico'" (*Puerto Rico* 1939:vii), the text does confront such matters as the island's limited development, outside interventions, and contemporary dilemmas:

> In spite of the remarkable increase in the percentage of children attending school today as compared with the Spanish era, this increase is in danger of being nullified by the tremendous growth of population. The tragic fact remains today that only about two- fifths of Puerto Rican children of school age have the opportunity of securing an elementary education. This places Puerto Rico in a class by itself among United States territories and will remain a present threat to democracy until such time as the American ideal of universal education can be made effective (*Puerto Rico* 1939:129).

The perception of a "Negro problem" proved especially critical for the projects set up in the southern states, where racial segregation and lack of support for projects about blacks eviscerated potentially important contributions to historical and social records. Despite the activities and guidance of Sterling Brown in Washington and the interest in folk culture of other project leaders such as John A. Lomax, blacks faced barriers as well as encouragements within the Writers' Programs.

Indeed, the WPA's incorporation of blacks reflected their participation in other government projects of the Roosevelt era within their distinctive social roles in southern states and northern cities. As Mangione has noted, this promoted advances in some areas:

> Perhaps the greatest beneficiaries of the Project were its black employees. As a result of pressures brought on the New Deal administration by a self-appointed "black cabinet" of Negro leaders, which included Robert Weaver, John P. David and William Hasty[10], the WPA was structured to provide hundreds of American Negroes with their first opportunity to exercise skills they already had or to acquire new skills. What was an economic disaster for the country became a liberating experience for many of them. This was especially true in the WPA arts program where, as Ralph Ellison noted, "writers and would-be writers, newspaper people, dancers, actors—they all got their chance" (1972:255).

Young authors such as Ellison and Richard Wright received early support from the Federal Writers' Project. An older generation from the Harlem Renaissance, including Hurston and Arna Bontemps, found refuge in Florida and Illinois, respectively (Mangione 1972:254–68; Hemenway 1977). The massive project to interview former slaves picked up on the independent work of black scholars, developing into a nationwide resource (Perdue et al. 1980; Yetman 1984). Blacks participated in the preparation of the volumes discussed from Louisiana, New York and Nebraska as well as individual works in Illinois and Virginia (*Cavalcade of the American Negro* [1940]; *The Negro in Virginia* [1940]).

Discussed but voiceless themselves, black people appeared in other works, reflecting varied opportunities. Despite the strong black presence in the Florida project, other collectors in the South obviously were influenced by a long-standing tradition of white discrimination and held to traditional black stereotypes. Out of 4,500 total workers employed by the Writers' Projects in 1937, only 106 were black—slightly over 2 percent. Penkower notes that blacks were mostly employed in New York, Illinois, and Louisiana, while other states hired none, including southern projects such as Georgia. A black assistant editor in Texas was labelled insolent for trying to revise depictions of blacks in that state (1977:66–67). Even Sterling Brown found his scathing essay on black life in Washington, D. C., "bowdlerized" for a later edition of the city guide (Mangione 1972:210–11).

Moreover, separate but equal sections about blacks could reinforce white cultural viewpoints as well as social mores. This is exemplified in the white-composed introduction to "Negro folkways" in *Mississippi: A Guide to the Magnolia State* (1937:22):

> Different from the Louisiana folk Negro in speech and from the east coast Negro in heritage, the Mississippi folk Negro stands alone, a prismatic personality. Those who know him well enough to understand something of his psychology, his character and his needs, and like him well enough to accept his deficiencies, find him to be wise, but credulous—a superstitious paradox. He seems to see all things, hear all things, believe all things. But ask him a question and he will have neither seen, heard nor believed. He counsels with himself and walks his way alone. [11]

The distance between author and subject recalls Sterling Brown's objection, summarized by Mangione, that "although a good deal had been written about the Negro in America, he had invariably been treated as a problem, but not as a participant" (1972:258).

Even in such a classic volume of southern life as Georgia's *Drums and Shadows* (1940), the emphasis on survivals betrays an equation of black with primitive that breaks through into the text in this report of a worship service conducted by the charismatic preacher, Bishop C. R. "Daddy" Grace:

> Regular members and visitors from outlying districts crowd the lumber benches of the House of Prayer. The air is tense with excitement. Above the confusion can be heard the strident but rhythmic beating of drums. Bright splashes of color are given by the crepe paper decorations and the vividly contrasting costumes of members of the church organization. . . .
>
> The procession continues to the front of the church itself where, with much ceremony, the Bishop seats himself upon a lofty throne set far back on the spacious platform. The Queen stands at the Bishop's right, facing the congregation. The music blares forth with renewed intensity and the entire multitude, led by the uniformed guards, passes in single file before the throne. As members approach the Bishop, they pledge themselves to him by removing their hats and bowing low. In the midst of all this commotion "Daddy" sits, a remote, detached figure, his downcast eyes indicating that he is scarcely aware of this carefully planned reception (pp.46–51).

Portrayals of these services, despite their vividness, stress almost minstrel-like characterizations by white observers. Black observers in *The Florida Negro*, by contrast, prove more respectful and more reflexive in their participation in folk culture, although descriptions of "sanctified" churches sometimes still indicate a difference between subject and writer in class or education. Nonetheless, the willingness to participate and feelings of identification experienced by the educated middle-class black observer in a poor church suggest the complex readings that these African-American projects now demand.

Of course, not all projects created pictures of black stereotypes. Despite the paternalism of the texts, overtones of black resistance surfaced: James West Davidson and Mark Hamilton Lytle, for example, through their comparison of ex-slave narratives collected by white and black researchers in South Carolina, have pointed out the concealed knowledge that ex-slaves could hold back from white interviewers (1986). Equally striking is the attitude conveyed in the Illinois project's *Cavalcade of the American Negro*, which proclaims itself "the story of a brave people forced to become a part of the American scene, more often than not treated unjustly, generally discriminated against, and frequently persecuted; yet, despite these handicaps, a people who have contributed generously to American culture"(1940:9). This brief volume, prepared to accompany educational dioramas on black life in America, considers black history, education, religion, music and the arts, literature, labor, the press, and sports.

Perhaps the key text in situating *The Florida Negro* is the well-known *The Negro in Virginia*. Although suggested by some as the model for *The Florida Negro*, it is really a "sister" work, if a more polished one, which was successfully prepared for publication.[12] This book, which Gertrude Fraser considers in her afterword, was claimed by supervisor Roscoe Lewis as a publication of the "only all-Negro unit of a State-wide writer's project." It provides a carefully crafted academic and social-historical framework; indeed the weight of history is such that the text only reaches the events of Emancipation after two hundred pages, two-thirds of the way through the book. It also suggests the power of a black bourgeoisie in its scope, which focuses on history more than folklife, and its tone:

> Concentrating by necessity on the essentials of living, the Virginia Negro finds a measure of solace in the "intangibles." Whatever the intellectual level—the "happy" old woman improvising at a revival "shout," or the society matron entertaining her bridge club with her most recent "poem"— the inherent striving of the Negro for expression is a necessity in an environment that calls primarily for physical labor (1940:291).

Nonetheless, the text maintains a critical perspective, whether noting that "Negro entrepreneurs are prone to follow the white man's business practices without command of the white man's capital" (p. 301) or the observation that "Rural negro homes have become a gold mine for antique dealers" (1940:331). In all, it follows the pedagogical and polemic goals set forth by Lewis in his prefatory call to a challenging audience: "It is to the American Negro and to those who would seek to understand him that this volume is offered as the written record of a people who have helped build America—a people who are perhaps the most widely discussed and the least understood, though by no means the least important element in America's racial pot-pourri."[13]

The Meanings of *The Florida Negro*

The Florida Negro challenges the contemporary reader with the complexities of the Federal Writers' Project itself as well as the situation of American blacks in the 1930s and 1940s. Some of the book's most intriguing aspects, in fact, arise from the relationship of the text to the files and work of individual authors from which it was selected and compiled. [14] The extensive drafts saved in Florida archives indicate the individualism of the authors and show patterns of choice and editing that are rarely even suggested in other Writers' Project volumes. A number of significant themes arise from the text itself and compare interestingly with other work by and about African-Americans of the time.

The Florida Negro collection, in fact, includes several partial and undated typescripts. This edition follows what seems to be both the earliest and the only complete text.[15] It is apparent that this manuscript relies heavily on selections submitted in 1937 by Martin Richardson of Jacksonville as primary author, with chapters drawing strongly on the work and reports of Rachel Austin, James Johnson, Samuel Johnson, Viola Muse, Pearl Randolph, and some efforts of white folklorist Cora Mae Taylor. It appears that Richardson was the primary compiler and editor for the entire draft, although he seems to be an investigator for both Pensacola and Jacksonville, rather than an editor, in reports on file. There is little other personal information about him. A Martin Richardson appears in the *Jacksonville City Directory* of 1935 as a painter and in 1936 and 1938 as a teacher. Stetson Kennedy (personal communication, 1992) believes that he later became a journalist.

There may have been an earlier or missing draft, probably by Richardson, comprising roughly this same material arranged in a different order.[16] The most striking differences between this proto-version, now lost, and the current text include the movement of religious materials from a more prominent place before folklore and voodoo and elimination of a consolidated final section dealing with work opportunities that ends on the grim note of a visit to the Florida State Prison at Raiford. The completed text of the Raiford chapter, another report filed by Martin Richardson, is included in Appendix A.[17] The fact that this chapter was actually completed but abandoned in all later drafts suggests that this may have been an early outline dominated even more by Richardson, who made later concessions to a less overtly critical, more "uplifting" plan for the volume.

The relationship of researchers and editors proves complex in this as in other WPA projects. Ellen Tarry recalled her experiences as a participant in the New York project, which later became *The Negro in New York* (1967):

> The routine would be to go in each morning and I guess sign in and discuss our assignment and the progress we were making and then go back to the library. At least that was my routine. I think maybe some of the boys had a different one. A lot we were newspapermen and I guess could get restless with research. My memory's not sharp but I think we completed assignments in the form of an essay. I have the feeling that it was only in the last year or so that we were working deliberately on a history of the Negro in New York. . . . Even at the end of my work there, I was not aware of the overall plan (Ottley and Weatherby 1967:xii).

The New York project, with its strong black leadership, was considered "too startling for conservative taste," according to novelist James Baldwin in his preface to the 1967 edition (xv). While Richardson seems to have had similar social concerns, as historian Pam Bordelon notes (personal communication, 1992), white editors did not need to heed him since he held no formal editorial role.

Stetson Kennedy, in a letter to Corse of September 29, 1938, discusses his role in subsequent revisions that worked *upon the text presented here*. He notes that "in editing Part One I found considerable material out of place, and the entire section suffered from a lack of continuity and consistent style" (Kennedy, personal archives). He proposed a table of contents that would have clarified the historical chapters but would have altered even more the second, contemporary half of the volume, resulting in a focus on education and social welfare. This process would have strongly integrated the presence of a white editor (Kennedy) as well. The remaining fragments of this later edition, mainly the first chapters, are particularly notable in their more academic historical additions to the Reconstruction and post-Reconstruction political sections. [18] Whereas the first manuscript includes varied critical voices and folk expression, the second appears more consistently academic and historical.

Black author Zora Neale Hurston's taking of a rather enigmatic role as editor and supervisor after 1938 has suggested the possibility of still another version of the text. Unfortunately, this program does not appear to have been completed. Biographer Robert Hemenway notes that Hurston joined the

Federal Writers' Project on April 25, 1938, after the publication of *Their Eyes Were Watching God* (1937) and after completing the manuscript of her study of Haitian voodoo, *Tell My Horse* (1938).[19] She had been supported in Haiti by a Guggenheim, and when that work was finished she found a stable salary through the WPA, as had other black authors. She became a supervisor in June 1938, although Kennedy suggests that this was an honorific title that did not increase her salary. Hemenway adds that she lobbied for the project with Henry Alsberg, FWP director, that same summer (1977:249–52).

At the Jacksonville office, her work habits appear to have been erratic, if brilliant, and her style challenging. Kennedy, acting at the time as editor for folklore, oral history, and ethnic studies, has written:

> There we were, doing our very best to see to it that everything that went into the *Guide* was couched not only in staid Federalese but also in the specific guidebook jargon set forth in the FWP *Style Manual*; and there was Zora, turning in these veritable prose poems of African eloquence and imagery! What to do? Inevitably, the inferior triumphed over the superior, and not much of Zora, beyond her inimitable folksongs and tales, got into the *Guide*. We rationalized this tragedy by reminding ourselves after that, after all, the *Guides* were meant to be exemplars of the merits of collective authorship.
>
> Of course, over in Louisiana, author/director Lyle Saxon was putting his indelible personal imprint upon the *Louisiana Guide*, but then Zora was neither director nor white (Kennedy 1991: 65).

Hemenway concludes, "Her reputation on the project was that of an actress who loved to show off, a woman of remarkable talent and spirit, a loner, an uncooperative co-worker, an editor who hated to stay inside at her desk" (1977: 249–52). Hurston left the project when federal sponsorship ended in July 1939 to go to a teaching job at North Carolina College for Negroes (Hemenway 1977:252–53). At this point, in fact, chapters on blacks from Corita Doggett Corse's files were being processed in Washington.[20]

Hurston's work for the project included both collecting and writing, especially with regard to the project's interests in folklore and music. She made visits to the Everglades and worked with collectors such as Stetson Kennedy and Robert Cook. She also contributed to the general guide with pieces such as her description of her native Eatonville (Mormino 1988:399–403; *Florida* 1939:361–62).[21] Project files include her contributions to the general guide and individual pieces; her notes and manuscripts remain rich sources.[22]

Yet Hurston's collected material, including versions of children's games and references to mythical places, songs, and religion that have been cited by later scholars, do not fit any existing outline of a planned text nor do they form an alternate final manuscript.[23] In a 1976 interview, in fact, Dr. Corse noted one of her regrets about the project: "I wish that we had given Zora Hurston, an outstanding Pulitzer Prize winner on Negro folklore, the editorial responsibility for the Negro book. In the state offices, it didn't occur to us, and neither was it suggested by Washington. But we would have had a book, an outstanding book, if we had done this."[24] Kennedy later concurred: "We saved her scripts, of course, thinking that the projected volume *The Florida Negro* would be an appropriate place for them, Black English and all"(1991: 66). But no revision of the materials of other collectors into a coherent text was completed.

A sense of what Hurston's voice in the project might have been like is conveyed by the rich opening of her folklore chapter, which appeared in neither the Florida guide nor the revisions of the Negro guide:

> Folklore is the boiled-down juice of human living. It does not belong to any special time, place, nor people. No country is so primitive that it has no lore, and no country has yet become so civilized that no folklore is being made within its boundaries.
>
> Folklore in Florida is still in the making. Folkation. Tunes, tales and characters are still emerging from the lush glades of primitive imagination before they can be finally drained by formal education and mechanical invention.
>
> A new folk hero has come to be in the Florida prison camps, and his name is Daddy Mention. It is evident that he is another incarnation of Big John de Conquer, the hero of slavery days who could out-smart Ole Mass, God and the Devil. He is the wish-fulfillment projection. The wily Big John compensated for the helplessness of the slave in the hands of the master, and Daddy Mention does the same for the convict in the prison camp.
>
> In folklore, as in everything else that people create, the world is a great, big, old serving-platter, and all the local places are like eating plates. Whatever is on the plate come out of the platter, but each plate has a flavor of its own because the people take the universal stuff and season it to suit themselves on the plate.[25]

Hurston's participation in the project had other problematic aspects. Notes by Stetson Kennedy on a conversation between Hurston and director Corse (Box 1, File 1/14 "Atrocities") raise questions concerning Hurston's attitude about the Ocoee incident. On November 3, 1920, in Ocoee, Florida, blacks became involved in fighting after trying to vote. A black man, Jules Perry, accused of killing two white men, was taken from a jail in Orlando and lynched the next day; a mob surrounded the black community and burnt it while keeping in residents with gunfire. Thirty-five blacks died. The Florida guide noted solemnly, "Since that time, Negroes have not been permitted to live in the town of Ocoee." While it may be significant, as some have charged, that this was not included in *Mules and Men* or *The Florida Negro*, it seems equally significant that it *was* included in the general guide.[26] Kennedy's notes, however, show Hurston opposing those who demanded more coverage:

> From Alsberg to the janitor they all talk and do nothing good. Mr. Phillips and Mr. McConkey [according to hand annotations, state Writers' Project employees] told them I had done very good work with the Negro book and with Negro material for the guide. I don't like to play dirty politics. Kellock [an FWP guidebook editor] told me to put a desk right in her office and deliver all material directly to her; not to submit it to even the Negro department; not to pay any attention to what Dr. Bois [Du Bois] said.

When Corse complimented her on her work in Washington—perhaps during the visit in the summer of 1938—Hurston was quoted as replying, "I sure went in and asked 'em to fight the thing out with all knives and razors out." Corse complained, finally, that "all Negro books are trying to discredit the Negroes and the South." Hurston replied, "They are biased, instead of true; written by plain crackpots. Negro information in Washington is most inaccurate. Particularly on the Ocoee incident. I told them I was an eye-witness; I gave them names, dates, etc." Ironically, Hemenway's biography suggests that she was actually enrolled at Howard at the time. Kennedy confirms that Corse was alarmed to find out that Hurston had presented herself as an eyewitness to events she had not actually seen and dispatched her immediately to Ocoee (Hemenway 1977:18; Kennedy, personal communication, 1992).

The central role of Richardson as editor and the complex renown of Hurston should not eclipse the others who constituted the Negro writers' unit and who participated in the collection and formation of individual reports and chapters in the manuscript. As Stetson Kennedy has reflected, "The ten job slots designated for Florida's 'Negro Unit' were seldom more than half filled, but the level of talent was exceptionally high (including a *magna cum laude* from Lincoln), and the quality of copy produced was quite beyond the capacity of the lily-white state editorial staff to improve upon" (1991:66).

Thirty individual authors are included in the files that I have consulted in the course of this project. Half of those contribute only one or two minor reports; this includes passing folklore notes or relevant interviews by white staffers in other units. A core group of repeated contributors includes six males and nine females: Rachel Austin, L. Rebecca Baker, Ruth Bolton, Paul Diggs, Alfred Farrell, Zora Hurston, James Johnson, Samuel Johnson, Viola B. Muse,

Pearl Randolph, Wilson Rice, Martin Richardson, and Portia Thorington. Though the files do not specifically mention race in this segregated project, indications are that all members of this Negro unit were black—despite the claims of the supervisor of *The Negro in Virginia* that his was the only all-black unit. Cora Mae Taylor and Modeste Hargis were white contributors, although they were not members of the Negro unit.

Some blacks also were employed elsewhere: after 1938 (according to dates on reports), Paul Diggs worked out of the Tampa office and Zora Hurston was on the main staff. Two women, Rachel Austin and Portia Thorington, are identified as secretaries despite their contribution of materials taken into the manuscript. However, Kennedy notes that "the typist at the Negro Unit was paid $5.00 per month more than Zora, by virtue of a higher urban wage scale" (1991:62).

Not all of these authors were equal in their tenure, either. Although the Federal Writers' Project nationwide only had 106 blacks (of which one was a supervisor) in 1937, in the early days the Florida program hired its full quota. Interviewers of ex-slaves in 1936 included Austin, Baker, Farrell, James Johnson, Muse, Randolph, and Richardson, while Portia Thorington contributed her only report and Grace Thompson and Wilson Rice worked on individual projects. [27] Yet while it is difficult to judge on the basis of submissions alone, it is clear that some of these contributors soon disappeared. After January 1937, the year's reports included only papers from James Johnson, Samuel Johnson, Viola Muse, and Martin Richardson (by this point working on the manuscript). Hargis also made contributions at this time as did Taylor from Miami.

Of these authors, only Samuel Johnson shows multiple reports for 1938, although James Johnson mentions the death of James Weldon Johnson (1938) in an undated paper. However, others came on board in 1938 and 1939. At that time, the extensive contributions from Paul Diggs and Hurston took shape. Diggs, through his prolific and varied writings, almost appeared to be proposing another collecting approach and topical focus oriented toward the black bourgeoisie. Ruth Bolton was also a contributor on black corporate organizations in this period.

These contributors developed clear stylistic bents within the overall work. Some were influenced by geography. As noted, Martin Richardson worked in the Pensacola area, where Modeste Hargis's interviews with Creoles also have been recognized as a historical resource (Coker 1989). Viola Muse concentrated on Tampa, writing extensively on its history and amusements. Most worked out of the main Jacksonville office, in the Clara White Mission, which was a world apart from the offices of white staffers (Kennedy, personal communication). Later, Paul Diggs focused on Lakeland and Tampa.

Other writers traced distinctive themes, although generally each of the early participants contributed topical sections on themes such as schools, history, ethnography, churches, art and music. Rachel Austin contributed a comparative review of Catholic churches in the state. Kennedy identified James Johnson, Samuel Johnson and Alfred Farrell for their yeoman work, from the gathering of slave narratives to field reports, while Pearl Randolph provided important contributions on superstition. The fact that men usually collected information on labor and worklore and women on cures, voodoo, and superstition suggests the presence of gender divisions within the project.[28]

Paul Diggs's documentation of an essentially bourgeois Florida black experience is noteworthy for its varied, if florid, tone. His lyrical, at times awkward, piece, "Follow Me Through Florida," seems to be a kind of itinerary for the Florida Negro driving through the state along the lines of the motor tours familiar from state guides. He also included in the files some drawings and a creative piece, a skit that he composed for the Lakeland Inter-Racial Commission for presentation by the WPA Household Aides. In a letter of November 4, 1938, Diggs mentions himself as vice-president of the twenty-four-member bi-racial commission. While the text is rather exhortatory and dramatically limp, a certain sly humor does creep into some of the black cook's comments to her apparently white employers. Nonetheless, his concerns with Boy Scouts, college fraternities, and civic projects suggest a different orientation from that of his earlier colleagues.

Despite the individuality of authors and projects, the compiled text still seems at times to present the synthetic, mass-market, and even romantic voice present in many other FWP guides. Nonetheless, a thematic analysis underscores some significant aspects of the work in progress that readers might pursue as well.

These include the geography of the project, which relies heavily on the developed, "southern" northern tier of the state. Jacksonville, with a population of 129,459, was at that time the state's largest city and a commercial center, as well as the location of the state office for the Negro project; thus the city's songs, institutions, and diversions figure prominently in the text. Historic St. Augustine, Eatonville (Hurston's independent black hometown), Daytona Beach, Lakeland, Tampa, Pensacola, and Orlando also appear frequently, as do some rural communities. The less-developed gulf and lower east coast regions play a much less important role. The relative absence of Miami is surprising. In part this reflects the settlement and development patterns of the state in this era, although the state guide does consider black populations in other areas. [29]

In the early chapters, a chronological picture of slavery and emancipation provided an overall framework for all extant versions. However, history never dominated the text as in comparable work in Virginia, nor did the authors posit the links to Africa that underlie more folkloric works of the period. Evidently, historical accuracy was an area of concern in a reediting of the manuscript that corrected some historical errors in the first drafts (such as identification of the Seminoles among early inhabitants of the state). Kennedy (personal communication, 1992) also mentioned the unsuccessful search for an expert advisor in this area. Within this history, slavery was clearly the dominant motif, both in data collected and in detailed and analytic discussion. Moreover, providing a sense of the experience of slave life was of more central concern than presenting chronology or documentation of changes. While this emphasis may reflect the limitations of interviews with aged ex-slaves as a primary source, it also reflects the investigators' desire to furnish social and cultural information that would balance more "objective" data. [30]

Manuscripts for Richardson's section, "What the Florida Negro Does," show that his first report included a much more extensive treatment of economic life, which took into account the depression and the entry of women into the marketplace. Much of this text disappeared from the completed manuscript, suggesting editorial pressure or attention to changing audience expectations. For example, the longer text notes the pressures for and against migration, as well as results:

> The time was early 1920. Every train that left the state carried in its Negro day-coach a load of former field hands, turpentine workers or laborers, bound for tobacco fields in Connecticut or steel mills in Pennsylvania. Manpower, since the war, was short in the North; Florida workers, used to the abnormal wages of the wartime shipyards and building jobs, were migrating to the higher-wage fields further North. Police orders, vigilante groups and other forms of terror did not deter them; they left in droves daily.
>
> Into the farms and fields of Florida, and indeed, into many other fields where men had been in short supply during the wartime years, went the women who could not accompany the men North. The women came into Florida labor, and children with her. They have both been an integral part of it ever since (Richardson p.36).

Such a portrayal hardly reflects well on local whites or on the imagery of Florida as a place that visitors and migrants should want to come to, rather than escape from.

The culture of work is evoked through descriptions of workers' experiences; thus folklore can be considered through the study of worksongs and calls like that of Jeremiah the fishmonger in Jacksonville: "Je'miah got fresh fish, /Je'miah got fresh fish, /He got mullets, he got shrimps,/ He got brims, he got trouts, /All Je'miah wants you to do is come out" (pp.48–49). Much of the material was collected by James Johnson, Alfred Farrell, and Samuel Johnson. The question is raised as to whether this juxtaposition results in a dilution of the depiction of economic inequality, or in an exploration of patterns of resistance and creativity within the world of labor.

Similar questions emerge from the chapters dealing with amusements, where more socially approved, "public" and middle-class opportunities and celebrations are placed beside the urban underworld of gambling. The chapter on bolita was transcribed, with minor editing, from a twenty-one-page report of August 17, 1936, by Martin Richardson. [31] The report is based, according to the author, on sources quoted in the text, reports of the Jacksonville "Crime Prevention League," observations, interviews, handbills, national black newspapers such as the *Baltimore Afro-American* and the *Pittsburgh Courier*, and visits to the Eureka Novelty House. In its vivid detail, it recalls oral narratives I have collected in Savannah and the writings on gambling in Hurston's *Mules and Men* and *Jonah's Gourd Vine*, as well as the later writings of Claude McKay on "numbers" in Harlem, which drew on materials from the New York WPA (Mangione 1972: 257; McKay 1940). This may be an early vision of urban folklore, not unlike Hurston's New York sketches such as the "Story in Harlem Slang" and "Glossary of Harlem Slang."[32] Nonetheless, in the proposal for further revisions of the manuscript in 1938, the intention seems to have been to moderate the exuberance in this chapter and to reduce it to a minor passage on black urban folk life. Such a shift echoes the restrained tone of *The Negro in Virginia*, which relegates gambling to a few late paragraphs (1940:341).

Folklore occupies a central position in the text, and is of special interest to readers drawn to the manuscript by Hurston's contributions. Chapters on superstition, hoodoo, and the conjure shop provide unique data from the period, drawing both on slave interviews and collections by Pearl Randolph and Portia Thorington. Again, the reader must ask if this is a representation of rural blacks as "primitive," as in *Drums and Shadows*, or if it reflects an interest in matters of everyday life, which were made accessible by black researchers gathering materials from other blacks. According to Stetson Kennedy, authors such as Richardson and Johnson had deep concerns about social conditions in Florida that they were not encouraged to pursue; the first outline and its ending at Raiford prison strengthens this interpretation. Is it possible that women provided a different research agenda?

Equally significant are the chapters devoted to modern achievement, whether in community affairs, education, religion, or the arts. Here, a folkloristic image of black life is balanced by a note of sophisticated pride. Again, the table of contents for the subsequent 1938 version suggests that this perspective would have become even more dominant in a later version, with more extensive chapters on schools and colleges, from Stanton High School in Jacksonville to Florida Normal in St. Augustine and Florida A & M in Tallahassee. Many more notes for an incomplete chapter on education remain in the files.[33] Nonetheless, the chapters printed here convey a sense that communities such as Eatonville could be examples to other blacks, as Hurston had already suggested in her works through a combination of folklore and sophistication. Richardson's reporting of the complex ethnic relations in Pensacola provides an interesting ethnographic vision of language and cultures in urban melting pots.

Some of the biographies nonetheless seem to reflect access to information rather than consistent criteria. Jonathan Gibbs, Zora Neale Hurston, and James Weldon Johnson, however, remain important figures in modern Florida's black heritage. The reports from local investigators on art, literature, and music that provided primary sources for this selection were much more extensive, including accounts of individual craftsmen, minor authors, and even schoolchildren. One of the most striking omissions is Mary McLeod Bethune, founder of Bethune College (later Bethune-Cookman) and a vital figure in black participation in New Deal reforms (two later portraits of her appear in the files).

The chapter on Durkeeville, while scant, brings in another important aspect of some reports that might have become stronger in later revisions: the impact of agencies of the Federal Emergency Administration and the Works Progress Administration on the black community. There are some interesting editorial omissions, including the absence of comparable materials for Liberty City and the deletion of statistics on black health problems. Note of WPA intervention is made in the longer version of "What the Florida Negro Does," including mention of WPA sewing-room employees in Miami and Jacksonville (p.39). Later, Paul Diggs also devoted various reports to WPA projects.

Perhaps the most confusing aspect of the text published here concerns the limited final chapters on religion and spirituals. Again, materials in the files are much more complete, although many of the songs in the list for chapter XVI were collected by the white folklorist Cora Mae Taylor. Part of an earlier chapter on religious music, in fact, has been combined with the chapter on religion, perhaps to parallel the organization of the work chapters. Why these chapters are so skeletal remains an enigma.

As a modern reader, informed by study of both archives and editorial selections surrounding this text, I would agree neither with critic Christopher Felker that the text(s) "lacked a unifying structure and was overly burdened by sociological prose" (1991:148) nor even with editorial comments cited above. I recognize some shortcomings of style,[34] fact, omission, and argument in the text which other modern readers also will see. At times, stereotypes are presented in what seems to be an appeal to white readers of the period; at others, a more critical voice is raised, even if a cogent argument for change is scarcely voiced. But it is not the consistency of the text that I have sought to present so much as the varied stages and opinions present throughout the project concerning who the Florida Negroes were and what they stood for. In this sense, one might also juxtapose the liberal ambience of Illinois, for example, with the difficult context of collection, even by black fieldworkers, in Florida, in terms of themes omitted or debated over time. Florida Agricultural and Mechanical College, for example, merits a short chapter, but the notes on what could be done with the subjects of education and social issues suggest more extensive and critical ambitions. The labor section was edited so that the emphasis is on menial trades, but how can this be linked with professionalism, on the one hand, and the ambiguous world of bolita, on the other? And what of lynchings or other incidents like Ocoee? Where are the press and the politics of Reconstruction, underscored in the 1938 revisions?

Such problems might be approached in the future through comparison not only of black portrayals and volumes in the Federal Writers' Project but of other texts prepared with a strong ethnic input and autonomy in the project. *The Italians of New York*, for example, at times has an almost boosterish tone that ignores any problematic social adaptations in its community.[35] In this sense, *The Florida Negro* seems to be a more human volume, even a more honest one. But more research and reading need to be done to achieve a final interpretation.

Moreover, this manuscript and introduction should be seen as the basis for future readings and interpretations that draw out its tensions. The struggle of

black voices, straightforward and ironic, against white domination is important to the reading of this text, as is the gendering of materials and subjects.
Equally striking is the tension across generations concerning historical knowledge, most deeply evident regarding oral traditions and culture versus writing
and mass media reproduction, such as in the impact of the phonograph on
music. And questions of rights and responses permeate the text as an historical
document (Young 1991). Gertrude Fraser, in her afterword, already suggests
other paths that readings may take, now that the text is at last brought to life.

The creators and themes of *The Florida Negro* situate it in a unique category,
then, both in its viewpoints and its condition as a WPA volume in progress. A
document that presents something between an impersonal voice and a black
conversation, a comprehensive cultural geography and a jarring collage, views
of "primitivist" folklore and pride in contemporary accomplishments, *The
Florida Negro* challenges us to think about the black world that many once
failed to listen to but we now can hear again.

Conclusions: A Call for More

No introduction should overwhelm its text, particularly one that represents
such an interesting historical and anthropological recovery. In fact, since few
other guides were extensively footnoted, it seems overbearing to do so even if
only to correct or comment on later work. In these notes, then, I have attempted to situate *The Florida Negro* within the interests and variety of the
WPA projects of the 1930s and 1940s. I have also suggested, by reference to
these volumes as well as the notes in the files of the Florida Historical Society,
themes to which we might pay special attention in reading this recovered and
reconstructed text, and I have provided general information as well as some
modern references. Each reader will bring more to this rediscovered text.

Yet this rediscovery and the richness of our readings underscore the importance of Writers' Project resources that have not yet been developed. Jerre
Mangione has noted that material from the Chicago Negro project "gathers
dust in the archives of Chicago's Hall Branch public library" (1972: 240).
Moreover, among the unborn books of the last years of the project were the
following:

> six regional guides with the general title *Hands that Built the Nation,*
> which were to be a collaborative project by the Arts and Writers' Program
> based on the Index of American Design; *America Eats,* a regional treatment
> of custom and tradition for serving and preparing food; *The Western Range:
> the Story of the Grasslands,* which was to tell the story of the vast open-range

country of the West in terms of its Indians, Spanish *rancheros* and *vaqueros*, American frontiersmen, cattle barons, sheep men, and modern ranchers; and *Indians of the United States*, a contemporary picture and historical account of what happened to the first Americans under the rule of white people (1972:346).

In conversations and in archives over the past few years, my inquiries have produced similar stories of materials lost, tossed out, or left to decay. Nearly twenty years ago, after decades of nearly-total scholarly neglect, Jerre Mangione observed, "The situation is changing; the memory of the Writers' Project is gradually coming to the fore" (1972:372). James Baldwin, in his 1967 preface to the long-delayed Harlem project, was more cynical: "That the information in this book should be startling is an interesting comment on the conservative, that is to say, the prevailing, attitude toward American history. If so many people did not find the information in this book 'startling,' they might be less at the mercy of their ignorance, and our present situation would be healthier than it is" (Ottley and Weatherby 1967:xv).

I believe that the Federal Writers' Project can still provide anthropologists, historians, and other social scientists, as well as interested readers, with a significant guide to the questions and dreams, visions and failings of a past American, as a whole and in its parts. Since I am completing my part in project, my hope is that others will recognize the possibilities and go forward.

Gary W. McDonogh

NOTES

1. Edited by Henry G. Alsberg (1937), the general American guide was a later compilation of materials from the guides, published by Hastings House in New York in 1949. After a complex search for financial sponsorship, the first state guide, Idaho, was published in 1937 and publication continued for years thereafter. My guidance in reading the WPA has come primarily from Mangione (1972), including its extensive bibliography of WPA materials by Arthur Scharf, and Penkower (1977), as well as my own collection of FWP materials. I have also been interested in the newer approaches to other aspects of the WPA in Barbara Melosh (1991). Finally, this project has also received support from my wife, Cindy Hing-Yuk Wong, from my student and research assistant, Geoffrey Mohlman, from my colleague, Justus Doenecke, and from specialists in Florida history including Nick Wynne and Gary Mormino of the Florida Historical Society, Pamela Bordelon, whose forthcoming work on the Florida project will further illuminate this manuscript, and Stetson Kennedy, who shared his memories and archives.

2. *Seeing St. Augustine* (1937); *A Guide to Key West* (1941); *Planning Your Vacation in Florida* (1941); *Seeing Fernandina* (1940); *Birds in Florida* (1942?); *The Spanish Missions of Florida* (1940); *Seminole Indians of Florida* (1941).

3. These files include Florida files in boxes A54, Correspondence; A55 Counties,

Dade, Ethnic Studies; and A62 Negroes; A591 Folklore Project/Traditional Folklore; and Negro Project Files in A877, A878 and A879, as well as slave narrative files in A897 which I did not examine there.

Pam Bordelon (personal communication, 1992) has suggested that the Tampa files actually encompass the files of the Florida Negro Writers' Unit.

4. The ex-slave narratives remain one of the richest, if at times most controversial, legacies of the WPA, as discussed in Yetman 1984. The entire Library of Congress collection was published by Rawick (1972) in nineteen volumes, and they have been published in part or as composite sources in a range of works including Botkin (1945); Yetman (1970); Killion and Waller (1973); Tyler and Murphy (1974); Perdue, Bardon, and Phillips (1980). Paul Escott (1979) applied a more quantitative approach, while Norman Yetman has provided a reflective overview (1984). Questions about how these materials may be used by modern historians are also considered in these articles, as well as in critical works by Blassingame (1977), Soapes (1977) and Bailey (1980). More general approaches that have shaped my consultation and reading of these materials include S. Smith (1974), Butterfield (1974), Foster (1979), Starling (1981), Olney (1984), Andrews (1986), and the overviews in Davis and Gates (1985).

5. Lois Dwight Cole to Zora Neale Hurston, May 11, 1939, The Florida Negro Papers, "Manuscripts, Correspondence" Box 4, File 1/7. The absence of an actual review is echoed in the companion letter from the Christopher Publishing House (Arthur J. Christopher to Zora Neale Hurston, May 10, 1939). While Hurston had collected pieces and songs and drafted a chapter on folklore, she is probably referring to the 1937 manuscript and 1938 revisions, primarily composed by Martin Richardson and edited in part by Stetson Kennedy before she joined the project.

6. My interest in the manuscript was sparked by Robert Hemenway's biography of Hurston (1977) as I began research in nearby Savannah, Georgia, shortly after I began teaching at New College. After discussion with then-director of the Florida Historical Society, Gary Mormino, I was encouraged to begin the project, profiting from Mormino's organization of a 1986 Florida Endowment for the Humanities Conference on the Federal Writers' Project, which included talks by Hemenway, Stetson Kennedy, Jerre Mangione and others, and by Mormino's work with "Florida Slave Narratives" (1988). I could not pursue it at the time. In 1988, the new FHS director, Nicholas Wynne, again encouraged me to undertake the project in conjunction with the University Press of Mississippi. Seetha A-Srinivasan has proved to be a supportive editor there throughout this process.

Among the basic resources for this work have been the FHS and USF collections, the P. K. Yonge collection of the University of Florida and holdings of the Library of Congress as well as Atlanta University. The FHS and UF collections, according to Stetson Kennedy represents the planned archival deposit of materials by director Corita Doggett Corse. Those donated to the FHS were later arranged according to the system I have used that was devised by Paul Camp. P. K. Yonge materials were bound in volumes around themes that also reflect an imposed, if interesting, ordering of project materials.

7. We await the detailed discussion of the history of the Florida Federal Writers' Project assembled by Pamela Bordelon in her 1991 Louisiana State University dissertation, "The Federal Writers' Project's Mirror to America: The Florida Reflection." I also recognize Dr. Bordelon's generous assistance to me throughout this project.

8. All I have located from these projects, however, are two volumes on Jews in New York, published in Yiddish (*The Jewish Landsmanschaften of New York* [1938] and *Jewish Families and Family Circles in New York* [1939]) and a late volume, *The Negro in New York: an Informal Social History*, compiled by Roi Ottley and William Weatherby (1967). Other New York projects ranged from *A Maritime History of New York* (1941) to *Who's Who in the Zoo* (1937).

9. This criticism also came up in conversation with Stetson Kennedy about the Florida project.

10. As well as Florida's Mary McLeod Bethune through her friendship with Eleanor Roosevelt.

11. Guides from four southern states—Alabama, Arkansas, Louisiana, and Florida—do not include a separate section for blacks; although it is not clear whether there is any unifying feature that has led to this. Information on blacks may still be segregated within the texts (e.g., a summary of information on "Negro education" within a chapter on education), but in general these recognize that blacks participated in many aspects of the state's life. Eight southern guides—Georgia, Kentucky, Maryland, Mississippi, North Carolina, South Carolina, Tennessee, and Virginia—include a separate chapter called "The Negro." In Texas, blacks are included in the chapter "Racial Elements," while in Maryland, a chapter of that title deals with British, Germans, Irish, French, Poles, Czechs, Italians, Lithuanians, Jews, Greeks, and Amish; there is a separate chapter titled "The Negro" (*Maryland* 1940: 49–54, 55–61). This suggests a transition to the method of organization used in guides for some northeastern states, in which there are chapters such as "Ethnic Groups and their Folkways" (*Pennsylvania*.1940: 59–70), "Foreign Groups" (*Rhode Island*. 1937: 98–105), and "Racial and National Groups" (*New Jersey*. 1939: 118–25).

However, the extent to which segregation could be taken is evident in the general introduction to the Georgia volume. The Georgia project apparently had no black members, and the writers evidently presumed that the "typical" Georgian was white. The overview notes that with younger Georgians, "[t]heir attitude towards the educated Negro, for instance, may be different from that of their elders who still prefer the old-fashioned, unlettered kind," and continues, "But, however kind he may be toward the cause of Negro education, the Georgian is usually kind to his own servants and not a little apprehensive of hurting their feelings" (*Georgia* 1940:6). Penkower cites a 1968 interview with director Carolyn Dillard, in which she recalled, "Looking at the matter from the viewpoint of 1968, I wonder why we did not have Negro representation on our State staff, but in the 1930s it didn't seem so urgent, *if indeed we even thought of it*" (1977:67).

12. *The Negro in Virginia* (1940). Zora Neale Hurston's biographer Robert Hemenway notes that "the Florida book was patterned after this Virginia volume" (1977:252). This is echoed by Christopher Felker in his "Adaptation of the Source: Ethnocentricity and 'The Florida Negro'" (1991). Yet the text was generally complete by 1937 and Stetson Kennedy (personal communication) did not recall discussion of other projects or comparison with them, although general guidelines may have suggested new trajectories.

Perhaps equally important was the WPA reception to progress on the extremely folkloristic *Drums and Shadows*, in which Charles Joyner notes, "The Savannah Unit's concentration on African survivals rather than on black acculturation in Georgia found itself in conflict with the vision of the national office, which felt that *Drums and Shadows* promoted a racist theory of cultural evolution in which cultural traits might survive from earlier, more primitive stages of culture but would eventually disappear under contact with more advanced cultures" (1986 edition). Evidently, this was an early thrust of supervisor Mary Grainger, as well as a reflection of the interests of her anthropological advisor, Melville Herskovits. Hence, although the manuscript of the study was not published until 1940, it could have been a discussion point underlying a 1938 shift in the Florida project—and perhaps an influence on the 1940 *Negro in Virginia* as well. The question of influences and shifts among volumes and programs demands future research.

13. Jerre Mangione notes that the Virginia project selected from a wide range of materials not included in the final text, citing thirty boxes of unpublished folklore left in the University of Virginia archives. Although reviewed in search of folksongs, "The larger part of the collection, consisting of ghost stories, superstitions, herbal lore and so on . . . remains unclassified" (1983: 269).

14. In the case of *Drums and Shadows*, for example, it appears that all but fragmentary pages of the original interviews and documents have disappeared (Georgia Historical Society, personal communication, 1985).

15. Now found in files 3/4 and 4/4.

16. The table of contents and sample pages from each chapter are to be found in WPC (LC) files A879, "Florida Miscellaneous Material." The outline includes these chapters (asterisks mark omitted or moved chapters): History; The First Slave; Slave Days in Florida; Ex-Slave Stories; Religion*; Music in Negro Churches*; Spirituals*; Folklore; Hoodoo Voodoo and Naningo; Amusements and Diversions; The Conjure Shops; Bolita; What the Florida Negro Does; Workaday Songs; A Day at Raiford*.

17. Richardson's collection of prison songs was included in the worksong chapter, and his materials on Daddy Mention, apparently collected at the prison, also figure in the text.

18. The FHS files, Manuscript 3/4 contains the later typescripts, which include handwritten revisions of the first part of the primary text, evidently by Stetson Kennedy. Later, after omitting chapters III and IV, it simply recopies the first text. This was evidently the basis, in turn, for the next, as yet incomplete manuscript of file 2/4, which covers seventy-one typed pages of heavy stylistic, organizational, and even factual revisions of the earliest text, incorporating handwritten changes on Ms. 1/4. The Kennedy letter cited above and conversations with him as well as the proposed "tables of contents" included in the file "contents" (Box 1, File 11/14) elucidates the relation of these manuscripts. Two sheets, which present the outline of chapter titles and sub-titles corresponding to MS. 3/4–4/4 are annotated "as was before 1938 summer revisions." A second set of chapter titles, without a date, refer to the revised manuscript 2/4. Significant differences are noted in annotations.

A grammatical stylistic reading was also done by Isaac Fischer, Department of Research and Publications, Florida A & M.

19. Mangione 1983: 257 suggests that these two texts were published while Hurston worked on the project, profiting from its support as did other authors. She probably did use part of the time to work on *Moses: Man of the Mountain* (1939), as Hemenway notes.

20. Letter from director Henry Alsberg to Corita Doggett Corse of June 3, 1939, in the WPA-LC files (A54, "Florida Correspondence, 1939") notes, "We are interested in learning the status of various Negro books. Please let us know what progress is being made on the Florida Negro and if it would be possible for us to see some completed chapters if the entire manuscript is not at present available." Apparently Hurston's folklore chapter was sent.

21. Hurston is mentioned by name as a Florida author in the State Guide (*Florida* 1939:147) among a series of black authors from the state, and her novel, *Their Eyes Were Watching God*, is cited for a description of migrant labor (1939:475).

22. Unfortunately, neither the manuscript nor the general guide includes a full list of contributors, nor are the Negro writers' unit's authors cited as consultants in the guide, even if Hurston and James Weldon Johnson are cited in the bibliography (*Florida* 1939).

If anything, Hurston's impact may be apparent in a final and barely projected manuscript, of which only sections are preserved, which moves *The Florida Negro* back from its academic stance to a more popular position. This is represented in her article on folklore, "Go, 'gator and Muddy the Water." Smaller texts on Eatonville are included as examples in the appendix and more are in preparation by other scholars (Bordelon, personal communication, 1992).

23. It is clear that no more final version of the entire text was prepared; although the P. K. Yonge Library labels the 1937 manuscript as the work of Hurston, this is clearly a mistake.

24. Interview by Mrs. Nancy Williams, New Smyrna Beach, Fla., March 18, 1976. Now in manuscript in the P. K. Yonge Library of the University of Florida.

Felker (1991) argues a complex case for Hurston's understanding of authenticity and professionalism in her WPA work which, while provocative, does not seem to correspond to details of the extant manuscripts at the FHS.

25. "Go 'gator and Muddy the Water," p.1. The Daddy Mention material had already been collected for Richardson's version of the manuscript.

26. Hemenway notes this omission in *Mules and Men*, all the more striking since Eatonville and Ocoee were Orlando neighbors (1977: 220). Stetson Kennedy augments the WPA report in *Southern Exposure*, directly blaming the Klan (1946: 112).

27. In his introduction to the collected slave narratives, historian Gary Mormino cites the presence of black women in this project:" Black women constituted one-half of the unit in 1936–1937, an unusually high number. On a national level, Jacqueline Jones notes that 'less than 20 per cent of all WPA workers were female, and only 3 per cent of all WPA workers were black women'" (Mormino 1988). The Florida unit seems to have employed a remarkable number of black women over the course of the project, but it is difficult to tell how long and in what capacity, especially after the first cuts.

28. Use of these contributions was not limited to the Negro project alone, however. The general Florida guide includes material from Negro unit workers dealing with bolita and bolita superstition, voodoo, and jook in its folklore section (131–33), while black authors from Jonathan Walker to James Weldon Johnson and Zora Neale Hurston are discussed under literature (146–47). The individual reports on cities and sites also drew on these files: the description of black Jacksonville includes data about authors and musicians as well as a specific reference to Durkeeville (193; see chapter XIV) and the Church of God and Saints (193), about which James Johnson had written a report. The

Pensacola report reverberates with Richardson's ethnography of a multiracial community (236–37), and prominent figures from black Florida history such as J. Gibbs received mention in the general guide as well (100, 272–77).

29. The files include large sections on Miami's black figures (primarily preachers) and other contributions from white folklorist Cora M. Taylor that did not find their way into the final volume (Box 1, File Biography). The files also include an extensive piece on the Bahamians of Miami, which was slated for inclusion in later tables of contents; Hurston collected materials from this group as well.

30. Some indications of secondary sources are included in the annotations on chapter I. Kennedy has written me, "A letter from Robert Cornwall to me dated 8/9/41 states that the FWP was seeking to hire Prof. J. C. Langhorne at FAMU to edit the Florida Negro. To the best of my knowledge, he was never hired. Langhorne said to be friend of Sterling Brown's" (personal communication, February 13, 1992).

31. FHS, *The Florida Negro*, Box 2, File 8/12.

32. "The Story . . . ," apparently including the glossary, was published in *American Mercury* 56 (July 1942), 84–96. It is notable that such items as her Florida magical place, "Diddy-Wah-Diddy," collected for the FWP, reappears in the glossary as "another suburb of Hell, built since Hell wan't no bigger than Baltimore" (Hurston [1985]:82–98, esp.92).

33. In his letter of September 29, 1938, to Corita Doggett Corse, Stetson Kennedy asks, "Is Zora Neale Hurston doing any historical research? Of course, I am also writing the chapter on education" (Kennedy, personal archives).

34. Style problems include minor spelling errors and punctuation errors that have been corrected here and that may actually be typographic errors. In general, I have kept to the manuscript.

35. Indeed, these are almost specifically rejected in that text's chapter titled "Problems of Social Adjustment" (50–58).

A NOTE ON ILLUSTRATIONS

All planned illustrations were separated from the original files, although many exist within the more general photograph and picture postcard collection of the P. K. Yonge Library at the University of Florida in Gainesville, from which a selection has been reproduced with permission of the library. Those chosen not only correspond directly to titles but bear indications of placement in pencil on their reverse. This selection, provided in an insert (not unlike most published WPA volumes), proves evocative rather than exhaustive and certainly does not do justice to a wider range of WPA illustrations to be explored in these files. Numbers refer to original number in sequence and suggested page placement.

1. Parade, Bethune-Cookman College, Daytona Beach (Illustration #3 in planned collection, for p.14)

2. Negro Masonic Temple, Jacksonville (#5, p.17)

3. Alice Stokes [The original figure 9 was Home of Alice Stokes at Mandarin—Sunday School pupil and servant of the author, Harriet Beecher Stowe (47)] (#10, p.47)

4. N.A.P.E. Convention (#16, p.67)

5. Negro Boy Scouts at Camp Lincoln, New Berlin (#20, p.94)

6. Hecksher Gymnasium and Swimming Pool, Florida Normal and Collegiate Inst., Jacksonville [Actually, St. Augustine] (#21, p.98)

7. Music Festival at Florida Normal Institution, St. Augustine (#22, p.98)

8–9. Durkeeville (#31–40, pp.171–73) [Collages]

10. Bethel Church, Jacksonville (#41–42, pp.174–75)

Listed below are some other photographs that exist within the collection but have not been included generally because of poor quality for reproduction. This is especially true of the overexposed and small originals for all conjure and bolita photographs from Jacksonville and of James Johnson's photos of Alice Stokes's house (it appears that at least one writer doubled as a photographer when necessary). Others proved impossible to identify. Asterisks mark those located in the P. K. Yonge collection, while page numbers indicate suggested original placement.

1. Esther, slave on Ft. George plantation (p.10)

2.* East view of campus, Florida Normal Institution (p.14)

4.* Stanton High School, Jacksonville (p.17)

6.* Wilder Park Branch Public Library, Jacksonville (p.21)

7. Tuberculosis Hospital, Orlando (p.23)

8. Charles Coats, oldest Negro in Florida (p.23)

11. Oak of Earlston (p.50)

12. F. E. R. A. Farm (p.64)

13. Scene at Flower Show (p.65)

14. Display of Florida Farmers' Co-operative Assn., Tallahassee (p.66)

15. Central Life Insurance Company, Tampa (p.66)

17. Scene at American Beach, Fernandina (p.88)

18. Dance Scene (p.89)

19. State Tennis Meet at Lavilla Park, Jacksonville (p.93)

23.* The Big House—Bolita House, Jacksonville (p.99)

24.* " " " " (p.100)

25. Naningo Dance (p.130)

26. 27, 28, 29.* The Conjure Shop, Voodoo Shop (p. 136, 136, 137, 137)

30. Choral group at Agricultural and Mechanical College, Tallahassee (p.150)

The Florida Negro

I

History

Introduction

In Florida today there are some 462,205 Negroes, constituting 29.1 per cent of the State's population.[1] They have schools, churches, and many business establishments separate from other races. Their characteristics are mainly the same as those found among Negroes of other southern States.

In their history, however, there are definite indications that they differ in many ways from their usual neighbors. This is because from the arrival of the first known Negro in the State to the post-Reconstruction era, the history of the Negro in Florida has been linked with momentous historical events unlike the course of events in other states.

Direct cause of wars costing millions of dollars and hundreds of lives, partial reason for the formation of a great State, central but unwitting figure in critical issues of careers of generals, cabinet members and even presidents, the Florida Negro has come through a long series of major national milestones as he has toiled in the fields which have been home to him for more than two and a half centuries.

The First Slave

Perhaps the earliest mention of a slave in Florida occurs in the account of the expedition of Narvaez in 1528.[2] It will be recalled that after the ruin of that expedition Cabeza de Vaca and three companions, after almost six years of incredible suffering, reached Mexico. According to De Vaca's account, one of his companions was Estevan, a blackamoor of Asemmur on the West Coast of Morocco. The Negro was the guide of Fray Marcos de Niza in 1539, being sent ahead of the Coronado expedition to report the character of the country. He met death at the hands of the Zuñis in the present N. Mexico.[3]

Negro slaves of the Spanish King were sent to Florida in 1581, and a small party of them were employed for two years in making wooden platforms for the artillery of the old fort at San Agustin. [4]

With slavery a widespread institution in Europe, it would be surprising if there had been no slaves in the New World. In point of fact, there were Negro slaves in St. Augustine, probably from the very first, but their number was negligible.

We have a record of a Negro slave at the friary at St. Augustine in 1589. In 1594 the governor of Florida asked the governor of Cuba for a number of soldiers and a "few slaves." In the first hospital in the United States, built at St. Augustine in 1597, a Negress in the royal service tended the sick "soldiers, Indians, and Negroes." In 1603 there were 32 Negro slaves in St. Augustine, five of whom were women. It is very likely that these Negro slaves were used for personal services, and not for hard labor; for this the Spaniard used the Indian, a most recalcitrant worker. No wonder that the arrival of Negro slaves for field work was hailed with joy.

A shout went up as the ship of Don Juan de Aila came to anchor in the harbor of St. Augustine in 1687, a shout that was the beginning of a celebration lasting all day. For, on the ship of the Don, in addition to the usual cargo, was a black slave, one out of 12 that the Spaniard had hoped to bring.

To the Spanish colonists of the new Florida the slave meant food; someone to raise crops on the farms near St. Augustine. The new slave had no companions because the Spaniards were strict; in addition to other qualifications a slave must be a Catholic before he could be transported to Florida.[5]

The slave of Don Juan was not long to remain alone, however; in the years that immediately followed he was joined, at St. Augustine and other parts of the State, by numbers of others who sought the protection of the Spaniards when fleeing from their owners, the colonists of the Carolinas.

It was during this period of the first Spanish occupation of Florida that the connection between the Negro and the Seminole Indian is first noted; Indians, like Negroes, had been enslaved in the Carolinas. Many of these Indians were of the Creek and Yemassee tribes, who occupied a wide territory in what was later to be Georgia. The Seminoles were a branch of the Georgia Creeks.[6]

Both Indians and Negroes frequently escaped from their masters in

Carolina; often they made their way southward to the Spanish territory of Florida. Here the Spaniards had erected for the Negro refugees a fort near their own San Marcos. This fort, called Fort Moosa, was built sometime between 1687 and 1695; it consisted of a large square with breastwork and four bastions. In and near this fort the escaped Negroes lived in comparative freedom, and apparently there were numbers of them.

The constant escape of Negro and Indian slaves from Carolina to Florida contributed to the creation of the Georgia colony; in Georgia ownership of slaves was at first forbidden, as it was felt that a free state between the two colonies would greatly reduce the number of slave escapes. Georgia remained free only eight years, however. The need for Negro labor in the fields brought about the change.

By June 1740 the number of Negroes occupying Fort Moosa had become large enough to become a factor in the threatening hostilities between the Spaniards and governor Oglethorpe. Learning that the Englishman planned an attack, the Spanish governor, Montiano, strengthened both Forts Moosa and San Marcos. A band of 80 Scotch Highlanders, however, captured Fort Moosa in the early days of the Oglethorpe invasion of St. Augustine, and it was later retaken only after several hundred Spaniards, Indians and Negroes had been hurled against it. In this engagement, Colonel Palmer, leader of the Highlanders, was killed, and many of his men were imprisoned at the St. Augustine Fort.

The Seminoles Increase

The infiltration of Georgia Indians into Florida was greatly increased about 1850 when a chieftain of the Creeks in Georgia, Seacoffee, left the Creek tribes and, with a large following, moved into Florida. They mingled with both the Negroes and the Miccosukee Indians who had preceded them to Florida, and enjoyed all the privileges of free Spanish citizenship.[7]

With the turning of Georgia into a slave-holding province the number of Indians and Negro runaways increased rapidly, to the extent, finally, that in 1776 the Council for Safety of that colony requested a large force of troops from Congress "to prevent their slaves from deserting their masters."

Sometime about this date it became known that Indians and Negro runaways had settled in numbers around the Suwannee and Apalachicola rivers, in addition to the settlements they already had in eastern and central Florida. War between England and the American colonies, the largely unexplored condition of Florida as a whole, and the fact that between Carolina, North Georgia and

Florida's boundaries there were savage tribes of Creek Indians to be encountered, may have contributed to this brief spell of prosperity that the Negroes and Seminoles enjoyed—the last in their history.

The first serious threat to this peaceful breathing-spell came in 1783 when, at the close of the Revolutionary War, the Creeks of Georgia made a treaty with the authorities of the State in which they promised to restore any slaves residing among them. While the authenticity of this treaty was disputed, it was to affect greatly the escaped Negroes and Seminoles living in Florida.

The Second Spanish Period

In this same year the Negroes again came under Spanish influence, but it was with little of the former protection and freedom that the Spanish governors had afforded in the past.[8] For one thing, the Creeks of Georgia, who had never been on good terms with the Seminoles or their Negro allies, began a series of border raids on them, murdering and burning and taking prisoners. Interestingly, the first treaty made under the new Federal Constitution was made in reference to the Negroes involved in these border events. It was a concession of certain lands to the Georgia Creeks, with a repetition of the stipulation that Negroes were to be surrendered by the Indians. It was this surrendering that had set the Creeks to invading Florida so that they might have Negro captives to surrender. This treaty bore the date of August 1, 1790, and the signature of President George Washington.

The succeeding quarter of a century witnessed two interesting developments for the Negroes of west Florida and their Indian allies: an intensifying of the efforts of the officials of slaveholding Georgia to reclaim the growing number of free Negroes in Florida, and the tighter cementing of the bonds between Negroes and Seminoles. In the latter connection, the Indians and Negroes in 1812 were able to defeat an army raised by Georgia which penetrated about a hundred miles into Florida; they cut it off from its supplies, and sent it back nearly starved. In the former, the governor of Georgia, in 1811, ordered the formation of an army large enough "to reduce St. Augustine and punish the Indians."

It was not from the East Florida section around St. Augustine, however, ·that the exiled freemen suffered their first major disaster. An expedition did enter that section of the state, but after two years returned to Georgia with little to show for its efforts except casualties.

In 1814, several British vessels assisted the Negroes and Seminoles in the area around the Apalachicola River to erect a fort, stock it with ammunition and mount some eight guns on it. This fort was about 30 miles above the mouth of the river, on its east bank. That the Negroes and their Seminole friends believed that here at last was security seems evident from the fact that around the fort sprang up many farms and even plantations; the fields, one historian says, extended for more than 50 miles along the river. There were hundreds of Negroes and Seminoles in the area, and they had large herds of cattle and horses. The fort was generally called the Negro Fort, but its real name was Fort Blount.[9]

On the morning of July 24, 1816 the quiet of the fort was shattered by the booming of two 18 pound guns; General Andrew Jackson, in charge of the southern forces of the United States Army, had ordered Colonel Clinch and Captain Loomis to attack the fort, "blow it up, and return the Negroes to their rightful owners."

After four days of attack on the fort, by both land and water, a heated cannonball found a powder magazine inside the stockade, and all but 60 of the 334 persons inside the fort were instantly killed. There were only three who escaped injury. Two of the survivors, one Indian and one Negro, were executed as "leaders." [10]

Before the Civil War

On July 10, 1821 the Negroes in Florida saw the American flag raised over the State. To them, at least, it was an unwelcome innovation; it meant the almost sure enslavement of every Negro who could be captured. The Seminole also viewed Americans with disfavor, having fought against them in the Revolution, as allies of England.

The Second Spanish period[11] was one of significant development for Negroes. Although the British, departing from Florida after the American Revolution, took their slaves with them, many more were brought in by planters who moved to Florida to take up Spanish grants. From the new United States came also American adventurers who received grants and imported slaves directly from Africa, a practice forbidden in the U.S. after 1808, but countenanced by Spanish law. As a result, slaves were brought to Florida in great numbers, and the majority were smuggled across the American border where prices soared as the cotton plantations spread over the lower South.

The reaction of the Seminoles and the Negroes was to retire farther into the fastnesses of the Florida swamps and forests, and to begin a state of war against the government forces that was to become famous as the Seminole Wars.

Actually, there had been no peace between the Seminoles and their Negro allies on the one hand, and the government forces on the other since the destruction of Fort Blount. General Jackson himself with about 4,000 regular and volunteer troops had already defeated Negroes in several towns around Lake Miccosukee, the Seminoles in St. Marks on the Gulf, and combined Seminole and Negro forces along the Suwannee. Those who had not been killed or captured had fled to the Everglades region in the southern part of the State.

From the destruction of Fort Blount until 1842 the Seminole Wars went on intermittently. On August 14 of the latter year, General J.W. Worth issued an official order that "hostilities with the Indians within these territories have ceased." The intervening 26 years had seen the question of surrendering the Negroes postpone peace with the Seminole many times; had seen the question become a major issue first among army officials, then on the floor of the houses of Congress, and finally assist in the undoing of an attorney-general and the discomfiture of presidents Van Buren and Tyler.[12]

The campaign of the Seminole Wars made many historic figures not only among whites but Negroes and Indians alike. Because of the enslavement of his Negro wife, the young half-breed Osceola became one of the most feared leaders of the Seminoles. Coacoochee and his inveterate friend Louis—a former Negro slave who led a whole army detachment into ambush rather than assist in an attack on the Negroes and Seminoles—grew so terrible in legend that they were cheerfully granted permission to depart unmolested from Florida to the West. Micanopy, with his Negro Abraham, who twice interpreted governmental treaties so well that objectionable clauses had to be removed—these, and many others crossed Florida's history during the turbulent years of the Seminole Wars.[13]

For years after the close of the Seminole War scattered Indians were a source of annoyance to the settlers. Here is an account of the capture of the last Indian on Amelia Island:[14]

"Missis, you want to hear how dey caught de last Indian on dis Island? My grampa say dey kep' a-noticin' some one in de corn patch, de corn was break off, and trample. Marse Harrison say, 'some one stealin' my corn, and I believe it de Indians.'

"Dey notice dat dar only one set of tracks, but dey know dem tricky Indians. Missis, dey might be 40 or 50 of dem critters, but dey wouldn't leave but one set of tracks. One keep a-steppin' in de gracks ob de other one. We all afraid to try an' git dem Indians, not knowing how many dey be. So Marse Harrison plan dat de whole bunch of buck niggers surround dat corn field, and wait. If dey be a lot of Indians, we all gwine run, if dey be one or two, we gwine catch him. Treckly dark came out of dey woods, without no sound, came a Indian, one lone man, and he warn't any too big. He creep in the corn patch and start a-breakin' off de corn. Wit dat we all rush him. We aint afraid of one Indian. Dey took dat Indian an' take him to de plantation, and keep him dat under guard until de officer come and get him and take him to the Indian Reservation. An' dat was the last Indian ever seen on the Island of Amelia."

Among the Slaves

Simultaneously with the struggles of the Negroes and Indians to remain free, another chapter was being written in the history of the Florida Negro by the less fortunate brothers who could not escape to join in the fight for freedom. These were the growing numbers of slaves who belonged to the plantation owners, then increasing their holdings in the state.

Probably among the largest slave-holders was Zephaniah Kingsley on Fort George Island, near the mouth of the St. John's River. Kingsley was concerned with slaves in a number of ways: he employed them on his plantation, he brought them from Africa in his own ships, and he trained them on his plantation for sale in the slave markets. This training was many-sided; suffice to say that at the sales in the vicinity there were usually a number of slaves offered for sale who were described as "Kingsley's niggers," and they brought much more per head than any others, because of their training.

Kingsley's slaves, however, belonged to no unscrupulous pirate dealing in human flesh. Though he was a professional slave-dealer, he had unusual standards. At the height of his slave trade he wrote a book concerning the merits of slave holding as a means of disseminating certain benefits to heathens. And Kingsley married an African woman, stating in his will that he respected fully the African rites that had united them.[15]

In the vicinity of Jacksonville were other large plantations; Mandarin had a number, and in Mandarin, Jacksonville, and St. Augustine there were public markets where slave sales were held regularly. In west Florida, particularly in Columbia, Madison, and Jackson counties, plantations were in general larger than in east Florida. In Pensacola, there were dozens of liberated and semi-free slaves working on government forts and properties. One of the largest plantations in west Florida was El Destino, settled in 1828.[16] Cotton was the chief product of cultivation, but corn, oats, sugar cane, potatoes, and rice were also grown. In fact, the aim was to make the plantation self-sufficient. Relations between master and slave were excellent. Very few changes occurred, as the same names appear again and again in the tabulations and reports for about thirty years. Even the Civil War brought only a slight change among the hands, due to the fact that middle Florida was never occupied by Federal troops. Many of the ex-slaves remained to work the old fields on a crop-sharing basis. In 1919, the plantation was sold to descendants of the original owner for $70,000. It is 17 miles east of Tallahassee, much visited because of its magnificent oaks and shrubbery.

During this period the Hanson plantation near St. Augustine raised sugar cane, vegetables and fruit, employing a number of slaves. It occupied the exact site of the present Florida Normal Institute, one of the outstanding Negro colleges of the State.[17]

Life of the Florida Slave

Conditions under which Florida slaves lived varied greatly. From the kindnesses of the Kingsleys, Sandersons, and Blounts, all of whom were known to discharge overseers for beating slaves more than was absolutely necessary, treatment went to the extreme of the Lopez plantation near St. Augustine, where ex-slaves say they were beaten for several hours at a time by the master himself.

On some plantations reading and writing was permitted; on at least one, Kingsley's, it was part of the slaves' training; on one Pensacola plantation fingers were cut off when slaves were found trying to write.[18]

Religion was usually permitted; perhaps the still perceptible Spanish influence was partly responsible for this. Even after the emancipation of the slaves, there were, in St. Augustine, no churches for them but Catholic ones, and Protestant missionaries were beaten by Negro Catholics when they attempted to establish Baptist and Methodist congregations. Not until after the Civil War was there a Negro Protestant Church in St. Augustine. This was largely due to the suspicion that the missionaries were abolitionists. One abolitionist, Jonathan Walker, was branded on the hand at Pensacola in 1844.

Among slaves as among free Negroes, there were leaders during pre-Civil War days. One of these was Robert Meacham, who went about the plantation of his master, near Quincy, for long hours each night, with a candle and a well-worn book, teaching his fellow slaves to read.[19]

William Bryant of Tampa had cleared away many lots and built structures on them for his master before there was any talk of emancipation. Several slaves had been placed at the head of gangs of their fellows on the government reservation at Warrington because of their building ability; in Columbia county there was one who went into seven years of voluntary slavery to pay for a slave wife, and there were a number of slaves engaged in building, repairing and other necessary occupations in Tallahassee, Jacksonville and St. Augustine.[20]

One of the most interesting characters ever to settle in Tallahassee was George Proctor, a Negro who came to Florida from the Bahamas in the 1830's. He entered business as a contractor and builder; he built many of the present old houses in Tallahassee, among which three are known as the "Three Sisters," because of their similarity. Proctor and his wife Nancy had a family of six children. In 1849 he wanted to go to California in search of gold. He did not have enough money to finance the trip, so he mortgaged his wife and children. The mortgage was never paid, and the family was sold to George Rutgers, a banker. Proctor did not succeed as expected; occasionally he wrote to his family, and sometimes he sent them a nugget of gold, but he died before the outbreak of the war without ever having seen them again.

The Civil War

Negroes figured in the Civil War in Florida, as they did in other states; some of them on the side of the Union—there were as many as three battalions of Negroes known to be in the state at one time—and many performing individual feats on the side of their masters.[21]

In the latter category were many of the slaves of the Sandersons, at what is now Yukon; so loyal were they that when freedom was declared they voluntarily remained on the plantation and were later given a division of land on it, which some of their descendants still occupy.[22] Also at Yukon was the Mulberry Grove plantation of Mrs. Reid and the Amelia Island plantation of the Harrisons.

One Negro battalion, stationed in Jacksonville at a time when Federal troops were burning and leveling the city, came in for commendatory notice. In describing the destruction being wrought in the city an eye-witness wrote, "It gives me pleasure to report that the Negro troops took no part in this vandalism . . . they had nothing whatever to do with it . . . were merely silent spectators at a sad spectacle."

Another Negro detachment was stationed at Tampa Bay, and does not seem to have seen much action. Still another was engaged in the battle of Olustee, and was repulsed with great losses by Confederate forces. 192 Union men lost their lives, and there were 1806 Union casualties.

That there must have been numbers of Negro troops in the state is borne out by the historian's statement that "The Union forces were finally reduced to about 2,500 or 3,000 men, mostly Negroes." This was in 1864.

Reconstruction

The Reconstruction period brought the Florida Negro into prominence in several fields where he had not been heard of, or at best figured little, in earlier years of the state's history.[23] These included education, religion, politics, and to a small extent the cultural pursuits.

In education, the advent of the Freedmen's Bureau, with its free schools in Jacksonville, St. Augustine, and other cities, began the movement of the Negro to elevate himself. In Jacksonville the bureau, with the aid of local white citizens, established a public school. This institution later grew and expanded, and stands today as the Stanton High School, located at Broad and Ashley Streets.[24]

Cookman Institute, also in Jacksonville, followed in 1872. This was another of the Bureau's ventures, and has developed as the Bethune-Cookman College at Daytona Beach.

Third among the schools established after emancipation was Edward Waters College, a Methodist institution founded in 1873. Like the others, it is still in existence, though it has moved from Live Oak, its first location, to Jacksonville, where it has a student body of several hundred.

The State college for Negroes at Tallahassee was opened in 1887 as a land grant college. The opening of the school was made easier by the fact that by this time a Negro had served as both secretary of state and superintendent of education. The college has grown rapidly and now has an enrollment of about 1,500 students. [25]

The advance of the Florida Negro in religion, once freedom had removed barriers, was even more phenomenal. At the close of the War, there were already several congregations established; they had either been worshipping with their white masters, as with the Negro Catholics of Pensacola and St. Augustine, or were immediately ready to set up churches of their own, as with the Baptist congregation in Jacksonville that later became Bethel.[26]

This was one of the first congregations to occupy its own church during the Reconstruction era. Contemporary churches were the Methodist Episcopal Church in St. Augustine, founded in 1864, and the African Methodist Church in Jacksonville, called Mount Zion.

In politics the advance was possibly greatest, due to the fact that northern politicians found the Negro voter a convenient figure to exploit.

One of the most outstanding of the early Negro politicians was Jonathan Gibbs. He was a young Philadelphian, who came to the state shortly after the conclusion of the War, and almost immediately entered the political life of Florida via the Freedmen's Bureau and its associated enterprises.

His rise was almost phenomenal; in 1868 he went to Tallahassee as secretary of state, a position he held for four years under Governor Reed. During this period an attempt was made to impeach the governor and it was thwarted only when Gibbs buried the State Seal, necessary to give legality to the papers in the action.

In 1872 he began a term as the first State superintendent of education, but he did not complete his term. After two years he died under somewhat unusual, and some say suspicious circumstances. However, he had given the State its first practical system of supervised public education.[27]

During the reconstruction period there were as many as 19 Negroes in the State Legislature at one time. They included such men as Davidson of Pensacola, Scott of Jacksonville, Meacham of Tampa and others.

In local politics, Negroes played leading roles in some communities. John R. Scott, Sr., was leader of a large group in Jacksonville that once had so many representatives in the city government (1872) that the entire form of government was changed by an executive act at Tallahassee; in Tampa there were Negro police, council members, and other officials; there was a collector of customs in Jacksonville, St. Marks and Key West, a postmaster at another south Florida city, and various major outposts occupied by Negroes at Pensacola.

The gradual assumption of political control by the Democrats, however, and the lessening strength of the carpetbaggers and other Republican factions from the North brought a slow decrease in the political prominence of the Negro until by 1920 only one city, Ocala, had a Negro in any important office (city treasurer); there were none in the State machinery.[28]

Contemporary Life

Florida's 462,000 Negroes today present many evidences of the progress they have made in the 250 years they have been in the peninsula.[29] They have businesses ranging from the small bootblack stands and restaurants found in every city to two large insurance companies, one having assets of more than a million dollars. Each city has from one to several undertaking establishments, real estate offices, doctors, lawyers, and other professional men, in addition to a variety of smaller enterprises.

Some cities, like Miami, Tampa and Jacksonville, have entire city blocks where Negro businesses are the only ones to be found. There are eleven Negro newspapers in the State (weeklies), several large hotels, gas stations and movie houses.

There are several beaches and pleasure resorts operated as private ventures, with at least one of them a resort for Negroes of several states. Business and office buildings, owned by individuals or organizations, are found in large cities.

The 103,536 Negro children, youths and adults who attend public schools in the State do so in 936 schools. 2,377 teachers instruct them, and there are four Negro supervisors. There are 54 Negro principals in the State, in addition to those employed in private institutions. Brick, frame, and other buildings housing the pupils total 769.

According to the last census there are 43,108 Negroes of high school age in the state, of whom 4,894 are enrolled in the high schools. These high schools are in operation in 37 of the State's 67 counties.

Five of the public high schools are accredited, as are the high schools departments of two of the private colleges. One of the high schools, the Booker Washington school in Miami, has an enrollment of more than 2,000 with a faculty of 45. Stanton High in Jacksonville has an enrollment of 1,500.

There are eight colleges and private institutions up to or above high school grade. Largest of them is the State college at Tallahassee, called the Florida Agricultural and Mechanical College, with an annual enrollment of more than 1,000 and a large faculty. The school was originally vocational, but now carries full liberal arts courses; graduate work is offered in some fields.

The Baptist church has two institutions in the State: the Normal and Industrial College at St. Augustine with an estimated annual enrollment of about 300, and the Florida Memorial College at Live Oak, with an enrollment of about 250.

The Methodist Episcopal church has a junior college at Daytona Beach and a junior college at Jacksonville. Also at Jacksonville is the school operated by the African Methodist church, Edward Waters College. The Roman Catholic and Protestant Episcopal churches conduct parochial schools at Tampa, Miami, Jacksonville, and Pensacola.

In music, Florida has given the world several Negro composers and artists, at least one of whom has become internationally famous. James Rosamond Johnson,[30] born in Jacksonville in 1881, has written the musical score for a number of musical shows popular on Broadway, also a light classical operetta and a number of songs. Among the best known of his compositions was *Under the Bamboo Tree*, a great success early in the century. His *Negro National Anthem* is sung at every Negro patriotic gathering.

Choirs of unusual merit are found in a number of Negro churches in the larger cities, and several school groups have become nationally noted. There are annual song festivals at two of the colleges.

In literature Florida has produced two outstanding figures, both still living and active. Foremost is James Weldon Johnson, brother of Rosamond, whose *Autobiography of an Ex-Colored Man* went into several editions, and who has contributed, in addition, several other books. T. Thomas Fortune, born in Madison County, was one of the best known editors early in the century; for years he was editor of the *New York Age*.

Zora Hurston, born in Mandarin, has written three books which will perpetuate the folklore of her race; *Jonah's Gourd Vine*, *Mules and Men*, and *Their Eyes Were Watching God*.[31]

A prominent sculptress is Augusta Savage, born in Green Cove Springs. After a period of study abroad, she opened a studio in New York City. Among her well known works are busts of *Henry M. Flagler*, *Old Woman*, and a life-sized group idealizing Negro womanhood.[32]

Social

In his customs, lore and legend the Florida Negro does not differ greatly from his brother in other states, except that a large number of racial and national influences have colored his history.[33]

First of these, of course, is that of the Seminole, whose influence is readily detected in some of the ethnological types found in the State, particularly in the west Florida and Everglades region, and in the legends and myths of the Florida Negro. These are a combination of the matter of fact, simple tale of the Indian and the humorous, imaginative story of the Negro. Negro versions of some legends, found in the work of writers like Zora Hurston, have almost exact duplicates in the legends of the Seminole Indians, as for example, the story of how the rattlesnake got its rattle.

From the Indian races the Florida Negro has borrowed much. There are numerous hoodoo practices that have come from the superstitious natives of Haiti and Nassau. Among these is naningo, an extreme form of voodoo, characterized by a music of its own, a frenzied dance, and seances that some-times last as long as three days. Several instances of the naningo practice have been found in Tampa and Key West areas in recent years, and attempts are being made to record the music used in the weird ceremonies.[34]

In Miami, where the West Indians at some periods outnumber even the Negro population, West Indian customs are predominant in Negro sections. Bahamians, in their dress, customs, and religious practices, have an unusually strong influence.[35]

With one or two notable exceptions, the Florida Negro lives in Negro sec-tions. These sections have one point in common; they are for the most part separated from other sections of the city by the railroad tracks running through the community. This is especially true on the east coast, of which it has been truthfully said that the Florida East Coast Railroad is the dividing line between the races. From St. Augustine to Miami Negroes live west of the tracks. The division is more clearly seen in Miami, where about ninety per cent of all Negroes live in an area five blocks wide adjoining the west side of the tracks.[36]

In Miami, the Negroes even more than the whites refer to their section as "colored town"; in Ft. Lauderdale there have been popularity contests to elect a "ruler of Darktown." In Key West, which once had a curfew law prohibiting Negroes from being out after dark, they composed and sang a song about the law. It would seem that the Negro is at least philosophical.[37]

Relations with his white neighbors are constructive and co-operative. Near-ly all the larger cities have inter-racial committees or commissions, where beneficial legislation is often formulated. In Orlando and some other cities there are interracial groups of ministers. Especially active in the State is the Association of Southern White Women for the Prevention of Lynching, which, in addition to its main objective, works closely with Negro organiza-tions in the attempt to ameliorate the lot of the Negro.[38]

It is estimated that there are 90 Negro congregations in the State which have no church of their own, but worship with white members or their denominations. In addition, amiable relations exist between Bethune-Cookman College and Daytona Beach, the former white and the latter col-ored. There are frequent interchanges of forum speakers, and occasional visits by students.

Social Welfare

In the field of social welfare the Negro in Florida is at a decided disadvantage. Not only is the incidence of some diseases much greater among Negroes than among whites, but hospital and medical facilities are inadequate. According to the 1936 health report of Duval county, deaths from pellagra were five and one-half times as numerous among Negroes as among whites, deaths from tuberculosis 20 times, and deaths from venereal disease three and one-half times higher. Duval county, it should be noted, has better free medical facilities than most of the other counties in the State.

In spite of this abnormally high prevalence of disease, less than a dozen counties in the State have any hospital facilities for Negroes; a few others have out-patient departments. There is a government hospital at Lake City where Negro war veterans are sometimes accepted. The State college has a small infirmary; Tampa has a clinical service.

In recent years, with the help of Federal funds, four small, well-equipped sanitoria for Negro tuberculosis patients have been built in Escambia, Duval, Palm Beach, and Hillsborough counties. The first State Sanitorium for tuberculosis patients, also built with the help of federal money, will soon be opened at Orlando; it will accommodate 100 Negro patients.

In Miami a white specialist, Dr. S. Jay Flipse, conducts an annual clinic for Negro doctors of the State; at the State school in Tallahassee and annual clinic in general practice is held. To it come Negro doctors from all parts of the country.

The Negro insane are cared for at the State Hospital at Chattahoochee. While this institution admittedly cannot and does not provide for the major part of the State's Negro insane, it did care for about 250 Negroes from 1931 to 1935.

Several private and semi-private institutions, some of them connected with such enterprise as the Community Chest, care for Negro sick and indigent. In Jacksonville there is an Old Folks Home, a Child Placement Bureau and a Juvenile Detention Home for boys. There is none for girls in the state. Tampa has a well-conducted day nursery for the children of Negro working mothers; two similar nurseries, operated by the WPA, and another supported partly by Community Chest funds, are in Jacksonville.

Negro state prisoners are confined in the prison at Raiford or in the various road camps scattered through the counties; other prisoners are lodged in the city and county jails. Conditions are best at Raiford; here there are well constructed buildings, regular occupation for prisoners, and some educational and religious services. The latter is in charge of one of the few registered Negro prison chaplains in the country.[39]

Conditions in the city and county jails vary with the different counties.

Miami, Jacksonville, and Pensacola have fairly well-kept jails, although in the matter of segregation old and new offenders and the care of women prisoners leaves much to be desired in all counties.

Until very recently there was no state provision for the care of indigent Negro mothers with dependent children; with the assistance of the Federal government a program of this kind has just been started (1938).[40]

II

Slave Days in Florida

By the turn of the nineteenth century the number of Negro slaves in the State, in the sense that slaves were considered in neighboring states, was still small.[41] For the most part they were runaways from the United States who had been accepted by the Seminoles as slaves. There were some hundreds in and around St. Augustine, some at St. Marks, Pensacola, and other smaller communities. Under Indian ownership they lived under a modified form of slavery; it was more a matter of payment of part of their farm produce, a tribute such as a medieval serf paid, than the stringent bondage of Georgia and the Carolinas.[42] Aside from this tribute, the life of the enslaved Negro was fairly comfortable. They had their own towns and livestock and led an unsupervised existence.

Though the number of slaves in Florida was increasing slowly, it was increasing by leaps and bounds on the southern border of Georgia. Originally settled in 1738 as a buffer state between the slave-holding Carolinas and the semi-free Florida, Georgia lost little time in becoming a slave state itself. Its huge plantations, with their hundreds of slaves, pushed steadily towards the Florida border.

The transfer of Florida from Spanish to American control early in the nineteenth century heralded the approach of slave-holding on a large scale. Agricultural expansion began; plantations appeared on the Apalachicola, Suwannee and St. Johns rivers; the section around St. Augustine saw several others. It is thought that the number of Kingsley's slaves reached into the hundreds. Jefferson, Leon, and other sections of the cotton-and-tobacco belt—they were not counties then—had their large plantations; there were others farther west and south.

Classification of Slaves

With few exceptions, the slaves of Florida fell into two major classes: the farm workers, who constituted the vast majority, and the house slaves, the few lucky men and women who tended the grounds and homes of their masters and occasionally acted as overseers.

A few were mechanics, blacksmiths, carpenters, and workers in other crafts. These, however were found in numbers only in such areas of Jacksonville, Pensacola, Tallahassee, and other large settlements; the raising of cotton, tobacco, and food engaged the rest.

As in other sections, both men and women worked in the fields. Their work began at sunrise; on some plantations the "woods horn," cow horn, or bell summoning them to the day's labor sounded shortly before sunrise. Work continued, except for a noon period that ranged from a few minutes to an hour or more, unto dusk; then another horn or bell informed the slave that he might drop his hoe or plow.[43]

"Git it an' Run!"

While the food that the slaves ate seems to have been about the same on most plantations, the conditions under which it was eaten differed greatly. Some former slaves state that when the work signal sounded they had to "Git an' Run," that is, snatch up a sandwich or chunk of bread they had prepared the night before and eat it on the way to the field or after arriving there.

Others were given adequate time for breakfast. Lunch on some plantations was eaten in the field, too, and in the greatest possible haste; on others, lunchtime meant a rest period of varying length in which the slave who could eat quickly could also rest for some little time before returning to his labors.

Supper, on most plantations, was the slave's only important meal. This was always eaten in his cabin, with whatever family he might be fortunate enough to have. It was cooked by his wife or mother, after her own duties were finished in the field or at the Missus' house; the children, tended during the day by a Negro woman, shared supper with their parents. Supper usually consisted of corn meal in some form, meat—white salt pork—on some occasions, coffee of parched corn, and sometimes potatoes or some green vegetable.

The corn meal might be mush or bread. In the former case it would be boiled, with whatever scraps of meat or vegetable might be available, in a large iron pot out of which the whole family was served. If corn bread, it would have to be baked in the top of an iron spider, a large pan with a compartment over it in which coals could be heaped.

Potatoes, when available, were wrapped in the large leaves of the tannin plant, or sometimes in green corn shucks, and roasted in live coals. Corn, in season, was sometimes given to the slaves in its green form; they used it for both vegetable and beverage.

While these were the rations that the master saw and knew about, there were others that did not so readily come to his attention. Among these was the wild squash once found growing in the woods of west Florida. Since it was a prolific growth, slave owners might have had little objection to its use by slaves, except that it required a trip into the woods to procure it, and this was often a risky matter.

Pilfered eggs were another common dish. Where stumps and underbrush were burned to clear or fertilize the land, the ground beneath the fire would turn a clear, clean white, holding an intense heat. When this point was reached, eggs from stolen nests would be surreptitiously buried near the fire; a few minutes later a loud crack would inform the slave that his baked egg was ready to eat. Potatoes, also, when not included in regular fare, would be stolen and cooked in this manner.

There were several substitutes for coffee. Most common was corn or corn meal, parched until dark brown, then boiled. When this was not available, okra seeds and even parched potatoes were used.

Sundays and special occasions would bring dessert as an addition to the slave's meal. This would sometimes be potato bread, made of sweet potatoes, boiled until soft, then mashed and combined with grease and corn meal and baked until brown.

None of the Florida ex-slaves report the use of sugar in their cabins; when sweetening of any kind was afforded, it was sugar-cane molasses.

The amount of meat eaten depended entirely upon the master; it was not an accepted necessity in the slave diet. Some plantations provided it at least once a day, and kept well-filled storehouses. Others parceled it out very seldom, and then only the unused parts of the hogs or cows killed for the master's use. Frequent disappearance of hogs was a consequence in the latter case.

Salt at a Premium

One commodity seems to have given both master and slave great cause for worry—salt; the master, because of the expense and trouble often necessary to secure it, and the slave because he so frequently went without it.

In many cases it was obtained from boiled sea water; so great would have been the cost of purchasing it that one plantation owner near Monticello used to take a team and a slave and travel 40 miles to the Gulf and there boil down a week's supply. The process was slow and laborious.

The slaves used other methods of obtaining it. On some plantations they would scrape the floor of the smoke-house at every opportunity. One slave used to wash the smoke-house floor, carefully saving his scrub-water; with this brine she would do her seasoning.[44]

No scrap of fat or drop of grease was ever wasted: the grease from the "big house" and the cabin alike was carefully kept in a special container.

At certain intervals oak or cypress wood was burned and the ashes placed in a vat or tub. The ashes would then be soaked in water for several days, then the water would be drawn off into a pot. In this pot would be placed the accumulation of grease, and the whole mixture boiled for several hours. The potash and grease mixture would be poured out to cool, after which it was cut into squares. The plantation then had its supply of soap.

Beef tallow, melted and poured into molds, provided the light for the plantation. Some of the slaves were adept at placing strings in the hardening tallow in such a manner that a creditable candle would result. On many plantations, however, only the master's house got the candles; the cabins were illuminated by fireplace.[45]

The oak tree came in for duty again when the leather was to be tanned. Oak chips or ashes would be soaked in water, as in potash making, and after the solution reached a certain strength cowhides were placed in it. After a few days the hides would be taken out and dried, later to be fashioned into shoes, harnesses, and other articles.

All Dye Together

Both mistress and maid during the Florida's slave period had a taste for gay color in dress. Cloth was made on many plantations by the women with the help of those children too young to work in the fields.

This white cotton cloth could be dyed in a number of ways. The indigo plant, once grown here commercially, is still found in a wild state and provided blue coloring; the poke berry gave a desirable red. Oak bark provided varying shades of brown and the walnut an ineradicable dark brown.

On some plantations, where the owners gave the women a white cotton dress once or twice a year, this method of coloring was effectively used to afford the slave woman a gay change of dress for her infrequent trips to "meetin'."

However, the dress of the slave was not generally colorful; the men wore simple pants and shirt, both coarse. The women wore tight bodices and full gathered skirts; those were the days of half a dozen petticoats. Occasionally a slave was the proud possessor of her mistress' discarded hoop skirt, but this was the exception. Hoops were expensive, but grape vines and bamboo served for home-made hoops of mistress as well as slaves.

Good Masters and Bad

Though a slave might know what kind of food and working conditions to expect on the plantation where he worked, he never knew what to expect if he changed masters. On some plantations there were special privileges given to the slaves, such as dances, visits and gatherings. On others, they would be forbidden to attend even the usual church meetings. At the hamlet of Sixteen, Florida, one woman saw her son killed for attending church, and was threatened with death herself if she did not stop crying over the incident.

There seem to have been fewer really "hard" plantations, however, in Florida than in Mississippi, Alabama, and other states where there were more and larger plantations. Some owners, like the Sandersons in Duval County and the Hansons in St. Johns, would carefully avoid separating families when buying or selling slaves; some almost never sold a slave and refused to employ overseers who beat slaves. One slave remembers that he never was forced to do any strenuous work as long as he beat the slaves of other masters at marbles; another was permitted to earn himself extra money by distilling moonshine. Several recall having been permitted to plant small gardens for themselves near their cabins. In Leon County one master's two daughters spent each Sunday teaching the slaves how to read and write. Thomas and Bryant Folsom, in Jefferson County, often staged rival parties to see which could give his slaves better times.[46]

That some of these kind masters may have been known to the slaves is evident in the fact that there are several instances of persons who voluntarily entered slavery in order to secure the freedom of others. One such instance occurred on the Cone plantation in Columbia County; another was a three years' slavery in the vicinity of St. Augustine. In this case the sum of $850 had to be paid in work.

In Columbia County, Cato Smith, a free Connecticut Negro travelling in Florida out of curiosity, entered into a seven year period of slavery in order to free the woman he wanted to marry. He was fortunate, however; within four years he had his wife together with a small income from his labors.[47]

Slaves reacted differently to cruel masters; some were thoroughly broken, while others resorted to retaliation, not always open, but sometimes quite effective. One woman, tiring of the beatings given to her by an overseer, hacked him to death with a hoe[48]; another killed the Negro overseer on her master's plantation when he goaded her too far, then went to her master and bade him to punish her as he saw fit. She says that he sent her to a cabin by herself and told her to "keep your mouth shut and only do whatever work your mistress has for you to do and behave yourself."[49]

"Parson" Andrews, nearing his hundredth birthday and full of reminiscences about early days in Florida, described the attempt of the "paterollers" to round up a group of slaves and return them to their plantations. The slaves, he says, were on their way back to their cabins anyway, but had stopped at the home of another slave for a brief visit. As they started to leave several of the dread paterollers burst in. One of the slaves reached into a pile of hot ashes with which a hide was being cured, and threw them into the faces of the patrols. In the resulting confusion all the slaves escaped and returned to their cabins.[50]

Escapes were much more numerous than reprisals. In describing the news of emancipation one west Florida Negro states that when the gun sounded—the signal that they were to get news of their freedom—slaves came out of all parts of the woods. Some of them had been in hiding for over a year.

Some of the escapes were dramatic. One slave was pursued by several bloodhounds, and when they tracked him to his hiding place in the creek, one by one the bodies of the hounds who entered the water after him came floating to the surface. He was not captured.

Some masters dealt summarily with slaves who attempted to escape; others regarded the desire to seek liberation as natural, and ever forbade the paterollers to punish their escaped slaves before or upon returning them. One slave escaped three times as a boy, returned voluntarily twice, and remained on his plantation as the most dutiful servant of his mistress when his master went to war. Another escaped, was captured, severely beaten and buried alive;

others slaves surreptitiously exhumed him, revived him and sent him on his way again. He was not recaptured.

The use of bloodhounds is recorded as early as 1837, when several of them were imported from Cuba and loosened in the St. Johns River area to regain a number of Indians who had escaped into the country occupied jointly by Seminole Indians and free Negroes. On that occasion the bloodhounds did not succeed in locating a single refugee.

Despite the fact that escapes were blamed on whatever free Negroes could be found in a section, many of them were aided or engineered by white people who were either abolitionists or desired slaves for purposes of traffic and used the escape method of securing them.

In Leon County, near the Campbell plantation, were several of the abolitionists, and they assisted many of the slaves of the vicinity to gain freedom. In Jefferson and Madison counties surrounding the Pamell and Lenton plantations, were poorer slave owners who would assist in the liberation of slaves from the larger plantations and sell them to itinerant slave traders who came through the section around the first of the year.

Among the abolitionists the case of the Hanson brothers in St. Augustine is interesting. Both brothers came to the state during the early days of the Seminole War to fight the Indians. One of them returned to his native New England, thoroughly convinced of the iniquity of the institution of human bondage; the other remained in the state and establishes a large plantation worked by slaves about three miles southwest of St. Augustine. Paradoxically, slaves would escape from one Hanson to be aided in reaching Canada by the other. The old Hanson plantation is now the site of a large Negro school.

Due to the friendliness of the Seminole Indians, the relative inexperience of Florida slave owners in practices of slavery, the number of Negroes who escaped or attempted to escape was still high in the State by about 1835–40; after that time, however, it was not unusual to see plantations employing the "buck and gag" rule for runaway slaves, a punishment wherein the slave was doubled about a hoe, shovel or board, tied, and allowed to remain in the sun part of the day. The "bell and stocks" system, where an iron halter was placed around the waist and neck of the slave and a loud bell attached to it, was another favorite method of punishment. And of course recalcitrant slaves could always be sold to masters outside the state.

"Slave raiders" were another product of these escapes. Florida Clayton, daughter of a white father and a free Negro mother, relates that a large covered wagon used to come periodically to her section near Tallahassee and remain for weeks sometimes; unfortunate escaped Negroes and sometimes Negroes kidnapped from plantations would be rounded up, bound, and placed inside it. Eventually it would drive away, after decreasing the Negro population in the vicinity. Florida recalls the names of "Mister Nimrod" and "Mister Sheehee" as leaders of the enterprise, which employed a number of hounds. She thinks the slaves were sold in Alabama.[51]

"The Paterollers"

The "paterollers," despite liberties that some of them took, were not usually slave raiders. Their duties were the return of slaves to their masters, and they were particularly active when the War took many of the masters away from their plantations.

Much of the fear in which the paterollers were held was due to the fact that they were accustomed to administer a beating to the slaves before returning them to their owners. This was the most dread factor the escaping slave had to take into consideration.

Self-appointed "paterollers" were not uncommon; sometimes they were thrill-seeking young hoodlums who saw in the patrol idea an opportunity to catch and beat unfortunate runaways, enjoying meanwhile a certain amount of esteem as well as a lucrative profit.

Eugenics to Order

The rapid breeding of more slaves, to replace deaths and natural retirement in some cases, and for purposes of sale and trade in others, was desired on most plantations. Thus we find women whose sole duty was that of "breeder." Their job was to have children, big healthy children, and they would be mated with the most promising of the men. It was not unusual for a breeder to bear twelve or fourteen children during her active life. Her daily duties were confined to light work around the house.[52]

Some of the better-looking women were mated with master or overseer; this resulted in the much sought after mulattoes, used as house slaves. They were thought to be less strong than other Negroes, and care was used in working them.

Another unique plantation job was that of "suckler." Her duty was to nurse the babies while their mothers were at work in the fields. On some plantations mothers gave up their babies to sucklers while they were less than a week old, and not infrequently did women leave the fields till their labor pains started.

Marriage Customs

Some plantations owners not only permitted but encouraged the marriage of their slaves. When both parties lived on the same plantation, they might be given legal and religious ceremony to seal their union; if one party lived on another plantation, such a master might even intercede for the purchase of the other party.

On other plantations, though, the marriage ceremony took the form of "jumping over the broom." This was performed after work hours in some cabin. In the presence of a few slaves a broom was placed on the floor or slightly above it, and while various words were mumbled, the bride would leap across the broom, then the groom. They were then married.

By 1859 religious service had become an indispensable part of the activities of the slaves on most of the Florida plantations. There were few owners who did not permit their slaves to listen to service in either the white churches, the colored meeting-houses on some neighborhood plantation, or both.

Reasons for this appear to have been both economic and spiritual, since the preachers, whether white of Negro, generally based their texts on the theme of "Love you master . . . don't steal . . . be obedient," in return for which "The Kingdom of Heaven will be yours when you die." The natural inference was that it would be quite another kingdom while the slave lived if he failed to obey these profound religious preachments.

At the services in the white churches, to which the slaves were often allowed to come, they would sit in some part of the church especially reserved for them. This was sometimes in the back, sometimes in the front, and sometimes in the gallery. In some churches a special sermon would be preached for the slaves after the regular service.

Thin Dresses and Cold Water

At periodic intervals baptism services were held at or near the larger plantations. After several weeks had been spent preparing the slaves to "accept Christ," a large enough group would be ready to hold a "christ'nin'." Robed in a single dress-like garment of white, the candidates, men and women, would be taken to some nearby stream. Here the preacher would go through an elaborate ceremony, accompanied by the singing and "falling out" of the witnessing slaves. "Falling out" was the working up of an emotional fever, ending in an unconscious fit, real or simulated. After a little excitement over the "falling out" the other slaves would continue their singing and shouting. A triumphal march back to the plantation would follow the immersion in the cold water of the baptismal candidates.[53]

Some plantations permitted regular Sunday school classes, sometimes taught by kindly young daughters of the master, and sometimes by house slaves who could read. Others made attendance at the Sunday meeting compulsory. One slave complains that "after we had worked in the field from half-past four to half-past six every day in the week, we would have to get up at seven o'clock on Sunday and listen to the preacher." At least one plantation is known to have a full time preacher, who wasn't too well liked "'cause he went 'round dressed up in a high hat all the time, whatchin' us and meddlin' an' tellin' the master ev'ything we done."

Beliefs, Superstitions, Cures

The constant efforts of the preachers to center the slaves' thoughts on the hereafter did not stop them from having an elaborate system of signs, beliefs, and cures for troubles here on earth. Many of their remedies for illness, like ipecac, were no doubt efficacious, though their potency was always given a supernatural rather than natural explanation.

An unusual help was the mixture of "graveyard dust and lightwood splinters that my Uncle Bob and Uncle July smeared on their feet when they run away, and Bob Amos' hounds couldn' break the spell and catch them." Cotton seeds sprinkled on the ground kept them from getting cold while they were hiding in the woods.

Hogs, according to the belief of the slaves, could see the wind with ease and it was always blood-red to them. On Christmas the wind would evidently be what the hogs would talk about because early on Christmas morning all the animals talked fluently.

The rind of a watermelon worn around the neck would eliminate all trouble for a child in teething, and a pearl button, if melons were not in season, would accomplish a fair imitation of the same miracle. A concoction of boiled wasps' nests and vinegar would aid the child who was slow in learning to walk; nursing occasionally at the breast by a child of two, three, or more years would save it from later trouble with its teeth and bones. Sheep droppings made an excellent remedy, used either as a liniment or a medicine, for a number of ailments, and the ipecac plant was a great favorite for any ailment of stomach or respiratory tract.[54]

Amusements

Plantation life was not always all work and no play. There were definite occasions for merriment and even celebration on many plantations; these ran from the usual visits of individuals or small groups to the large festivals occasionally staged. Mention has already been made of the two masters who engaged in friendly rivalry to see who could give his slaves the biggest party. There were others who let their slaves go to other plantations for affairs at certain times.

Christmas was the biggest of these occasions. On some plantations there would be parties at Christmas time with extra food allotments, meat and other goodies from the master's house, and numerous other presents for the slaves. No ex-slave remembers having been overlooked when it came to these Christmas presents. The men usually got new shoes or articles of clothing; the women were made happy with household articles or discarded, but welcome, dresses of the mistress. Several plantations gave their slaves, in addition, cash presents.

New Year brought a short day in the field or a holiday, and another gift of extra food, with the highly prized meat allotment. New Year's night, on some plantations, was spent in singing, dancing and visiting.

The end of a crop, like tobacco, cotton, or sugar-cane, was cause for celebration also. In at least a few cases there were celebrations that corresponded very closely to the Green Corn Dance of the Seminoles, though just how much the Seminole dance influenced the slaves is uncertain.

Occasionally, visits to neighboring plantations would be made on a large scale. These would bring forth carefully hoarded stores of molasses, meal, potatoes, and other foods; if there was much music on improvised banjos and much jollity, the master might even contribute a few delicacies for the entertainment of the visitors.

Singing and dancing around a fire in front of one of the cabins would last late into the night and any previously missed opportunities for courting were eagerly seized by the younger couples. Young husbands and wives, living apart, made the most of these occasions, and even children were sometimes allowed to participate.

Freedom at Last

At various times during 1865 freedom came to the slaves on Florida plantations. Few of them seem to have observed their day of emancipation at the same time; some were liberated upon the cessation of the war, others after their crops were harvested.

Nearly every ex-slave has a different experience to tell of his long awaited emancipation. To some it came with the crack of shooting guns, soldiers riding up to them and reading them long and important proclamations that they couldn't understand, even when blue-clad Negro soldiers came to the plantations to help them celebrate. To others emancipation was a guarded whisper from one to another, then a long wait for darkness so that they could slip away from the masters from whom they still expected harshness.

As in other states, many refused to leave their plantations. In Duval, St. Johns, Jefferson and some other counties, many of the slaves remained on the plantations where their descendants may be found today under a sharecropping arrangement; others were given tracts of land for their own use.

Many left immediately for the cities. In Jacksonville, where a number of northern soldiers were quartered, temporary houses had to be provided for hundreds of them. Confusion naturally resulted, intensified by the Negro's entrance into politics, religion, and other fields. Economic helplessness settled on the Negro's shoulders for a time.

Gradually, however, his situation improved, and today the descendants of the former slaves of Florida plantations and Negroes from other states live in a fair degree of harmony and progress.

III

Sidelights on Slavery

Perhaps no form of social life has been more violently defended and condemned than slavery. To some, especially when viewed through the softening haze of time, the institution of slavery seems like paradise on earth; to others it is just the opposite. What did the slaves themselves think of the system? Before it is too late American Guide field workers have interviewed a number of slaves and asked them to tell what they remembered. Curiously, the subjects of both the following interviews were women, whether because women live longer or are better talkers than men would be hard to say.[55]

Margrett Nickerson

Margrett Nickerson was born to William A. Carr on his plantation near Jackson, Leon County, many years ago.[56] She now lives in Jacksonville with her daughter.

"Mr. Kilgo wuz de fust overseer I 'member; I wuz big enuf to tote meat an' stuff fum de smokehouse to de kitchen an' to tote water an' git wood fur granny to cook de dinner an' fur de sucklers who nu'sed de babies, an' I ca'ied dinners back to de hans."

"On dis plantation wes 'bout a hunnert haid. We done de cookin' in de fiahplace in iron pots, an' de meals wuz plenty of peas, greens, cornbread, burn' co'n fur coffee. Sometime de marster bot coffee fur us; we got water fum de open well. Jes 'fore de big gun fiahed dey fotched my pa fum de bay whar he wuz makin' salt; he done hear dem say de Yankees is comin' an' he sure wuz glad.

"We done had rice an' cotton an co'n an' taters what got to be tended, an' cowhides to be tanned an' thread to be spinned. They done made de thread into ropes for plow lines."

"Ole Marse Carr done feed us, but he didn' care what an' whar, jes so you made money, an' when you made five an' six bales o' cotton he say you ain' done nothin'.

"When de big gun fiahed on a Sat'day me an' Cave an' Minnie Howard wuz settin' up co'n fur de plowers to come 'long an' put dirt to em; Carr he read de free papers to us on Sunday an' de co'n an' cotton dey had to be tended to. Marse Carr he done tole us he gwine gi' us de net proceeds"—here she chuckles—"what turn out to be co'n an' cotton stalks. Den he ask dem whut would stay wid him to step off on de right, an' dem dat wuz leavin' to step off on de lef'."

"My pa made soap fum ashes when he clean de new groun'; he done take a hopper to put de ashes in, made a li'le stool 'side the house, to put de ashes in an' po'red water on it to drip. Den at night when he git off fum work he done put in de grease an' make de soap. I done make it myself sometime, an' I makes it now."

"My step-pa uster make shoes fum cowhides fur de farm han's on de plantation an' fur ev'ybuddy 'cep ole Marse an' his fambly; deys wuz diffunt, fine."

"My gramma Phoebe Austin—my mother wuz name Rachel Jackson an' my pa wuz name Edmun' Jackson; my mother an' uncle Robert an' Joe wuz stole fum Virginny an' fetched here. I don' know no niggers dat 'listed in de War. I don' 'member much about de War, only when dey started talking 'bout drillin' men; Joe Sanders wuz a Lootenen'. Marse Carr's sons, Tom an' Willie went to de war.

"We didn' had no doctors, only de grannies; we mostly used hippecat (ipecac) fur medicine.

"Lak I done tole you, Kilgo wuz de fus' overseer I ricollec', den Sanders wuz nex' an' Joe Sanders atter him; John C. Heywood came in atter Sanders, an' when de big gun fiahed ole man Brockington wuz dere. I never saw a nigger sol' but dey ca'ied 'em fum our house an' I never seen em no mo'."

"We had church wid de white preachers an' dey tole us to mine our masters and missus an' we would be saved. Dey don' never tole us nuthin' 'bout Jesus."

"When de big gun fiahed Ole man Carr had six sacks uf Confederate money whut he wuz ca'ing wid him to Athens, Georgia, an' all de time if any uf us gals whar he wuz done ax him, Marse, please gi' us some money"—here she raises her voice to a high pitiful tone—"he say I aint got a cent, an' right den he would have a chis' so full it would take a whole passle uv slaves to move it. He had plenty of co'n, taters, pumkins, hogs, cows evything, but he didn' gi' us nothing but strong pain close and plenty to eat; we slep' in ole common beds an' my pa made up li'le cribs an' put hey in dem fur de chillen."

"Now if you wanted to keep in wid Marse Carr don' drap you' shoes in de fiel' an' leave 'em or he'd beat you. You mus' tote you' shoes in de fiel' he'd say, you gin haided debbil, droppin' you' shoes an' everything over de field."

"Now jes lissen, I wanna tell you all I kin, but I wants to tell it right. Wait now, I don' wanna tell no mistakes an' I don' wanna lie on nobody. I ain' mad now an' I know taint no use to lie. I'se taking my time, I done prayed an' got all de malice out o' my heart an' I ain' gwine tell no lie fer un, an' I ain' gwine tell no lie on um. I ain' never seed no slaves sole by Marse Carr; he wuz allus tellin me he wuz gwine sell me but he never did; he sole my pa's fust wife, though."

"Dere wuz Uncle George Bull, he could read an' write. Chile, de white folks didn' lak no nigger whut could read an' write. Carr's wife, Miss Jane, useter teach us Sunday school but she didn' low us to tech a book wid us hans. So dey useter jes take Uncle George Bull an' beat him fur nuthin; dey would beat him an' take him to de lake an' put him on a log an' shuv him in de lake, but he allus swimm' out. When dey didn' do dat dey would beat him tel de blood run outen him an' den trow him in de ditch in de fiel' an' kivver him up wid dirt, haid an' yeres, an' den stick a stick up at his haid. I wuz a water toter an' done stood an' seem um do him dat a wat more'n once, an' I done stood an' looked at um tel dey went way to de udder rows an' den I grabbed de dirt offen him an' he'd bresh de dirt off an' say t'ank-you, git his hoe an' go on back to work. Dey beat him lak dat an' he didn' do a t'ing to git dat sort of treatmen'."

"Some uv de slaves run away, lots uv em. Some done got caught an' when dey ketched em dey put bells on em; fust dey would put a iron ban' aroun' dey neck an amunder one aroun dey wais' an' rivet em together down de back; de bell would hang aroun de ban around dey neck an' it would ring when de slave walked an' den dey wouldn' git away. Some uv em wore dese bells three an' four month, an' when dey time wuz up dey would take em offen em. Jake Overstreet, George Bull, John Green, Ruben Golder, Jim Bradley an' a host uv others wore dem bells. Dis is whut I know, not whut somebuddy else say. I done see dis mysel'. En mussus, when se big gun fiahed, de runaway slaves comed out de woods fum all d'rections. We wuz in de fiel' when it fiahed, but I members dey wuz all glad.

"Atter de war, we work' but we got pay fur it."

"Ole man Pierce an' some others would call some kine uv a perlitical meetin, but I couldn' never understan' whut dey wuz talkin' bout. We didn' had no kine uv schools an' all I knows bout dem is I sent my chillens in Leon an' Gadsden county.

Mama Duck

"Who is the oldest settler, white or colored, that you know of in Tampa?"

"See Mama Duck," the grinning elevator boy told us, "she bout a hunnert year ole."[57]

So down into the scrub we went and found the old woman hustling about from washpot to pump. "I'se mighty busy now, cookin breakfas," she said, "but ef you come back in bout a hour I'll tell you what I kin bout ole times in Tampa."

Her dust-covered dog met us with elaborate demonstrations of welcome on the return visit.

"Gwan away f'm here, Spot; dat Gemman aint gwine feed you nuthin. You keep yo' dirty paws offen his close."

Mama Duck sat down on a rickety box, motioning to us to another on the shaky old porch. "Take care you don' fall thoo dat ol' flo'," she cautioned. "Hit bout ready to go to pieces, but I'se way behin' on de rent, so I caint ask em to have hit fixed."

"I see you have no glass in the windows—doesn't it get you wet when it rains?"

"Not me, cause I gits ovah on de udder side o' de room when hit rains. Didn't have no do', neither, when I moved in. Young folks round here used to use hit fo' a co't house afo' I come."

"A what?"

"Court'n house. Kep a-comin atter I done move in, an' I had to shoo em away. Dat young rascal comin yonda, he one of em. I claiah to goodness," and Mama Duck raised her voice for the trespasser's benefit, "I wisht I had me a fance to keep folks outa my yahd."

"Qau-a-ck, quack, quack," the dressed-up young Negro mocked, as he passed on, grinning.

"Dat don' worry me none; I don' let nuthin worry me—worry makes folks gray-haided," the old woman said, as she scratched her thinly covered dome. Three braids, about the length and thickness of a flapper's eyebrow stuck out at odd angles, and there were not more than a dozen gray hairs streaking the rusty black."

"I sho' had plenty chance to worry effen I wanted to," she mused, as she sipped ice water from a fruit jar foul with dirty fingermarks. "Relief folks got me on de black list. Dey give rations to young folks what's wukkin an don' give me narry a mouthful."

"How's that?"

"Well, in de fust place, dey wanted me to go to de po' house. I wanted to take mah trunk 'long, an dey wouldn' let me. I got some t'ings in dere I be'n havin' nigh into a hunnert year. Got my ol' blue-back Webster, onlies' book I evah had, 'scusin' mah Bible. T'ink I wanna thow dat stuff away? No-o suh!" Mama Duck pushed the dog away from a cracked pitcher on the floor and refilled her fruit jar. "So dey black-list me, cause I won' kiss dey feets. I aint kissin nobody's feets—wouldn't kiss my own mammy's."

"Well we'd all do lots of things for our mothers that we wouldn't do for anyone else."

"Mebbe you would, but not me. My mammy put me in a hickry basket when I was a day an' a half ole with nuttin on but my belly ban' an' a di'per. Took me down in de cotton patch an' sot de basket on a stump in de bilin' sun."

"What in the world did she do that for?"

"Cause I was black. All de othah young uns was bright. My granmammy done hear me bawlin' an' go fetch me to my mammy's house.

"'Dat you, Mammy' she say, sweet as pie, when granmammy poun' on de do'."

"'Don' you nevah call me Mammy no mo',' granmammy say. 'Any woman what'd leave a po' li'le mite lak dis to perish to death aint fittin to ve no datter o' mine.'

"So granmammy tuk me to raise. I aint nevah seen my mammy sence, an' I nevah want to."

"What did your father think of the way she treated you?"

"Nevah knew who mah daddy was, an' I reckon she didn' neither. I was bawned at Richard, Virginia, Mah sister an' brothah be'n dead too many year to count—I de las' o' de fam'ly."

"Do you remember anything about the Civil War?"

"What dat?"

"The Civil War, when they set the slaves free."

"Oh, de fust war, you mean. I reckon I does—had three chillen, boys, bawned befo' de war. Mah fust mastah didn' make us wuk none when we was chillens. All I done is play. When I was ole enough to wuk, dey tuk us to

Pelman, Georgia. I nevah wukked in de fiel's, not den, dey allus let me nuss de chillens. Den I got married in granmammy's kitchen an' went to us own log house. By an' by mah mastah sole me an' mah baby to de man what had de plantation nex' to ours—his name was John Lee. He was good to me, an' let me see mah chillens.

"No, I nevah got no beatins f'm mah mastah when I was a slave. Onlies' t'ing I evah got was a little slap on the han', lak dat. Didn' hurt none. But I'se seen cullud men on de Bradley plantation git frammed out plenty. De whippin' boss was Joe Sylvester, a white man. He had pets 'mongst the wimmen folks, an' used to let some of 'em off light when dey 'sarved a good beatin'."

"How would he punish his pets?"

"Sometimes he jes bop em 'crost de yere wid a battlin' stick.."

"A what?"

"Battlin' sick, lak dis. You don' know what a battlin' sick is? Well, dis yere one. Use hit for washin' close. You lif' em outa de wash pot wid de battlin' stick, den you lay 'em on de battlin' block, dis yere stump. Den you beat de dirt out wid de battlin' stick."

"Great guns, that stick would knock a horse down!"

"Nossuh, wan't nigh as bad as some o' de othahs got. He had pets 'mongst de mens, too, but dey got hit a li'le wusser dan de wimmens. Effen dey wan't too mean, he jes strap em 'crost de sharp side of a bar'l an' give em a few right smaht licks wid a bull whip."

"H'm—they did get off light, didn't they; and what would he do to the bad ones?"

"Well sometimes dey try to run away; den he mek em cross de han's, lak dis. Den he tie a rope roun dey wrists an' thow hit ovah a tree limb. Den he pull em up so dey toes jes touch de groun an smack em on de back an' rump wid a heavy wooden paddle, fixed full o' holes. Know what dem holes was fur? Ev'y hole mek a blister. Den he mek em lay down on de groun whilst he bus' all dem blisters wid a rawhide whip."

"I should think that would kill any man."

"Nevah heard o' nobody dyin' f'm gittin' a beatin'. Some couldn' wuk for a day or two. Sometimes dey thow salt brine on dey backs, or smear turpentine to make it git well quicker."

"Well I suppose you're glad those days are over."

"Not me. I was a heap bettah off den I is now. Allus had sumpin' to eat an' a place to stay. No sech t'ing as gittin' on a black list. Mighty hard on a pusson ol' as me not to git no rations an' not have no reg'lar job."

"How old are you?"

"I don' know, 'zackly. Mebbe—wait a minute, I didn' show you my pitcher what wuz in de paper, did I? I caint read, but somebody say dey put how ol' I is under mah pitcher in dat paper."

Mama Duck rummaged through a cigar box and brought out a page of a Pittsburgh newspaper, dated a year ago. It was so badly worn that it was almost illegible, but it showed a picture of the old woman and below it was given her age, 109.

In answer to the question regarding the length of her residence in Tampa she said that she didn't remember. "Come here when dey was only one sto'," she mused. "Hit b'long to Ol' man Mugge. Dey raised cotton where Plant City is now. I picked some cotton dere, den I come to Tampa an' atter a while I got a job nussin Mister Perry Wall's chillen. Cullud folks jes mek out de bes' dey could. Some of em lived in tents tell dey could cut logs an' build houses wid sticks an' dirt chimbleys."

Judging only by the appearance of this wiry old woman, it is hard to realize that the Massachusetts lawyer, John Quincy Adams, virtual author of the Monroe Doctrine, was serving as this country's sixth president when Kate Bennet left her unwanted black baby in a Virginia cotton patch. An interesting study, this patient old crone resigned to unpleasant circumstances over which she has no control, curbing her temper in the face of petty annoyances, sitting in a dusty alley with her cur dog, as she stolidly waits for the last curtain to fall on her long drama of life.

A Slaveholder Speaks

Mention has previously been made of a slaveholder by no means unfavorably disposed towards the Negroes, since he married a Negro woman and left her his property. Perhaps his opinion of slavery is as impartial as any we can have, and it has the merit of being practical and not theoretical. The following excerpt is from the *Patriarchal System of Society*, by Zephaniah Kingsley, a book which ran through four editions:

> About 25 years ago, I settled a plantation of St. Johns River, in Florida, with about 50 new African Negroes, many of whom I brought from the coast myself. They were mostly fine young man and women, and nearly in equal numbers. I never interfered with their connubial concerns, nor domestic affairs, but let them regulate these after their own manner. I taught them nothing but what was useful, and what I thought would add to their physical and moral happiness. I encouraged as much as possible dancing, merri-

ment and dress, for which Saturday afternoon and night and Sunday morning were dedicated; and, after allowance, their time was usually employed in
hoeing their corn and getting a supply of fish for the week. Both men and
women were very industrious. Many of them made 20 bushels of corn to
sell, and they vied with each other in dress and dancing, and as to whose
woman was the finest and prettiest. They were perfectly honest and obedient, and appeared quite happy, having no fear but that of offending me;
and I hardly ever had occasion to apply other correction than shaming them.
If I exceeded this, the punishment was quite light, for they hardly ever failed
in doing their work well. My object was to excite their ambition and attach-
ment by kindness, not to depress their spirits by fear and punishment. I
never allowed them to visit, for fear of bad example, but encouraged the
decent neighboring people to participate in their weekly festivity, for which
they always provided an ample entertainment themselves, as they had an
abundance of hogs, fowls, corn, and all kinds of vegetables and fruit. They
had nothing to conceal from me, and I had no suspicion of any crime in
them to guard against. Perfect confidence, friendship, and good understanding reigned between us; they increased rapidly. After a few years, this pleasant and profitable state of harmony was interrupted by the revolution of
1812. A war party of Seminole Indians attacked the plantations in my absence; caught, bound, and carried off, or killed 40 of them, whose reluctance
in going with the invaders may be imagined from the following circum-
stance. The wife of a young man they had tied and were driving off, that her
husband, that were too strong to be handled and who had his young child in
arms, might follow; but that his master should never say that he was a
runaway negro; upon which the Indian shot him, and he died the next day.

IV

What the Florida Negro Does

It is estimated that more than a quarter million of Florida's 459,000 Negroes are normally employed at some gainful occupation.[58] Seasonally both figures are higher, due to the influx of thousands of workers who come to the State in winter following the tourist industries, and due also to the relatively higher percentage of available work during the tourist season.

In the past seven years this number of gainful workers, as in the rest of the country, has suffered a sharp reduction. Relief work, odd jobs, small businesses and part-time employment, however, have partially made up for the lowered total of normal workers.

There are few fields of skilled or unskilled labor that these workers do not enter. Among the skilled trades there are carpenters, bricklayers, locomotive firemen, building contractors, electricians and even a bridge builder. The unskilled laborers, of course, comprise the vast majority of Florida's Negro workers. These include many hundreds in citrus work—picking, packing, tree culture, etc. that make up the unskilled or less skilled branches of this work— thousands in the tourist industries, and farm laborers, turpentine workers, logging-camp laborers, and many others.

Women are conservatively estimated to constitute at least one-third of the gainfully employed Negroes in the State. Their work is largely domestic, although there are thousands employed in the few factories that have thus far employed them. These factories include citrus plants, cigar factories and other light industries. There are large numbers employed in the laundries of the

State, and among unusual occupations, a few grade phosphate rock in a central Florida quarry.

It is difficult to ascertain any exact figures in the increase of employed Negroes in the State during tourist season; a good season will double and even triple the Negro population of some communities, while a bad season will see relatively few enter the State. It is known, however, that for the past five years Miami's Negro population from November 1 to April 1 has been more than double its usual 30,000 population; Orlando boasts a doubled population beginning at the same time, and the cities of the lower east coast receive the bulk of their transient Negroes in the wake of the tourists in the fall and early winter. In 1937, during the winter season, the Negro population of the State is believed to have been increased by at least 100,000.

Where the Negro Employment is Heaviest

The bulk of the employment for Negro males falls into three categories; agriculture (exclusive of citrus), domestic employment, and commerce (including shipping). Agriculture, with its many different types of work, is generally the largest of the three major divisions, although seasonal increases often bring the domestic total above it. Domestic employment, which includes the tourist industries, is normally second; then comes the hauling of the State's imports and exports on docks, railroads, trucks to warehouses and factories. Following closely are turpentining, often classified under agriculture, the lumber industries, and the building trades.

This division of Negro labor makes a geographical grouping easy. Agriculture's thousands, for instance, are largely employed in the truck farm regions of the lower east coast and the Everglade margins, the central, south-central and north-east Florida tomato, cucumber, celery, and potato regions, and the tobacco, peanut and cotton areas in the northwestern part of the State.

The domestic fields center around the lower east coast, with central Florida—Orlando, the lower St. Johns River and the Florida lake region—showing increasing growth. A few cities on the Gulf share the seasonal tourist industry increases, but with the possible exceptions of St. Petersburg, Pensacola, and Tampa, these increases are not pronounced.

Commerce and shipping confine their labor largely to the seaport cities or those which have wide railroad facilities. In Tampa, for instance, which handles the bulk of the State's phosphate shipping, much of the lower Florida vegetable shipments and a considerable volume of citrus, there are 3,000 longshoremen employed more or less regularly, with an additional 2,000 or more occasional workers. Jacksonville, with its imports for the State, exports of general Florida products, and the handling to lumber, naval stores, and scrap iron, has a few hundred more than Tampa working on the docks or in the railroad shops. Pensacola is the third city in the state for shipping workers, with more than 2,000 registered in labor organizations or known to receive employment on the docks regularly. Miami is fourth, and Ft. Lauderdale, Fernandina, Port Tampa, Ft. Pierce, Key West and other cities also employ considerable numbers.

The Economic Status of the Florida Negro Laborer

The Negro laborer in Florida enjoys an economic status similar to that of his brothers in other southern states. Some Florida industries afford him good working conditions, fair wages, and reasonably steady employment. This is true of general labor in cities like Pensacola, where neither the seasonal visits of tourists nor the unsteady income from crops contributes to the laborer's income. It is likewise true of such industries as shipping, dock work, warehouse, and factory labor, except citrus and other seasonal employment.

In the tourist industries there is reasonably good money for the worker during those months given to tourist traffic. In some cities these wages are such that the prudent worker can earn enough in six or seven months to support himself for the year. Hundreds of workers successfully do so.

At the other end of the scale are the low-wage farm sections, turpentine camps, and phosphate mine camps and similar enterprises. To the evil of low wages in the State must be added that of forced labor, of which there are indisputable evidences remaining, and the infamous "commissary system," in which a worker is forced to make all his purchases of foodstuffs and commodities from a commissary operated by the owner of the farm on which he lives or the camp in which he works, at prices generally far above those charges elsewhere. Forced labor has been reported at frequent intervals in turpentine camps in Baker, Duval and Clay counties; the commissary system exists in many counties. Workers in one turpentine camp were so terrorized that they refused pointblank to be seen talking to field workers of the American Guide; at least one record, and several verbal reports, were obtained on the commissary system.

An interesting sidelight on economic conditions in the cotton-tobacco-peanut belt of west Florida was provided by several small sharecroppers, who reported that although they had raised and sold several acres of peanuts, after they had paid all the so-called debts against their crop they could not even buy peanut oil, the cheapest frying oil in the section.

The fact that citrus workers live in settlements and communities rather than scattered over wide areas make their living conditions somewhat better than those of the share-crop and tenant farmers, but how much better can best be described by an excerpt from an investigation made by federal officials in 1935. A citrus worker is describing his existence:

"When it's de season we eats all we can buy an' dat's 'bout enough. But in de summertime, dat's diff'ent; it's jes' pertatoes den."

In the same report another laborer said that he had his water cut off, so that he could get back his deposit and buy food. Caretakers in the big groves earn about $50 a month the year round; pickers average $1–1.50 a day for not more than a three month season.

Though conditions are slowly improving, there are still grave problems of sanitation, housing and health in many counties of the state, and even in some good-sized cities. The Negro section of Winter Haven, in the heart of the citrus belt, was recently described by health authorities as "overcrowded and with a high rate of mortality from the prevalence of venereal disease and tuberculosis." Few homes in rural districts of some counties, like Jackson, Gadsden, Broward, and Marion, have any sanitation facilities; often even schools have neither running water nor toilets.

The Trend Towards Civilization

The Florida Negro laborer is taking some steps himself to improve his wages, conditions and surroundings. In several industries in the cities trade unions have been formed and are drawing increasing numbers of workers; in some counties the co-operative idea is being developed by the residents of the rural areas. Beginning with the farms, the co-operative move has spread to the point that plans were under way in 1936 to establish a co-operative canning plant for the women of Marion and Levy counties.

Longshore workers have led the way in trade union organization. Pensacola has the oldest union of this kind in the state, but in 1936–7 Tampa, Jacksonville, and Miami, in the order named, saw longshoremen's unions organized. Pullman porters, cigar workers, taxicab drivers and building trades laborers have unions in some cities; a state-wide organization of the unemployed has its headquarters in Tampa. In Jacksonville baggagemen have a co-operatively owned shoe store; in the same city one of the largest churches is attempting to organize the wives of laborers among its members into a cooperative house-wives' league.

The Outlook

Three readily apparent factors are making the outlook for Negro labor in Florida more hopeful than it has been at any time in recent history. First to be noted is an improvement, natural and gradual for the most part, in working conditions; this may in part be due to growing enlightenment. The trend is noticeable in citrus areas, in the employment of more Negro women in the canning and packing plants, and of more men in groves that formerly did not hire them. The increasing number of former common laborers who are mov-ing into skilled classifications in celery in another evidence of this trend.

Education, the second factor, is certain to improve conditions in truck-farming, sharecropping, tenant-farming and other industries that have below subsistence wages at present. The co-operation of schools and colleges in spreading agricultural information is parallel with this improvement.

Last of the factors, and regarded by some as the most promising, is the trend toward wholesome, constructive organizational gains made by some trades can be carried over into agriculture and other fields, Negro labor will be able to lift itself into a position of prominence in the state's economic and social system.

Over a quarter of a million people are interested in the possible correctness of this view.[59]

V

Workaday Songs

The soul of the American Negro seems to find its most natural expression in music.[60] Wherever groups of men are performing a common task, wherever work is monotonous, singing lightens the drudgery. Though the phonograph and radio have had a profound effect on these workaday songs, they have not entirely quenched the Negro's original expression of his emotions.

In the following collection of workaday songs no attempt has been made to give the music, but only the words that the Negro composes during his times of sorrow, joy, work, and imprisonment. For the most part they are songs of the illiterate Negro, simple and spontaneous.

The following song was sung by husky stevedores unloading lumber:

> Uh huh, I went home last night, oh Lawd,
> Uh huh, I went home last night, oh Lawd,
> Uh huh, I went home last night, oh Lawd,
> Me an' my wife had a fight, uh huh, uh huh,
> Yes, Lawd, I went home last night an' knocked her down
> With this Joe Louis right. Yes, Lawd, uh huh

Here is the song of a fickle woman:

> Baby, did you hear about
> All you' men gonna leave you,
> On the nex' pay day
> Baby, did you hear about
> All your clothes gwine leave you
> Yes, Lawd, on the next pay day.
> Baby did you hear about

All your furniture gwine leave you,
Yes, Lawd, on my next pay day.
Baby, did you hear about
Me an' my sweetie is gwine away,
Oh, my Lawd on the next pay day.
Baby, baby, did you hear about it
Me an' my sweetie gwine ride
De Cherokee up de river.
Yes, Lawd, an' nary cent will I be the giver
Yes, I'm gwine up the St. Johns River.

On these same docks can be found the hero of the stevedore legend, Ol' Doc, as he was popularly called; he ranks with the immortal John Henry of chain-gang fame. He was a huge, muscular Negro, with long ape-like arms, his strength familiar to all dock hands, respected by his friends and feared by his enemies. He appears to have had a sense of humor. One tale about him tells of the time when a large piano was being hauled aboard the old S.S. Mohawk by means of a steam winch. The piano had been hoisted above the hatch, when suddenly the winch rope gave way. Ol' Doc, who was bossing the job, looked down the hatch and saw a gang of stevedores three decks below. There was no time to yell; Doc hurled himself upon the parting rope in time to be jerked 20 feet into the air by the falling piano, but he held on until his body reached the top of the pulley. He was doubled into a knot, and the sound of his body hitting the wooden top of the pulley could be heard all over the docks; yet this modern Hercules held on until the pulley was lowered. Bruised and bleeding he reached the deck, jumped up without a moment's pause and shouted "Why de debbil don' you niggers get back to work, you lazy, blank-blankity-blank good-for-nothing blankity-blank-blanks." And all set to work immediately, Doc included.

During the periods of inactivity around the docks, when hundreds of stevedores lounged lazily or slept on the wooden piers, the sound of the Clyde-Mallory steamers coming round the bend with the three loud toots of their whistles was the signal for Ol' Doc to arouse the stevedores. Walking from man to man he would barely touch them as he sang this original song:

Buddy, buddy, come jump right up,
It's not quite time befo' things get rough
De ol' lady's in bed sleeping so well
Better git right up or you'll be catchin' hell.
De boss is mad for calling dese piers junk
Yet sleepin' all over 'em like day was bunks

De work aint hard and I aint mean
Come on, git on up befo' I hit you on you' happy haid bean.

The other day a group of Negroes were taking up the street car tracks on Davis street in the Negro section of Jacksonville. An old man began to sing:

Annie Weaver got de fever, aint you sorry
You got to leave her, can't you shake it
Can't you line it

In de mornin' when I rise, got to shake it
Shake it by my side
Can't you heave it, can't you hold it
Annie Weaver got de fever.

Down on the Merchants & Miners docks the stevedores like to sing:

Mary went to Mobile, Lawd, I tol' her not to go,
Mary went to Mobile, Lawd, I tol' her not to go,
Mary went to Mobile, Lawd, I tol' her not to go,
Now she got to sleep in dat col' icy snow.

Gimme my dollar, keep you' lousy dime,
Gimme my dollar, keep you' lousy dime,
Gimme my dollar, keep you' lousy dime
'Fore I have to sleep on dat col' icy groun'

Ev'y mail day, Lawd, I gits a letter, son come home,
Ev'y mail day I gits a letter, son come home,
Ev'y mail day I gits a letter, son come home,
'Fore I have to sleep on dat col' icy groun'.

In the large cities the old workaday songs are gradually becoming lost. The young Negro sings very little in performing his hard tasks; if he does sing it is usually the latest popular song heard on the radio. Where the nickel phonograph made its appearance, the change was immediately noticeable in the songs that had formerly been more or less peculiar to the particular locality gave way to the "Pinetop's Boogie-Woogie," the "Mistreating Blues," and other favorites of the machines.[61]

Certain of the recorded numbers have an almost universal appeal in the State, being as popular with the phosphate mine workers of Bartow and Mulberry as with the truck farm laborers of Clewiston and Ft. Lauderdale. The vocal recordings have the most widespread appeal. These are usually recorded either by loud throaty sopranos or by male singers accompanying themselves on a piano or stringed instrument. In the cities, orchestral recordings are sometimes favored, but the outlying sections prefer the vocal records.

The song on the phonograph record soon becomes the music of the work-crew, but with this interesting change: the original words and music are modified to satisfy the tastes of the community's own singers. Out of a record called "Troubled in Mind," for instance, tie-choppers near Palatka made this local revision:

> Mama, I sure am blue,
> Seems like I'm gwine lose my min'
> Sometimes I feel like laughin'
> Other times I feel like dying'.
> I'm gwine lay my head
> Out yonder on dat railroad line,
> Jes to feel dat Special
> Runnin' cross my min'
> My yaller gal done quit me,
> An' my min' is in a mess,
> I try to sleep at night,
> But my heart won't let me res'.

Some revisions are not mentionable in polite society; in the case of some records they are unprintably vulgar. In several parts of the State a recording called "Boogie-Woogie" was found to have been revised with a particularly lewd phrasing, but men and women alike were laughingly singing their changed edition. Just what the meaning of "Boogie-Woogie" is must be left untold; no one could be found who knew the exact meaning of the words, but for several years songs using them in their titles have been popular.

Some of the recorded music evidently is of Florida origin, although the songs are not recorded in this State. For some time one of the best known phonograph singers has been a man called "Tampa Red"; "Tampa Slim" is another favorite.

Titles of songs popular in work camps are of interest. Women, of course, provide the subject for many songs; blues is a close second. Here are some favorite titles: Tee-nincie Mama; Walking the Streets; Mistreating Mama; Gambling Woman Blues; I'm a Gambling Woman; Standing at the Bedside; Bad Blood Blues; I Wonder Who is Booging my Woogie Now; No Good Woman; The Running Swing; Stop Trucking; Gully Blues. And among pho-nograph records available at the Camps Concrete Company's settlement in Hernando County are these: Jesse James Blues; the B & O Bus Line Blues; Baby, Come Back to Me; The Nashville Blues; the Kidnapper Blues; Drinking My Blues Away; Kind Hearted Woman; Blue and Evil; Rattlesnake Daddy.

Two other records in this last collection were orchestral music, thoughtfully inserted for dancing. Not that this is essential, however; the dwellers in the "quarters" and those who frequent the beer gardens and restaurants in the smaller communities can do the most intricate "Lindy-hop" or "Susie-que" perfectly to the rhythm of Tampa Red's guitar, Bumblebee Slim's banjo, or the washboard of Washboard Sam.

The nickel phonograph has not yet entirely displaced the traditional piano player always found wherever a group of Negroes lives, and the often improvised jazz band. The piano player is usually a man, who plays loudly and insistently with no slightest guilt of reading any music for his renditions. His music is largely made on the bass keys of the piano, although some of the players achieve unusual "runs" and "breaks" on the treble keys.

A good piano player takes the place of a whole orchestra. There is little need for other instruments if he knows his "jook" music well. Much of his rhythm is accomplished by the unique use of the piano pedals; instead of using them to make his notes louder or softer he beats his foot on them to give the effect of a drum. If he does not sing his own choruses, as often happens, he has frequent and cheerful volunteer vocal assistance from the dancers. Sometimes these pianists work during the day in the sections in which they live; others make a fair living out of playing for the "parties" in the vicinity.

Jacksonville wood peddler:

> Dry load, dry load of pine,
> You git up dere, mule,
> Dry load, dry load going by,
> Make up your min' befo' dis mule cry,
> Make up your min' befo' I pass by,
> Now you git up dere, mule,
> Dis good ol' wood, jes f'om de tree
> Dis good ol' wood, jes f'om de tree
> Dome on, folks, an' help po' me,
> Dry load, dry load o' pine, dry load, oh, dry load,
> You git up dere, mule,
> Ah'll sell it to de rich,
> Ah'll sell it to de po',
> Ah'll sell it to de yaller gal standin' in de do'
> Dry load jes gone by, dry load, oh, git up dere, mule.

Jacksonville, Jeremiah the fish peddler:

> Je'miah got fresh fish,
> Je'miah got fresh fish,
> He got mullets, he got shrimps,

He got brims, he got trouts,
All Je'miah wants you to do is come out,
Je'miah got fresh fish, Je'miah got fresh fish.

Jacksonville, Snow, the ice cream peddler:

Vanilla, choc'lit, peach cream
Dat surely freezed by de steam,
It was made in de shade,
An' is sold in de sun.
Ef you aint got a nickel,
You can't git none.

Jacksonville, Negro laborers on Moncrief Road to the lazy water boy:

Water boy, water boy,
Bring dat water roun',
Ef you don' like you' job,
Set you' bucket down.
You can bring it slow,
You can bring it fast,
Ef you don' bring it now, you can't last,
Hey water boy, hey water boy.

Foley Negro wood cutter:

I'm a gonna drink my licker ev'y place I go, uh huh.
I'm a gonna drink my licker ev'y place I go, uh huh.
It make me feel good fum my haid to my toe, uh huh,
It make me feel good fum my haid to my toe, uh huh,
I'se so bad I don' never wanna be good, uh huh,
I'se so bad I don' never wanna be good, uh huh,
I'se goin' to de debbil an' I wouldn' go to hebbm, uh huh,
No, I wouldn' go to hebbm ef I could.

Jacksonville, Negro workers hoisting a safe at Masonic Temple:

Heave away, heave away,
I rather court a brown skin gal,
Dan work for Colonel Kay,
Heave away, heave away,
I really wanna go, yes, Lawd,
I gonna take my baby to de show, uh huh,
Lawdy, Lawdy, won' you ketch my groan, uh huh,
Dis ol' world done make me groan,
Dis ol' world done make my groan, uh huh,
Heave away, heave away.

Jacksonville, Negroes working in a sugar patch:

> Oh, Mary Brown, where have you been so long?
> Oh, Mary Brown, where have you been so long?
> Say you been to town, my sweet high brown,
> Say you been to town, my sweet high brown, uh huh,
> Aint no blade in dis vere town
> Dat cuts like mine, baby, baby,
> Dat cuts like mine, uh huh,
> I ask Mister police to turn me loose
> I said I aint go no money but a good excuse, uh huh.

Turpentine Negro's song:

> When I left de State of ol' Virginia
>   I left in de winter time,
>   Where you gwine, nigger?
> I'se gwine to Florida, I'se gwine to Florida
> Gwine to Florida to work in de turpemtime
> Den dey give me a hack an' a stock,
>   An' put me in a crop,
> An' say, Ol' Nigger,
> Ef you wanna see dat double line,
>   You shorely got to chop.
> Gwine to Florida, gwine to Florida, I's
> Gwine to Florida, to work in de turpemtime
>   See dat ol' woodsrider
>   He rides to de pine,
>   An' he peeps
>   An' he say, ol' nigger,
>   You better chip em deep
> Gwine to Florida, gwine to Florida, I's
> Gwine to Florida, to work in de turpemtime.
>   Den dat ol' bookkepper
>   Say to de boss,
>   I'll bet, bet what
>   Dat nigger left in debt
> Gwine to Florida, gwine to Florida, I's
> Gwine to Florida, to work in de turpemtime.

Dock laborer:

> Hundred days, a hundred bucks—
> Hundred days, a hundred bucks—
> Hundred days, a hundred bucks—
> My yaller gal is playing in luck.

With this somewhat cryptic description of the length of time he must work, the amount he receives for it, and his intentions towards the spending of his money when he gets it, the Negro dock laborer on the Florida waterfront lightens his labors as he loads cross-ties, barrels or boxes into the holds of ships.

Unfortunately conditions of work and an increasing complexity in the problem of living have taken away much of the colorful singing and play during worktime of the Negro laborer in Florida, but the traditional singing has not yet entirely disappeared. When gangs of men work at the same jobs there may still be heard many of the old melodies that were at one time so prevalent in the State.

The songs at work are of a wide variety. On some occasions they are light, gay, and often humorous. On others they are sad and drearily expressive. Usually they are begun as a solo; it is seldom, however, that they are not joined by a chorus of workmen after a few strains have been sung by the leader. In the stanza quoted above several men loading cross-ties into a ship were singing it; occasionally snatches of it from far inside the hold of the ship were heard blended with the voices of the men on the dock.

Many of the songs still heard are based on work conditions and pay. The song about the hundred days and the hundred bucks referred to the actual wages that were paid at that particular dock for the tie handlers. Another that is sometimes heard is this one:

> The work aint hard,
> The man aint mean,
> The food's alright,
> But the cook aint clean.

This is sometimes paraphrased to state that the work IS hard, and that the man (the boss) IS mean; other variations are heard.

There are several types of jobs in Florida where songs are heard most frequently. These include the dock labor, mentioned above; the saw-mill gangs, where the sound of the singing is freely punctuated by the whine of the huge circular saws; the turpentine crews, where dozens of men work in the woods within a small area, and where the singing sometimes is pitched to carry long distances through the forests; the log-chopping gangs, who sing as they swing the adzes and axes on pine and cypress logs; the truck garden and farm laborers, road repairing crews, and others.

It is not unusual to hear a song of this type where a log-cutting or trimming crew is working:

Oh ho in the morning,
Oh ho in the evening,
Oh ho hallelujah
Aint gwine be here all my days.

The "oh ho" is pronounced as though it were spelled "wo ho" and following each repetition of it the axe or adz is buried again in the log. The song does not appear to have many more words than those quoted; it is often sung for long periods, however, and sounds very melodious when there are several choppers singing it at the same time.

The workers in the turpentine sections have one song that is apparently general among them. This is more of a shout than an actual song; it has little melody itself, though it is often made to sound lyrical by the men singing it. It runs:

Boss man's a-ridin' by,
Boss man's a-ridin' by,
Boss man's a-ridin' by,
Look out, boy, look out.

The song evidently started as a warning to those who might be "taking a little time out" while supposedly at work. It is sometimes sung to a tune similar to some of the Negro spirituals like "Swing Low, Sweet Chariot" or "My Lord's A-Riding All the Time."

Two sources that always used to prove fertile for the person seeking Negro work-songs were the old railroad section gangs and the convict squads working along the highway; these groups appear to do little singing now, however.

A large phosphate rock mining camp near Brooksville made this contribution to Negro work songs:

Mama, mama, mama, why do you treat me so?
Mama, mama, mama, why do you treat me so?
Mama, mama, mama, why do you treat me so?
I'll tell you why, mama:
It's 'cause my bucks are low.
Listen to me, Mama, I'll tell you something you don' know,
Listen to me, Mama, I'll tell you something you don' know,
Listen to me Mama, I'll tell you something you don' know,
You better take me back, Mama,
'Cause I'se making money now.

There are several stanzas to the song, which may be extemporaneous, composed as the singer goes along. One in particular, that may be part of another song, but it is included in the same melody, goes:

De boss man he is evil, de job is hard as hell,
De boss man he is evil, de job is hard as hell,
De boss man he is evil, de job is hard as hell,
But I'm gonna stay wid it
On 'count o' my big brown gal.

The "mama" referred to is the common Florida Negro term for sweetheart; the "evil" boss-man is one who is mean or hard on his men. A unique feature about the song is that no matter how many extra words its singer wants to include in a verse of it, he always finds room without impairing the melody.

One innovation of recent years is greatly affecting the originality of the Negro songs of the State: the mechanical, nickel phonograph. These machines have found their way into the farthest removed places; it is not unusual to find them at remote turpentine, logging, phosphate, and other camps.

Typical Prison Songs

Great big bars,
Cast iron locks;
But ef I try to leave
I'll get the box.

Bed is hard,
Work is too;
Beans all week,
Sunday stew.

In this vein, and with as many verses as there are complaints on jail life, the tenant of Jacksonville City Prison Farm, or to the initiate the "Blue Jay" sings his passive protest.[62] The song has so many stanzas that a person hearing it for the first time might think that the singer is composing it as he goes along; this idea dissipated, however, if he chances to listen to it in the dormitory during a rainy day or a Sunday rest period. Here he may hear as many as twelve of fifteen prisoners singing it together, each placing the correct stanza in its proper place with a little break in the monotonous rhythm of the few bars that constitute the song's tune.

The melody is not greatly different from the tune found in many of the popular "blues" numbers that have been sung, played, and recorded in the recent past. In fact, vague suggestions of parts of the St. Louis Blues and similar airs may be found in the song.

When sung while the prisoners are at work, the song has a long grunt at the end of each line, as have most of the work songs that are heard at the prison.

This grunt sometimes marks the swing of an axe by the logging and grubbing crew, an extra swipe of the hoe by the wood-cutting or potato-digging gang; with the grunt it sounds like this:

> Little corn, uh huh,
> Yaller gal, uh huh,
> Little fight, uh huh,
> Lotta time, uh huh

It is worthy of note about the concluding grunt to each line that although there may be only one person singing the song out of a gang of 30 or 40 workmen cutting weeds or hoeing potatoes, within a very few minutes nearly all of the hoes or axes will be swinging in time with the "uh huh" of the singer.

If the song has a name, nobody remembers it. All that any of the prisoners profess to know about it is that other prisoners have always sung it, and that it is heard in the road camps of Polk County, the County Jail at Jacksonville, and the State truck farm at Belle Glade; wherever, they tell you, "that colored folks gits in jail."

Very popular at the jails and prisons in the vicinity of Jacksonville is the song "Louise." Just who the lady is or was, none can tell you, but there are few prisoners who do not sing a stanza or two to her during the day. The song seems a localized version of a ditty that was recorded for phonograph some years ago, and still has a wide popular appeal on the nickel phonographs in Negro neighborhoods; in the form in which it is heard around the prison farms, however, there is little resemblance to this, or any other, original.

The melody of "Louise" is unique; it has nothing of the stereotyped form of the usual Negro spiritual or blues song. It is essentially a chant, but there its resemblance to anything else ends. It begins on a high note, extended for several beats; its beginning always seems to be the continuance of something that was broken off some moments before. Some singers run the preceding stanzas into the following one because of an apparent difficulty in starting a song "in the middle" of itself.

Louise, according to the songs dedicated to her, must have been the final word in versatility; she veers sharply as the song goes on from a ruthless pursuer to an impelling force and then to a dispenser of satisfactory love in abundant quantities; in another stanza she is the center of some unexplained fishing industry. For instance:

> Lou-u-u-ise! sweetest gal I know;
> She made me walk from Chicago
> To-oeo-o- the Gulf of Mexico.

Ef I had a million dollars,
An' she asked me for a dime,
I'd give her all my money Ev'y dog-gone time.
Lou-u-u-ise! sweetest gal I know,
She made me walk from Chicago
To the Gulf of Mexico.

I had a dozen women,
Had 'em big an' small,
But when I met this Mama
Right then I quit 'em all!

Big ship in de water,
Try'n to make de lan'
Ef if don' git some steam up
It'll never touch the san'

Somebody's been a-fishing,
Where I fished befo'
Ef I cin ever catch 'em
Dey aint gonna fish no more.

Lou-u-u-ise! sweetest gal I know,
She made me walk from Chicago
To the Gulf of Mexico.

"Louise," like most of the other Blue-Jay songs, is often sung as a work chant, and when sung in this manner has the characteristic "uh huh" at the end of each line. When sung by some prisoners the grunt is also interposed at various points in the body of the line, as:

Lou-u-i-ise u huh, sweetest gal I know, uh huh,
She made me walk from Chicago, uh huh,
To the Gulf, uh huh, of Mexico, uh huh

There are a number of other songs that the prisoners sing; some of them are apparently original, or at least peculiar to the prisons of the section, and others are obvious parodies of songs heard on phonographs, radio, or other medium. Still others are made up as their singers go along. Whatever the origin or source, there are few occasions that a visit can be made to the Blue-Jay without the visitor's hearing a number of these typical songs.

VI

Amusements and Diversions

In the large cities of Florida, the Negro's diversions are not markedly different from those of his white brother.[63] If the younger folks tend more to movies, dancing and promenading, and the older ones to activities connected with the church, all are equally ardent devotees of bolita. Even the large cities are noticeably deficient in community resources for both white and Negroes; for example, though Florida has thousands of miles of seacoast, a bathing beach and bath house for Negroes is the exception, rather than the rule.[64] In general there is little provision for diversion for this underprivileged class, a situation especially unfortunate in the case of children. It may be responsible, among other things, for the large concentration of crime in Negro areas.

Nevertheless, the Negro is a cheerful individual. To a visitor who sees large groups of Negroes for the first time, it is always a matter of surprise that the least favored class in the community should be so care-free and happy; he is apt to conclude that the Negro is a natural-born optimist.[65]

At any rate, to observe the Negro at his less commonplace diversions, one must leave the city for the turpentine camps, the phosphate mines, and possibly the small saw-mill towns where the Negro is thrown upon his own resources for amusement.

Here diversions are few, but they are actively participated in. Dancing, for the younger element, is the most popular amusement. With it go widespread drinking of beers and wines, and not infrequently the potent "white mule" or moonshine. While work camps are often too far away from cities to permit attendance at movies or large parties, there are few camps that do not have their weekly, and not infrequently nightly "jooks," the popular term for any place of amusement.

The jook may be anything from a simple dance gathering, in which the nickel phonograph or piano gets a maximum of exercise, to the combination dance, card or dice game and get-together for young folks from neighboring settlements.

If the jook is a nightly one, the attendance is usually small, perhaps two or three dozen. There are apt to be more men than women present, and this contributes to the fights that sometimes arise. That these fights sometimes take on serious proportions may be gathered from the frequent "No Guns or Knives Aloud" signs that are found around the jooks. At Barker's Camp, near Lakeland, appears this sign:

TO WHOM IT MAY CONCERN Effective this date anyone shooting a gun in these quarters will be charged $5.00 and required to forfeit the gun, or go to JAIL. I will pay $2.50 for proof of anyone shooting a gun.

The notice is signed by an official of the company that owns the quarters. At another camp the walls of the jook bear this sign:

Everybody is welcome—but if you fight in hear you will go to JAIL.

That particular camp, however, may have fewer fights than others because of another sign on the same wall, just above the gaming table:

No wemen aloud in hear; this don't mean Bob, it means you.

This jook, located in a phosphate camp in Hernando County, 4 1/2 miles northeast of Brooksville, has several balls each week, but Saturday and Tuesday are the big nights. Then the men and women of the camp are joined by their friends from nearby communities and dancing, drinking and gambling are the favorite pastimes. The dance is the ordinary tightly-clenched shuffling found in most camps, with occasional "trucking" and "Susie-que-ing" thrown in.

The gambling, however, is far from ordinary. Stakes are larger than in many city games. A sign warns players that they may not even enter the game with less than three dollars; the cut to the house, that is the amount collected by the jook operators, is larger than many an entire stake in the usual city games. This is all the more remarkable because the men in the camps earn only about $1.50 a day, and the women ordinarily do not work.

This jook is called "Benny's Place"; on the special nights it serves in addition to the surreptitiously handled moonshine, fish, barbecued meats, and in season the ever-present Florida watermelon.

About a dozen signs on the walls help the guest govern himself properly—
should he be so inclined. Some of them, copied verbatim, are:

Ever Tuesday nite is Ball nite—everybody come.
You can DRINK in hear, but go outside to get DRUNK.
We take no advice from nobody.
Possible no cub win hear.

The last sign evidently refers to some technicality of the game.

Favorite games are dice, a card game called "blackjack," another called
"coon-can," and "skin," probably the most popular of all the jook games in the
State. In blackjack the player attempts to draw two or more cards totalling
the number 21, without going over that figure; he plays it usually against the
house, the owner of the jook. In coon-can the process is longer, and usually
two players participate. Skin is another game against the house, and the betting is often brisk and heavy.

Most of the camp communities have some kind of little church, with a
preacher who visits it once or twice monthly. In some camps the church
appears to enjoy popularity only with the women and older men of the camp;
others spend their day of rest in heated debate at the card table, while the
nickel phonograph lustily blares out a guitar-accompanied blues song. On
only one turpentine camp, also near Brooksville, was there a comparatively
large church attendance.

Where there is no "quarters" for the workers and their families, amusements
are sought in the city. This is particularly noticeable in towns like Orlando and
Winter Park, where there are numbers of domestic workers and farm hands; in
Palatka, the center of the logging and sawmill area, and in Quincy, Marianna
and other communities.

In these towns, for the benefit of the laborers nearby, there are many restaurants, beer gardens, and other places where the men and women may dance,
drink, and play—and of course fight. Such places are crowded nearly every
night in the week; it is not unusual to find people who attend them almost
nightly, staying as long as someone puts nickels in the phonograph, leaving
when the music stops, then going across the street or down the block to some
place where another phonograph has started playing. The custom may be seen
at its height in Quincy's Negro section and along Tampa's Central Avenue; in
the latter city the phonographs run all night and seldom play to empty houses.

In the outlying settlements the effect of the radio is not as pronounced as in
the cities. There are still communities where the piano and phonograph are the
major influences on music and amusement, and the songs of the Negro laborer

in the fields, on the roads, at his parties and church services cling to some semblance of originality, at least to whatever originality is possible in a fast growing state.

Organized Recreation

It is doubtful if organized recreation plays a large role in the life of the average Negro.[66] There is an occasional baseball or tennis club, a few special celebrations are conducted by the schools, but the great mass of Negroes is unaffected by these events, which are mostly confined to the large cities.[67]

A sport which interests Negro tennis players is the Tennis Tournament conducted by the Florida Tennis Association, which embrace cities of Georgia, Alabama, Florida, and the Bahama Islands. The annual tournament is one of the major tennis events among Negroes of the country. These tournaments alternate between Florida and the Bahama Islands. Matches have been held at Tallahassee, Miami, and Jacksonville. When the meet is in the Bahamas, it is held at Nassau, Providence Island, where an entire week is given over to a colorful series of activities. One of the largest hotels on the Island is usually reserved for the visiting players and their friends who attend the tournament.

Prominent individuals and business people provide trophies for the winners. Beautifully decorated boats ply the waters of the islands, carrying excursions for the visitors, and a gala time prevails.

Jacksonville also boasts a golf club, which goes by the name of the Lincoln Golf Club. Members and their friends keep this club going the year round. Besides golf, there is an opportunity for fishing in the waters of Six Mile Creek, which is on the grounds of the club. The course is located in the northwestern part of suburban Jacksonville, and may be reached by motor. Yearly tournaments are also held on the Lincoln Golf Course. The Hart trophy is much coveted by contestants.

The poor, crippled and blind of Jacksonville are provided amusement annually by the Clara White Mission. They are taken to Manhattan Beach in trucks and busses, and spend the day romping, surf bathing and eating the food which has been donated by kind-hearted merchants.

Washington's birthday, Lincoln's birthday, Frederick Douglass's birthday and Memorial Day are more or less celebrated in the various schools throughout the state. Another day usually celebrated by the schools is May Day. The plaiting of the May pole, along with various contests and games are part of the fun.

The large cities have scout troops for both boys and girls, and the usual scout activities are part of the program.

Tampa Celebrations

Aside from the regular celebrations carried out at Christmas, Thanksgiving, and New Years, Tampa Negroes also participate in the South Florida Fair, held in February of each year. On the fair grounds there is an exhibit building valued at nearly half a million dollars. The affair is an all-day event, and the second day is known as Specialty Day or Negro Day. People for miles around come to Tampa.

Negro schools close on that day and the children are admitted free when accompanied by teachers. The city recreation department promoted several racing events at the fair in 1936, and the Hungerford Academy ar Eatonville carried away most of the prizes. On Friday night before the close of the fair, the Lincoln-Douglas reception is held; this is not so much an activity of the fair, as an entertainment feature for the Negroes. More than 500 persons attended the last fair and paid a dollar admission. All money above expenses was donated to charity.

There is a golf club in Tampa composed of Negro members and they have had several tournaments. The man promoting these activities, Kid Mason, was once a caddy for white businessmen, and had a chance to learn the game. He no longer resides in Tampa, but his golf club still exists.

Tennis enthusiasts have organized the Alpha Tennis Club, which provides much wholesome activity for its members.

An annual celebration in which Negroes take part is the Gasparilla festival. This commemorates the exploits of Capt. José Gasparilla, a pirate, whose frequent visits to Port Tampa are believed to have been attended with much pomp and splendor. Long parades with colorful floats move up and down the streets of Tampa and the Negro is always present, since it is thought that Gasparilla had with him on his voyages Negro sailors and slaves. Floats reminiscent of the Negro in slavery upon the Gasparilla boats present an interesting feature, especially to the Negro populace.

National Music week and the annual May Day Festival occurring near the close of school are celebrated in the Negro churches with the combined choirs of the city giving elaborate programs in the municipal auditorium.

During 1936 WPA made it possible for Negroes of Tampa to enjoy band concerts at the recreation center on Central Avenue. The conductor, W. Carey

Thomas, had a well trained band, who presented classics as well as popular music. The public to appreciate the better type of music and looked forward to the concerts.

Pensacola

Pensacola, the largest city in the western part of Florida, is one of the oldest cities in the State. The Negro forms a large percentage of the population, and has always enjoyed a friendly relationship with the whites. There is perhaps less friction between the races at Pensacola that in any city of its size in the State, and Negroes feel free to take part in many of the celebrations which are promoted by whites.

The Mardi Gras Carnival, which is perhaps the most elaborate occasion of any at Pensacola, is anticipated with much joy by the Negroes. Two days are set aside for the carnival, the Monday and Tuesday preceding Ash Wednesday. The first day marks the coming of the King of the Mardi Gras, who of course has been previously selected by a committee for that occasion. A Queen is also selected at that time. The arrival of the King in an airplane is staged at the foot of Palafox Street Wharf attended by great pomp and ceremony, and a great crowd is on hand to witness it. A parade is held through the principal streets of the city to city hall, where the keys of the city are tendered the King. Then the noise and fun-making begin, culminating in a ball at night. Negroes have a ball of their own, usually at Odd Fellows Hall. Club rooms and places of amusement are gaily decorated and a general air of festivity prevails. Masquerades and confetti add to the carnival spirit. On Tuesday night another parade is held; this time many beautifully decorated floats represent fairy and legendary tales and mythical personages, instead of comical ones.

Emancipation Day[68] attracts Pensacola's largest Negro crowds, however. A parade depicting the progress of the race from slavery is a leading feature. After that a mammoth mass meeting is held and many speakers of interest and note are heard. This is followed by a banquet, made possible by personal donations, collections from churches and other sources. Any money above expenses is always given to charity. During one of these affairs the money collected was enough to extend the school term.

St. Augustine

In St. Augustine celebrations are not markedly different. There Florida Normal and Collegiate Institution always has a worthwhile program in honor of

Lincoln and Frederick Douglass. Many outdoor celebrations in the city, such as May Day and the Fourth of July are held at Manhattan Beach, which is within easy reach.

The Hecksher Gymnasium and Swimming Pool at the Florida Normal and Collegiate Institute offer much employment to the student body, both during the regular term and the summer session. It is open to the public, but little advantage is taken of it other than by students. St. Augustine also boasts a private Negro bathing beach, called Butler.

VII

Bolita

Few things give a clearer side glance at the makeup of the Negro than his almost universal addiction to the Cuban gambling game of bolita. In the following picture, incomplete though it be, can be seen something of his superstitious belief in the power of luck, his instinctive following of hunches, and his sanguine faith that sooner or later some stroke of fortune will overcome the economic insecurity under which he constantly lives.[69]

Beginning as a game of the street corner element—the gamblers, pool-room hangers-on, race-track fans and others—bolita has come to invade nearly every level of Negro life. In recent years, in fact, it has done more; its insidious influence has come to affect the white agents, collectors, policemen who have businesses in Negro neighborhoods; its playing public is now both white and Negro.

Furthermore, it is not a business confined to one city or one area. There is hardly a city in the country with any appreciable Negro population where the game, in some of its many variations, is not played heavily by the colored element, and in recent years, by a growing number of white persons. The *Baltimore Afro-American*, a Negro weekly, in its issue of July 4, 1936, quotes from the magazine *Business* that the money gambled on bolita and other similar games in 1935 totalled the staggering sum of $1,500,000,000 among Negroes alone. This sum included money spent on the Louisiana lottery and bolita in New Orleans, clearing house and policy in Atlanta and Memphis, clearing house in New York's Harlem, and bolita and policy in Tampa, Miami, and Jacksonville.

Bolita was imported to this country from Cuba well over a generation ago. It appeared in Tampa before the end of the World War; some say that it had been known there long before that. Apparently it came to Tampa from Havana, Cuba, where workers on ships and railway employees knew of it for several years before its actual apperance. Jacksonville had a somewhat crude version of it in 1911–2.

The Spanish word bolita means literally "little ball." The game's distinctive element, separating it from other gambling games of a similar nature, is the "throw and catch." In its simplest form, this consists of the tossing of a bag with numbered pellets from one man to another, and the selection of one ball caught by grasping the bag, as the winning number.

Several factors have contributed to the spread of bolita. The first, naturally, concerns the player and the sales technique to which he is subjected. It is safe to say that no Negro can walk for any distance along the business streets of his section without being continually importuned by hawkers with long, numbered strips of paper, who assail his ears with cries of "Big House, Mister! I got the Big House!" Numbers can be bought for one cent, though a good salesman averages from ten to fifteen cents for each sale. Indeed, a player does not have to walk the streets to find a "runner"; if he has played before, he will very likely receive a home visit sometime between 6 a.m. and 10 p.m.

The next figure to engage our attention in the bolita hierarchy is the runner. Each morning he is given a quantity of bound strips of numbered slips, with numbers running from one to 100, and with from ten to twenty numbers on each strip. The slips are given to him by some representative of the "big house" or he may get them from any of the number of "stations" in the city, or occasionally directly from the "big house." At the usual ten per cent commission, some sellers average six to eight dollars a day.

Next in the bolita racket comes the operator of the station, or neighborhood headquarters for the business. Although the purpose of these stations is known to nearly every resident in the area in which they operate, and although not a single city in the United States has legalized bolita, nevertheless the stations are almost universally immune to raids by the police. This is markedly true in Jacksonville and Tampa. In the Ybor City and central Tampa areas bolita stations are numerous;[70] Jacksonville has three stations on the west side of the city, two in the Florida Avenue section, and a large central station or general clearing house, called the "Big House" on East Bay Street, within five blocks of City Hall.

The neighborhood station receives the stubs of the numbers sold by the agents. These are later turned in to the Big House, and then ensues the juggling that always manages to net the players a loss and the operators a fortune. The truth of this last statement may be judged from the article previously quoted in the Baltimore Afro-American, which gives the total winnings collected by the players who spent the $1,500,000,000 as slightly more than $1,000,000—about one dollar won for every $1,500 played.

In Jacksonville the following stations were in operation in August 1936. Raymond's, owned by a man said to be the son of a former cigar manufacturer of the city, located at Ashley and Jefferson streets, in a store that uses a few bottles of wine and beer to present a more respectable front; Machin's Place, Beaver Street near Davis, no legal excuse given for its operation—merely known to all the neighborhood as a bolita station; Manuel's, Davis and Beaver Streets, where the major portion of the west side bolita business is transacted, the last step before the Big House; Machin's East Side, another frankly open bolita exchange at Florida Avenue and First Street; another Florida Avenue station of which many persons speak, but whose address is not generally mentioned because of a murder that occurred there, with considerable attendant publicity; lastly, the Big House itself, which occupies a whole building at the northeast corner of Bay and Catherine Streets.

Little activity or interest is to be found in the neighborhood stations except the endless transaction of the passing of money. The payoffs to the occasional winners are generally made here; the agents report their sales to the operators of the stations; disgruntled players bewail their complaints to deaf ears, and policemen occasionally saunter in for reasons best known to themselves. Manuel Rivera, a dapper Puerto Rican, may be found at the Davis Street place, his long green Auburn parked outside, his two ever-present guards never far away. Raymond, riding in a Packard coupe whose windows are plastered with political advertisements, is frequently seen at Raymond's Place on Ashley Street; Machin alone, of the big operators, is difficult to locate.

At the Big House, however, there is action. There are first the private conferences of station operators, which take from the 10 p.m. closing time for sales until the throwing at 1–2 a.m.; the throw and catch itself, an interesting spectacle, and lastly the sighs of the losers when the winning number is announced. Formerly throwings were small affairs, conducted simultaneously in different little houses by private operators; within the last few years, since the dramatic gang murder of "Doc Ellis," the business has become systematized and all operators work under the Big House, with one throwing to suffice for all.

It is a curious commentary on human nature that though all players seem to know of the many crooked devices used to fleece them of their pennies and dimes, none are deterred by such trivia. It is general knowledge that the mechanics of the throw and catch are invariably based on the sales for the day, and that after the sales have been completed at 10 o'clock a comparison is made by the operators to ascertain which numbers have been most heavily sold. Numbers having very large sales are discarded entirely; the lowest played numbers are then found and the throw and catch adjusted to them.

The throw and catch determines the winning number. One hundred balls, numbered from one to 100, are tied up in a sack before the spectators. The public, if not openly invited, is certainly not barred from this spectacle. The bag is then shaken thoroughly and thrown across the length of the room. A man at the other end catches it, and holds it finally by one of the balls, still enclosed. This ball is then tied away from the others by a third man, and then cut off from the rest of the sack. It is then unwrapped and announced as the day's winner.

Two ways of fixing the ball in the sack are well known. One is a method much used in the past, isolating a previously determined ball in a small hardly noticeable pocket in the lining of the sack before the throw is made, and catching the sack near this ball. A later practice, and one employed frequently in the small houses that operated before the Big House monopolized the game, was the "palming" of the winning ball by the man who cut open the sack. So swiftly and skillfully was it exchanged for the actual winning ball that spectators were never the wiser. If the present system used by the Big House is known to any of the players, it is not divulged. The only information obtainable is that the throw in some manner is still definitely fixed, and heavily played numbers never win.

Public sentiment some time ago caused the discontinuance of one of the favorite methods of cheating the players of bolita. This was the "house number" system, whereby one, two or more numbers were never sold to players, but were house numbers, i.e., numbers that the house played for itself against the players. Under this system, avoiding a heavy payoff was simple; whenever play was heavy all along the line, one of the house numbers won for the day. It was known to be a raw, vicious trick, of course, but the illegality of the game plus its control by the gangster element effectively silenced complaints. If a street corner crowd should happen to get excited, the call of "Big House, Mister," would very likely divert attention from complaints to sales.

In its generation or more of prevalence in the Negro section, play has become as much a part of the day's business as the sale of food or drugs, and no level of society is immune to the lure that a penny may bring 80 cents. With the more efficient organization of the business and the inclusion of a number of native-born white investors in the banking end of the game, as contrasted with the previous almost all Cuban and Negro set-up, the number of white players has increased until now many of the white businessmen with establishments in Negro neighborhoods, and many white citizens in other parts of the city, are rabid bolita players, losing their dimes as optimistically as the Cubans and Negroes. The growing interest of white players and investors in the game may be judged from the fact that one of the most sensational murders attributed to bolita during 1936 was that of a white operator by a white runner; it occurred in a section predominantly white. It may be added that the Big House itself is usually in a white section of the city.

That there should be experts who could, for any sum from ten cents to ten dollars, tell the player just what number to play, was inevitable. These experts range from the simple hoodoo woman of the neighborhood, to elaborate organizations like the one in Detroit, which does an immense business in picking winning numbers each day, and escapes the postal authorities by receiving and sending only telegrams. Its advertisements, which used to appear regularly in the *Pittsburgh Courier*, colored weekly, guaranteed at least one winning number for each five dollars sent. Other firms, more afraid of the law, sell worthless booklets and novelties, and send along a winning number with each purchase.

There are innumerable books that explain explicitly how to select a winning number. Some of these books interpret dreams and deduce numbers therefrom; some deal with what they profoundly call the science of numerology, and prove conclusively that a person born at such-and-such a time can be fortunate only in a wave of sixes and eights, and must always avoid elevens and twelves. The *National Policy Player's Guide*, author and publisher unknown, is a treatise of this kind which enjoys a large circulation.

Dream books, explaining the connection between dreams and winning numbers, also enjoy great vogue; there are even two books alleged to have been written by Moses, and inadvertently left out of his compilation. Here are some titles selected at random: *Pow-wows*, or the *Long Lost Friend*, by George Hohman, published first in the United States in 1820, and frequently since then. This book carries on its fly-leaf the promise that "Whoever carries this book is safe from enemies, fortunate at gaming, and cannot drown in any water, burn in any fire or have any unjust sentence passed upon him."

Three Witches Dream Book, a combination dream directory which boasts a complete list of dreams and tells the lucky number that each indicates.

The Silent Friend, which tells in detail "how to cut rich, or the great $50,000 secret, and a table for finding lucky numbers."

Crystal Gazing, a thorough course, so it is said, in the art of gazing into magic crystals and determining lucky, winning numbers.

Aunt Sally's Policy Players' Dream Book, an all-time favorite with gamblers, which professes to tell lucky numbers that harmonize, to interpret dreams and numbers to which they apply, tell the significance of cards dreamed of and the numbers to play from them, good combinations of numbers, table for finding lucky numbers, ladies' list of numbers, gentlemen's list of numbers, etc. The book sells for $1, and can be found in many homes.

If it were not for the fact that $1,500,000,000 is being taken annually from the pockets of the most impoverished element of the population there would be considerable amusement in watching the bolita player fasten his hopes of winning on his dreams. Some of the dreams that have a winning significance, and the numbers that should be played because of them are: alligators, play numbers 4, 9, 11; apes, play numbers 3, 13, 21; wild animals, 5, 7, 9; blood, 40; cats, 45; crutches, 53; drunkenness, 13; elephants, 35; hearse, 14.

The fact that few people can ever recall having dreamed of an alligator, an elephant or a camel plays no part in the bolita players' belief in this book. The *Black and White Luck Book*, from which the above examples were taken, has almost entirely replaced almanacs and other booklets distributed by drug stores.

There is little need to describe the charms, talismans, magic preparations and drugs that aid the bolita player in overcoming the wiles of Lady Luck; they are practically the same as those used in any other kind of charm-casting. Incense that leaves numbers in its ashes and "7-11 holy oil," which, when sprinkled on the money with which bolita slips are to be purchased are sure to make them winners, are additions to general superstitions regarding good luck.

The psychology of the bolita player is difficult to understand, but it is possible that the widespread publicity given to every winning, and the natural reluctance that players feel in emphasizing losses, is responsible for much of the unflagged interest in a form of gambling that would have made even Barnum ashamed of himself.

In Tampa in the spring of 1936, for instance, a young white man was observed walking at a brisk pace down Tampa Avenue, a sheaf of bills in his hand.

Above: Parade, Bethune-Cookman College, Daytona Beach; *left:* Alice Stokes

Opposite, top: Negro Masonic
Temple, Jacksonville; *above:*
Hecksher Gymnasium and
Swimming Pool, Florida Normal
Institution, St. Augustine; *left:*
Music Festival at Florida Normal
Institution, St. Augustine

Negro Boy Scouts at Camp Lincoln, New Berlin

N. A. P. E. Convention, Jacksonville

Scenes from Durkeeville

Scenes from Durkeeville

Bethel Church, Jacksonville

Every few feet he would stop someone and tell him that he had caught the "Cuban end" for $40, the first time he had played. The field worker to whom he told this followed him from Scott Street to within a block of the post office, a distance of ten blocks, and noted that in every block at least two or three people were given this glad, if purely personal, bit of information by the happy winner.

In the case of scoffers who refuse to believe the bolita success stories, there are always kind souls to point to well-known examples of fortunes made by the game. That these fortunes have been made by capitalizing on the gullibility of players rather than by attempting to beat a mathematically impossible gamble, is a fine distinction omitted from the stories. The Cutliffes of Atlanta, phenomenal bolita successes in Toledo, Pittsburgh, Detroit are pointed out to the skeptical as proof positive that buying a number of pink or blue or white slips on Monday morning is an assurance of fortune before Tuesday night.

Lowlier, and therefore more readily believed, are the stories of women like "Mother Jones," who played a nickel on a number to oblige a friend, and hit for nearly $30. She played 10 cents later as an experiment and won $54. Convinced that there was an infinitely better method of earning a livelihood than the domestic work that had hitherto occupied her time and talent, Mother Jones played 25 cents, and won for the third consecutive time in less than two weeks. But this time she did not get the $135 coming to her, for her "writer," secure in his conviction that no one could hit three times in a row, had neglected the little detail of turning in her stub, and had spent her quarter in a manner best known to himself. So although she won, she could not collect.

Somewhat sadder, but with no less effect on those people who are almost persuaded to play bolita and need only a story of winning to push them into the game, are the stories of the Pullman porter, and the mistake made by a New York woman's children; both stories are well known in bolita circles.

The porter had run for years on the Kansas City to Jacksonville run, and had religiously purchased his little blue tickets at the end of each run. These he bought in amounts that frequently ran as high as two and three dollars. Before leaving for Missouri on one occasion, he bought a certain number rather heavily, on the hunch that he would win, and he told several friends about his feeling. Still he was very much excited when he received a wire at Kansas City telling him that he had hit and was the winner of several thousand dollars. Naturally he was overjoyed. He was now wealthy, and he occupied his time on the trip down to Florida cussing out those of his superiors that he did not like.

He knew that he was fired, be he didn't care; wasn't he well off now? But alas, the wire was merely the brainwork of a practical joker, and the porter found himself out of both job and money.

The woman in New York sent her children to the corner store to buy her some number 23, a rather large play of it; then she went to work. Returning in the afternoon, she asked her children for the slips. Much to her annoyance, she found that instead of 23 they had bought some other number, whereupon she began beating them, and did not stop until a neighbor came running to tell her the winning number for that day. It was the number the children had bought, and she was now richer by a few thousand dollars.

Her fortune did her no good, however; within a few days after receiving the largest sum of money she had ever seen in her life, she went completely insane. It is presumed that this disconcerting climax to the usual bolita success story has not deterred a single player from his daily purchases.

Whatever the good or bad points of the Cuban game of bolita, it remains in Jacksonville, Tampa, Miami, and a number of other Florida cities, one of the largest, if not the very largest, enterprise in the entire Negro section of the city. It is doubtful if even foodstuffs surpass it in net income in the course of a year. Except for the heavy deduction for protection, it is a business that is almost 100 per cent profit—a profit divided entirely among a tight little group in each city. It is money of such importance that men have been killed because of it, not to mention the deaths indirectly attributable to it.

Its greatest significance to Negro life, however, is the economic one: the butcher may have to close shop because of falling sales; the rent man may dispossess in vain; even churches may pass into the hands of outsiders because of unpaid mortgages; but Manuel, Machin, and Raymond in the Big House do an increasingly larger business each year. It is they who are responsible for the cry of "Big House, Mister! I got the Big House!"

VIII

Folklore

Out of a past colored with superstition that was his religion the Negro has developed certain practices relative to cures and beliefs that are peculiar only to himself.[71]

Concerted health drives and increased educational advantages have done much towards his enlightenment, but a surprisingly large number of Negroes still cling to these old superstitions; no doubt they have contributed to the high Negro death rate.

Cures

Poor eyesight—Many Negroes bore their ears in the belief that part of the virtue will be transferred from their hearing to the sense of sight.

Tuberculosis—Alligator tail, especially prepared, and water that has accumulated in pine tree stumps are given many sufferers. The meat of fattened dogs killed by stealth is used in some cases. Often the house of a tuberculosis victim is converted into a community prayer center, as many Negroes believe the disease is a favorite form of punishment meted out by God for sins, and that recovery is dependent upon His complete forgiveness. If the sufferer is a child, the sin is attributed to some of its forbearers.

Still others believe this disease to be incurable and in their terrible dread of it, use all sorts of preventives when visiting a victim. Special "conjure balls," properly prepared by a favorite witch doctor are often used to ward off the disease. Anointing the palms and nostrils with iodoform, turpentine and asafetida are common practices. Others believe that they become immune to contagious diseases by reading the Psalms.

Night sweats—A bowl of water secretly placed beneath the head of the sufferer for nine nights is thought to many to be an effective cure.

Poor complexion—Bathe the face in fresh chamber lye (urine) every morning before uttering a word to anyone.

Falling hair—The combing of the hair by a person of the opposite sex or by one subject to cramps of the hands. Never say "thank you." If the hair is too thick, comb it with a fork.

Any affliction—Visit the corpse of one you have known in life and who has been pleasantly disposed towards you, and while no one is looking whisper the name of the deceased and request that he carry your ailment with him. If there is some external growth, such as a wart or wen it is considered more advisable to rub gently the afflicted part on the face of the dead.

External ailments—Persons of posthumous birth may cure any of these by simply blowing three times upon the afflicted area, saying after the first breath, "In the name of the Father," after the second, "And in the name of the Son," after the third, "And the Holy Ghost, A-men."

Whooping cough—Fried crow meat, or a tea made of sheep manure.

Fever blisters—A dried eel skin tied around the affected parts and left on until the wearer loses it. The person picking it up will take onto himself the discarded complaint.

Mumps—Vigorous rubbing with the marrow obtained from the jowl of a hog. Sardines are also a standard cure. They are eaten by the sufferer and the oil is used to rub the affected parts.

Nose bleed—Drop a bunch of keys down the back.

Hiccoughs—Place two brown straws on the "mould" of the head in the form of a cross.

Headache—Rub table salt onto the "mould" of the head.

Weak limbs—If a young child, massage limbs in greasy dish-water each morning. Burying in the sand for several hours is practiced on old and young.

Any complaint not understood or affected within a reasonable length of time by a physician is looked upon as some form of conjuration. Almost invariably the sufferer is prevailed upon by friends or relatives to visit a voodoo man, who will tell a colorful tale of the enemy and the methods his uses. Then he prescribes treatment. This usually consists of the wearing of charms, incantations at sunrise, reading of the Psalms, and the taking of various herb medicines concocted by the "doctor."

Bolita Superstitions

Few bolita players will admit a woman into the house on Monday, if she is the first person that has called that day; some purposely call in a man the first thing in the morning so as to avoid offending a woman caller. A man caller on Monday is considered a lucky omen. His host will often ask his age and play that number on his purchases of bolita tickets. For a person who does not play the game to dream of numbers is considered a sure sign that some "house" will "throw" them. If one is buying numbers and any of them fall from the hands of the seller to the floor before being caught, these are considered lucky numbers.

Garbage cans and sidewalks of some neighborhoods are always littered with bolita tickets, as it is considered bad luck to burn them. Some Negroes will not even tear them up. It is also considered unlucky to tip the ticket seller out of one's winnings; better to borrow money from a friend.

Play the age and favorite number of someone who is dead. It is thought that the spirit of dead will cause such numbers to fall.

Powdering the face at bed time or burning the soles of old shoes are thought to be conducive to clear dreams. All numbers dreamed should be played for three days. Some persons play the first number seen in the morning.

Ghostly Superstitions

Persons born with cauls, commonly called "veils," over their eyes, are credited with supernatural powers such as healing and being able to see ghosts.

To see a ghost coming towards your house is regarded as a sure sign that someone will be ill; if going in the opposite direction, there will be a death.

If a ghost is seen more than once and you do not wish to see him again, swear at him and inquire his business; he will immediately give the reason for his visitation and will never trouble you again.

If a house is haunted, a piece of new lumber should be nailed in a conspicuous place; ghosts have new things. Horse shoes are also nailed over the door to ward off evil spirits and bad luck.

It is a common belief that murderers are always harassed by the spirits of their victims and often forced to confess their crimes. There are numerous instances of murderers being apprehended by the spirits of their victims. Many murders have pointed to Negroes by the fact that the body was lying on its face because it is thought by them that a victim will not haunt its murderer placed in this position.

Ghosts are generally believed to frequent the places where they lived and died.

Child-birth Superstitions

Many Negro women believe that a midwife can better serve at delivery of babies because being women they can understand their misery. It is considered immodest to have a man, even a physician, at the bedside during delivery.

An expectant mother is never without some old articles of clothing in the layette, believing that too elaborate preparation will frighten the infant's spirit and cause death at birth or during early infancy.

It is considered unlucky to name a child after a deceased child.

An expectant mother should never raise her arms above her head, as this is supposed to tie the navel cord around the neck of the unborn child, strangling it.

If a little boy shows liking for the expectant mother, she will have a girl, and vice versa.

A baby born near midnight will be able to see ghosts.

Babies born on the full of the moon will be larger than those born at other times. Midwives expecting babies at such times decrease the mother's diet.

Hang pants over the bed at night for easy delivery.

Presence of the child's father will help to alleviate the pains of childbirth. Some women wear the husband's hat or other garment at such times.

The new mother is fed on a diet of tea and crackers for at least three days after delivery. To eat fish is considered extremely dangerous. Nothing from the inside of an animal nor oysters is allowed.

Never step over a baby under one year old, as this is said to stunt its growth.

Sugar was administered locally in one case to ease the pains of child-birth. In another case the physician called in was told that the midwife had simply stared at the stars, saying that this would alleviate the suffering. Jeering at the woman about to deliver is a common practice; it is thought that to arouse her anger will hasten delivery.

When the baby is one month old he is carried around the house by the most estimable friend or relative; this is supposed to influence his character.

If the child's fingernails are cut before he is a year old, the child will be a thief; hence they are bitten off by the mother or some other member of the family. To cut a child's hair before he is a year old will affect his speech.

Many will not wash the mould or top of the baby's head as this is believed to give them colds. If a child has spasms or convulsions the piece of clothing next to its skin is snatched off and burned. Then he is never supposed to have another of these spells.

John Henry, 1937 Model

Just when or where Daddy Mention came into being will require some research; none of the guests at the Blue-Jay seem to know. Only one thing is certain about the wonder-working gentleman: he must have existed, since so many people claim to have known him.[72]

Not that any of his former friends can describe Daddy Mention to you, or even tell you very many close details about him. They agree, however, that he has been an inmate of various and sundry Florida jails, prison camps and road farms for years and from the stories told of him he must have enjoyed an almost unbroken stay in places of incarceration.

In fact, it is this unusual power of omnipresence that first arouses the suspicions of the listener: was Daddy Mention perhaps a legendary figure? Prisoners will insist that he was in the Bartow jail on a 90-day sentence, "straight up" when they were doing 60. Then another will contradict and say it must have been some other time, because that was the period when Daddy was in Marion County, "making a bit in the road gang." The vehemence with which both sides argue would seem to prove that Daddy was in neither place, and that very likely he was nowhere.

Legendary though Daddy Mention may be, however, the tales of his exploits are vividly told by the prisoners. All the imagination, the color, and the action of the "John Henry" stories of other sections are duplicated in Daddy's activities; it is peculiar that the exploits, far-fetched though they may seem, seldom fall on unbelieving ears.

Daddy Mention's Escape

"Daddy Mention liked the Polk County jails alright, all except the little jug outside of Lakeland. He told 'em when they put him in there that he didn't think he could stay with them too long.

"They had locked him up for vagrancy, you see. And Daddy Mention didn't think much of that, because jes like he had told them he had been picking oranges, and just had too much money to work for a week or two. He tried to tell them that he would go back to work as soon as he got broke, but you know you can't say much in Polk County.

"So they locked Daddy Mention up; gave him ninety straight up. (Ninety days with no time off for good behavior.) He went on the stump-grubbing gang. Soon he got to the Farm.

"It was afternoon when Daddy Mention started to work, and he made the first day alright. He fussed a little, kinda under his breath, when he saw what the prisoners et for supper, but he didn't say much. Then next morning he et breakfast—grits and bacon grease, but no bacon—with the rest of us, and went out to the woods.

"Before it was 10 o'clock—you know you start at 6 in Polk County—Cap'm Smith had cussed at Daddy two or three times; he didn't work fast enough to suit em down there. When we went for dinner he was growlin' at the table: 'Dey aint treatin' me right.'

"After dinner, when we lined up to go back to the woods, Cap'm Smith walked over to Daddy. 'Boy,' he hollered, 'You gonna work this afternoon, or you want to go to the box?'

"Daddy Mention didn't say nothing at first, then kinda slow he said: 'Whatever you want me to do, Cap'm.'

"Cap'm Smith didn't know what to make of that, and he put Daddy in the box in a hurry. He didn't go back for him that day, neither. He didn't go back till the next day. 'You think you want to come out of there and work, boy?' he asked Daddy Mention, an' Daddy Mention told him again: 'Whatever you want me to do, Cap'm.'

"I didn't see Cap'm Smith then, but they tell me that he got so hot you could fry eggs on him. He slammed the box shut, and didn't go back for Daddy Mention for another day.

"Daddy Mention didn't get out then, though. Every day Cap'm Smith asked him the same thing, and every day Daddy Mention said the same thing.

"Finally Cap'm Smith figured that maybe Daddy Mention wasn't trying to be smart, but was just dumb that way. So one day he let Daddy Mention come out, and let him go with another gang, the tree-chopping gang, working just ahead of us.

"Daddy Mention was glad to get out, 'cause he had made up his mind to go to Tampa. He told some of his gang about it when the Cap'm wasn't listening. But Daddy Mention knew that he couldn't run away, though; you can't do that down there. They'd have you back in jail before you got as far as Mulberry.

"Oh, no! Daddy Mention knew he had to have a better plan. And he made one up too. None of us knew much about it, 'cause he didn't talk about it then.

But we begin seein' him doing more work than anybody else in his gang; he would chop a tree by hisself, and wouldn't take but one more man to help him lift it to the pile. Then one day, when he was sure his Cap'm saw him, he lifted one all by hisself and carried it a long ways before he put it down.

"The Cap'm didn't believe any man could grab one of them big pines and lift it by hisself, much less carry it around. He call Daddy Mention and make him do it again, than he make him do it so the other guards kin see it.

"It wa'nt long before the Cap'm and his friends was picking up a little side money betting other folks that Daddy Mention could pick up any tree they could cut. And they didn't fuss so much when he made a couple of bumpers (nickels) showing off his lifting hisself.

"So it got to be a regular sight to see Daddy Mention walking around the jail yard carrying a big tree in his arms. Everybody was getting used to it by then. That was just what Daddy Mention wanted. One afternoon we came in from the woods, and Daddy Mention was bringing a tree-butt with him. The Cap'm thought one of the other guards musta told him to bring it in, and didn't ask him nothing about it.

"Daddy Mention took his tree-butt to the dining room and stood it up by the wall, then went on with the rest of us and et his dinner. He didn't seem in no hurry or nothing, but he jes didn't have much to say.

"After dinner he waited 'til nearly everybody got finished, then he got up and went back to his log. Most of the Cap'ms an' guards was around the yard then, and all of em watched while Daddy Mention picked up that big log.

"Daddy Mention clowned around in front of the guards for a minute, then started towards the gate with the log on his shoulder. None of the guards didn't bother him, cause who every saw a man trying to escape with a pine butt on his shoulder?

"You know you have to pass the guard's quarters before you get to the gate in the Lakeland Blue Jay. But Daddy Mention didn't even turn around when he pass, and nobody didn' say nothing to him. The guards musta thought the other guards sent him somewhere with the log, or was making a bet or something.

"Right on out the gate Daddy Mention went, and onto the road that goes to Hillsborough County. He still had the log on his shoulder. I never saw him again till a long time after, in Tampa. I never did figure out how he got into Hillsborough County from Polk, with watchers all along the road, after he left the Lakeland Blue-Jay. So I ask him.

"He say, 'I didn' had no trouble. I jes kep that log on my shoulder, an everybody I pass thought it had fell off a truck, an' I was carrying it back. They knew nobody wouldn' have nerve enought to steal a good pine log like that and walk along with it. They didn' even bother me when I got out of Polk County. But soon's I got to Plant City, though, I had enought money to RIDE to Tampa. They aint gonna catch me in Polk County no more.'"

Daddy Mention and the Mule

"Daddy Mention git a log trip to Raiford once. Dey wuz a lot up people workin' on de Canal near Ocala, an' dey wuz makin' good money. Daddy Mention, he wuz makin' better money dan dey wuz, though. You see, he wa'nt workin' 'xackly on de Canal; he wuz sellin' a little whiskey on the side to dem dat wuz.

"Dey didn' let the Ocala police arres' nobody on de Canal. De county cops didn' bother you much, neither. Dere wuz some special men could bother you, but ef you didn' raise a ruckus, de wouldn' care.

"But Daddy Mention uster have to go to Ocala whenever his liquor run out. He wuz smaht, though; he uster git one of de white men on de camp t' drive him in an' bring him back. Dat-a-way de police in Ocala didn' had a chance t' git him.

"It uster make de cops mad as a stunned gopher to see Daddy Mention come ridin' right into town wid dis yere white feller, den go ridin' back to de Canal agin, an' de couldn' git dere han's on him.

"But one time Daddy Mention done jes git his little load o' likker an' dey had started back when de white feller he see somebody he knowed. So he git out o' de truck an' tole Daddy Mention to wait a minute.

"He didn' have to tell him dat; de cop came an' put Daddy Mention where he cin wait a long time, real comfortable. De policeman he wait a long time for a chance to lock Daddy Mention up. So he think he would have a li'le fun wid him. So he stahted pretendin' to joke with Daddy Mention, an' kiddin' him about allus ridin' in to town wid dat what man: 'You mus' t'ink you as good as white folks,' he told Daddy Mention, an' laugh.

"Daddy Mention he think de cop wuz really playin' wid him, so he stahted tellin' stories. He tole him 'bout how de Lard wuz makin' men, an' put all de dough in de oven. 'He take out de fust dough,' say Daddy, 'an' it wa'nt nowhere near brown; it wuz jes yaller. So he set it aside, an' later it become it dem folks what lives in foreign countries, dem Turks an' all. Den He take out a real brown batch uf dough.' Daddy Mention tole de policeman how dis batch look, well-done an' season' jes right. 'Dese wuz de cullud folks,' say Daddy. De policemans dey all laugh; Daddy didn' see dem winkin' at each other.

"'What become of de rest of de dough?' de ask Daddy. 'Oh, dat,' say Daddy, 'dat what wuz lef' over, dey done make all de policeman in de world outa dat.' Den Daddy Mention he laugh as hard as he could, an' de policemans de laugh too.

"I don' know ef de jedge done laugh, though. He give Daddy Mention two years de nex' day. Dat's how Daddy git to Raiford an' git to know Jinny."

"It take Daddy Mention a long time to figure out he really in de Big Rock for two years or better. When he finally git it through his haid, he begin tellin' folks he wouldn' stay dere no two years.

"You can' beat Cap'm Chapman's Jinny, dey try tell him. But Daddy Mention he laugh; he ax em how, ef he done drown houn' dogs in de swamp an' done dodge guards wid double-barrell' Winches' kin a mule stop him?

"Lotsa other prisoners dey try to tell Daddy Mention, but he wouldn' have it no other way but he mus' try to escape an' make it to de Okeenokee Swamp up de other side o' Olustee."

"So one mornin', soon as dey let us out in the yard, Daddy Mention ups an' runs. He wuz in good shape, too; he beat dem shot guns a mile."

"When he git a chance to look back over his shoulder he sees one o' de guards put his finger to in his mouth an whistle. But didn' no dog come out; out come trottin' a little short, jack-ass lookin' mule, and she back' into a li'le drop-bottom cart wid nobody techin' her.

"It don' take but a minute to hitch dat Jinny into dat cart an' by de time de harness wuz on her all uf de dogs wuz in de bottom of de cart an' it was flying down de fiel' atter Daddy Mention."

"Daddy Mention wuz smaht; he had stole one o' de other prisoner's shoes befo' he lef', so when he git to de woods he take off his shoes an' put on dese. Den he throw his shoes in de ditch, to fool de dogs. An' it done fool im too. Daddy he had time to fin' hisself a good big oak tree an' kivver hisself in it befo' de dogs come an' lost his trail. So he wuz doin' a lot of laughin' to hisself when dey went on across de ditch an' kep' on barkin' and runnin' furder away. De cart that Jinny wuz pullin' de dogs in wuz standin' a li'le ways off fum his tree too."

"Daddy Mention he wuz busy watchin' de dogs an' figurin' when could he come down and hit it fer de swamp, when he feel somepin grap at his pants. Befo' he kin figure out what is it had tore de whole seat out of em, an' maybe a li'le bit of Daddy Mention too. Den he see it wuz Jinny. She has two feets on de bottom of de tree an' wuz reachin' for another piece of Daddy Mention's pants. He try to hurry up a li'le higher, an' one of his feets slip' down a li'le. Dat when Jinny show him she et leather too."

"Daddy, he didn' know what to do. He go round to de other side o' de tree, an' jump' down to run. Jinny she come right on behim' him. he have to keep goin' dat same way, cause de dogs wuz still runnin' roun' de other way."

"Befo' Daddy knowed it Jinny had done chase him right back to de prison fence. But he think even gittin' back inside'd be better'n git et up by day wil' mule, so he lit out fer de top o' de fence. Den jes as he git almos' over, Jinny bit again. Dis time dere wan't no pants for her to bite, so she jes grabbed a mouthful o' Daddy Mention."

"An' dat's where he be when Cap'm Chapman come, right dere, wid a good part o' him in Jinny's mouth. It wuz a long time befo' he kno sit him down to eat. Dat don' worry him so much, cause in de box where he wuz you don' eat much, anyway."

IX

Hoodoo and Voodoo

Many learned books have been written on the part that myths and superstitions have played in the life of man. We like to believe that only primitive and savage races are afflicted with this form of ignorance, but who of us is really free from superstition? Who would dare to walk under a ladder, make the thirteenth at a table or rummage in Tutankamen's tomb? It is a small wonder then, that the Negro, with his meager opportunity for education, should be even more credulous than we. The wisest of the ancients recorded his observation that good fortune was not the result of superior desert; perhaps, so the primitive mind reasoned, good fortune is in the hands of some capricious power who one must try to propitiate.[73]

Conversely, ill-fortune—illness, loss of money, domestic trouble, poor luck in love—must be the malicious work of some enemy or demon, and with the proper charms his power can be nullified. Hoodoo, voodoo, and naningo, the names are interchangable, are the rites and practices that experience has found useful in exorcising ill fortune. Naturally, certain men, the witch doctors or the hoodoo doctors, are more expert in this field than ordinary men, and it is to them, as to the Devil in Faust, that it is advisable to go.

One of the most colorful figures in the realm of hoodooism in Florida and one who could easily be classified as the peer of them all, was Henry N. Abraham, a tall, copper-colored Negro, standing six feet tall, with a voice that roared like Niagara, and full piercing black eyes that held his visitor spellbound. His fame spread far and wide as a master of black magic. He was said to heal any type of physical infirmity, remove "spells," give policy numbers, and remove any kind of ill-luck.

Abraham was born in Manning, South Carolina, 63 years ago, of poor parents who earned their livelihood working on plantations. He received practically no schooling, and spent his time working with his parents. At the age of 24 he married Malvinia Stuke, a childhood sweetheart. He obtained work on a locomotive, and later in a large saw mill as timber cutter.

One day a Negro from Florida named Hamp Miller came to Manning to recruit men to work in a turpentine camp for one Russ Edwards of Lawtey. Miller approached Abraham and some other men with this proposition, offering them higher wages than they were getting. Being a thrifty man, and having an eye for business, Abraham consented to go. Taking his wife and his new baby daughter, he arrived in Lawtey to live in the quarters of the turpentine camp. This was 35 years ago. Little did he know at that time that Fate had a certain niche in life for him to fill, not as a laborer in a turpentine camp, but as the "Hoodoo Doctor of Lawtey."[74]

He worked hard in the turpentine camp and at odd jobs for 20 years. He now had two children. With the years he grew in the esteem and confidence of his boss until he was given the job as recruiter, considered the plum of all camp jobs.

Once, on a trip to Georgia to enlist men, he promptly succeeded in getting a truck-load to come to Florida, but at the last moment they began to grumble and refused to go. Abraham had a habit of holding two pebbles in his hand which he would rub together as he talked, just as others twist a watch chain or stroke their chins. Suddenly he had an inspiration; looking steadily at the balky Negroes, he said: "Niggers, you see dese two stone in my han'? Ef you don' git in dat truck right now I'll rub em together an' throw the worstes' spell on you you ever done hear about." No doubt to his surprise and certainly to his joy the terrified Negroes crowded into the truck and Abraham carried them to their new jobs.

From that time on he became conscious of powers that he had heretofore known nothing of. His fame gradually began to spread as that of a man who could "fix you." After he had saved a little money, Abraham bought a few acres of land and began farming. His health was not very good, and physicians diagnosed his case as Bright's disease and heart trouble. As he walked behind the plow trying to till his land, his wife noticed that every few moments he would stop and rest, always complaining of shortness of breath.

One day as he was plowing under the parching sun, he suddenly stopped, his face bathed in perspiration. Calling his wife he said, "Honey, I jes can' do dis yere work; I has a feelin' God's done called his chile for higher t'ings. Eber sence I been a boy I had dis yere feelin' but I jes didn' obey. 'Quench not the spirit'; saith de Lord." Throwing down his plow Abraham left the field, never to return to it as laborer.

He at once began his holy work. People came to him with all sorts of diseases and "spells," and they said he helped them all. At first he set no particular fee, his motto apparently being, "Give what the spirit moves you to give"; as time passed and his services grew in demand this motto changed to "The laborer is worthy of his hire." "Ef yo give something yo git something, ef you give nothing you git nothing," he used to say.

He traveled through the country-side in his horse and buggy ministering to the sick and the spell-bound. As he accumulated money he bought and paid cash for 200 acres of additional land, fenced it, and built six 4-room houses, covered with corrugated iron. These housed the families who cultivated his extensive holdings. He paid them $1.50 to $2 a day when other employers were paying $0.75 to $1.

Strawberries, string beans and corn were his chief products. He was now known as one of the biggest strawberry planters in Bradford County, and shipped as high as a carload of strawberries to eastern markets a day. Laborers were afraid to refuse to work for him; they left any job at his request.

As money continued to pour in, he finally discarded his horse and buggy for a specially built Cadillac which cost $3000, and a de luxe Hudson. Both white and colored people visited him, some coming from places as far distant as California and Connecticut.

His method of treatment was as follows: as you entered the house he ascertained your name and how much money you had for him. This he bade you place in a large Bible lying on the living room table. He then rubbed the afflicted part with his large hands, while intoning some weird ritual, of which the only words comprehensible were the names of the Prophets. When he finished his incantations, he looked you straight in the eye and assured you that you were well, or would be so after a few more treatments. After this procedure cripples would leave, carrying their crutches in their hands; some who hadn't eaten a decent meal in years were able to devour anything that was placed before them.

Abraham often gave his patients a white muslin packet known as a "Christian letter" to be carried on the person at all times. These letters cost from $5–25, and were supposed to bring good luck and ward off evil spells and any form of disaster. To lose the letter meant that one was liable to fall under an evil influence and be tormented. In such a case one must hasten to Abraham to procure another, after paying him the customary fee. He also sold other "good-luck" pieces for small sums, for use in "little" cases.

One of his patients, Estella Barber, of Lawtey, has this to say about him: "In 1936 I was suffering with indigestion, couldn't eat nor drink. I suffered for two years. They I went to Father Abraham an' as soon as I got on his porch, chile, all my pains done disappear. He treated me an' I went to him three times; the last time I was cured. Haven't had it sence, an' I kin eat anything. One time I didn' think about eating—-I had high blood pressure and Father Abraham said for me to come an' he could cure that too, but you know I didn' had no money, an' I was skeered to, cause I done hear he talk so rough when you don' had no money. I giv him three dollars for curin' de indiges', you know. Yes, suh, Father Abraham was a good man." This seems to be the attitude of most of his patients; he did good but was rough if you brought no money.

After 15 years of this work, Abraham had risen from a poor turpentine worker to one of the wealthiest men, white or colored, in Bradford County. During his last illness, in June 1937, his wife insisted on calling a physician. He was reluctant at first, fearing criticism from his patients, for whom he never prescribed medicine, but he finally yielded. He healed others; himself he could not heal. Within a week he was dead. His funeral was attended by a throng of both races.

Abraham left his widow and two daughters about $4,000 in cash and $8,000 in real estate; he had suffered heavily from the failure of the Starke bank during the depression. One of his daughters has vowed to carry on his work.

X

Conjure Shop

Through the Days of Labor and Nights of Rest,
The Charms of Fairy Stones will Keep you Blest.

This quaint little saying hangs above the window of a small cubby-hole of a
store located just three blocks from the post office, two blocks from the second
largest Negro high school in the State, across the street from the largest Negro
fraternal building in the South, equally flanked by reputable business concerns, and, strange to say, situated on the leading highway to and from the city.
In other words, this hole-in-the-wall is located in the 400 block on Broad
Street, Jacksonville.

They call it the conjure shop. It is just an ordinary store from the outside,
but upon entering one is confronted by the exotic odor of soothing incense
that evokes visions of foreign lands. Roots, herbs, oils, magic powders,
charms, and spirit-chasing powders catch the eye among the thousands of
labels on boxes and bottles arranged in neat rows on the long shelves.

The white proprietor greets his customers with a cheery smile and asks,
"What can I do for you?"

It is hard to believe that this shop does a business running into the thousands of dollars annually, handling supplies for mediums, spiritualists, root
doctors and other believers. Nor is this business confined to the ignorant and
illiterate. The proprietor soon corrects such a misapprehension: "Some of the
leading business men and bankers come here regularly to purchase their secret
formulas." The usual method is to seek out mediums and pay for their advice;
then the medium refers the client to the conjure shop for certain herbs or

trinkets. About half the customers are white, but white or colored, all classes of society are represented.

Great is the proprietor's faith in the magic power of his wares. Several weeks ago, he says, an old colored woman came to him in tears, saying that she had just left the doctor's office and had been sadly informed that her "caked breasts" would have to be removed, else she would die. Some one told her of the conjure shop, and she asked the proprietor if he thought he could cure her without an operation. He did not fail her, he continues, but gave her some flour, to be made into flap-jacks and applied to the affected parts. Two days later the woman returned full of joy; she had been cured!

Most of his knowledge, says the proprietor, comes from the study of the Bible; this he supplemented with intense research work. Incidentally, he is a firm believer in the mystery of King Tutt's tomb, and the curses that have followed those who touched it.

Perhaps he may tell you the legend that connects the verse at the head of this chapter with Patrick County, Virginia. Fairies were playing there when news came that Christ had been crucified. So great was their sorrow that they wept bitterly, and as their tears touched the ground they formed perfect crosses. These are the fairy stones that are worn for good luck charms. Naturally, the proprietor of the conjure shop has a sufficient stock of them.

Among the products on sale in the shop are:

Queen's root: made in to a tea it is a cure for sterility in women.

Buckeye nut: carried in the pocket to ward off rheumatism.

Orris root: also known as love root; will bring love between two people if sprinkled on clothes by one of the sex who wishes to attract a person of the opposite sex.

Five finger grass: if hung over the bed will bring restful sleep and will ward off any evil that any five fingers can bring.

Lesser periwinkle: if the leaves are eaten by man and woman together it will cause love between them.

Teneka bark: carried in a bag around the neck to ward off diseases and for good luck.

Wahoo bark: used to uncross a person. Make a tea of it and while rubbing it on the head of a person, call "wahoo" seven times.

Grains of paradise: used as a stimulant. One grain to be taken in hot water in the morning. It is also used by some in witchcraft as a crossing agent.

Sang root: popular Chinese root used against all kinds of ailments.

Life everlasting: said to prolong life. Used as a charm against illness. Make a tea of it and drink a cup as hot as possible before breakfast. This will prolong life indefinitely.

High John, the conquerer: carried in the pocket to offset melancholy moods.

Devil's shoestring: place around the neck to ward off evil spirits.

Loving herbs: put some in a bathtub of water and bathe in it. It will cause pleasant and soothing effect on everyone with whom the person comes in contact.

Rue: this herb is said to keep maids from going astray in the affairs of love; it is said to make eyes keener and wits alert, to heal the bites of snakes, scorpion, wasps, and to drive away the plague.

XI

Unusual Negro Communities

There are two communities in the State where the life of the Negro is so out of the ordinary as to deserve special notice: Eatonville and Pensacola. It is not generally known that Florida has an all-Negro town, not to speak of a good-sized city where segregation is not on the rise.[75]

Eatonville has the distinction of being of being the only town in the state completely owned and governed by the Negroes. It was incorporated August 8, 1889. Although only a ghost of its former self and never boasting a population of more than 600 at the peak of its existence, this small community has continued through the years to adhere to its regular routine of self-government as provided for in its original charter.

The town has a population of 300, three small churches, the Hungerford Industrial School, the public school, and a full force of city officials. It is noted for its spirited elections.

In 1889 H. W. Lawrence, a wealthy white philanthropist of Maitland, Florida, donated a 27-acre tract of land to a group of Negroes for a townsite. Here he erected a church which was the first structure built in the town. This was the St. Lawrence A.M.E. Church, named in honor of the donor.

At Mr. Lawrence's request the town was christened Eatonville, in honor of a sea-captain friend of his, Mr. J. C. Eaton. This gentleman later engaged in citrus farming, and at one time employed almost the entire population of the town, always giving preference to its inhabitants.

Soon after its incorporation, the citizens of Eatonville held their first election, choosing Joe Clark, local merchant, as the first mayor.[76] The following mayors in order of their tenure in office have served since that time: C.H. Boger, Sr. (dec) two terms; C. H. Boger, Jr., now pastor of Mt. Olive church, Orlando, one term; Tom Pender, (dec) one term; Joe Clark (dec) two terms; John Hurston (dec), father of Zora Neal Hurston, two terms; C. H. Boger, Jr., re-elected, serving two terms; B. L. Perry, now agricultural instructor in Florida A & M College, one term. Eatonville is the scene of Zora Hurston's latest novel: *Their Eyes Were Watching God.*

Pensacola

Pensacola presents a situation found in few, if any, other Florida communities. Instead of a white section, a colored section, a Jewish section, and so forth, there are no sharp dividing lines at all; in the sections predominantly white, there are usually a number of Negro homes, and in the Negro sections are found many white families living in complete harmony with their neighbors.[77]

Residents of the city attribute this state of affairs to the friendliness and cooperativeness between the predominant races that existed long before the last vestiges of slavery were gone, and that survived even the dark days of Reconstruction, when carpetbaggers, scalawags, and others were successfully straining the relations between the races in nearly every other city.

While both races have their churches, it is not uncommon to find a generously interracial congregation in many of them. This is particularly true of the Catholic churches. One priest, in fact, conducted a Negro orphanage of his own next door to the parish house, and was noted for his little colored altar boys at Mass. He used to take his little black flock through the streets to the movies and other amusements, and was well loved by every racial group in the city.[78]

In Warrington a minister serves his white church in the morning and his colored flock in the afternoon. His week is spent calling on members of both groups. In many of Pensacola's largest stores Negroes have been employed as clerks, and often in even more important positions, for years. Among the more notable instances were the big Roberts Grocery Co., Green's, and others; John Gagnet was bookkeeper and accountant for the Harrison Bros. Furniture Co. for the greater part of his life.

Negroes have always served on the federal juries in the city, and the courts are especially impartial. Several years ago this was vividly illustrated when J. D. Thompson, a colored lawyer, successfully fought for white clients in two cases, one against the city of Pensacola in behalf of A. B. Cairo, the result of which made Thompson's client an independently wealthy man, and one against the Western Union Telegraph Co., where the result was an award of $17,000.

Two Negroes served as pilots in Pensacola and Escambia bays for a number of years, Charles Baker and Simon Jones. Both were licensed, and members of the Bar Pilots' Association. They achieved distinction and were well liked by their fellow pilots. Their fees were identical with those charged by white pilots.

A thoughtful and considerate amity between races, a fortunate absence of the bitter exploitation of slave by master so commonly found in regions purely agricultural during the early days of Florida, and the frequent changes of governments, are possible factors in the great contribution that the Negro has been able to make to the history of Pensacola.

Negro influence has been evident from the first days of Pensacola's occupation by Americans; white soldiers fought while, Negroes, free and slave, built breastworks; slaves sawed lumber for their masters and for themselves as building went on apace; families intermingled in a surprising number of cases with full benefit of clergy—and their joint descendants built a community that is freely conceded to be at this time one of the most progressive in the South. In construction, in war and defense, in solid American tradition, the Pensacola Negro has an outstanding part.

The establishment of one of Pensacola's largest and most prominent families—a family with both white and colored branches by the trick of a slave—is a surprising historical fact about Florida's western metropolis. Here is the story:

In Mobile, Alabama in 1864 a trusted slave named Willis was called into the office of his master during the early days of the Civil War. It was explained to him that the Union soldiers were expected in Mobile any day, and that when they arrived they were certain to confiscate all the horses, cattle, mules and other stock of his master.

To Willis, therefore, was assigned the task of taking the horses and mules, particularly the latter, to Pensacola, a safer place, there to hide them until the master could come with his family.

Apparently not all the trust placed in Willis belonged there. He brought the mules to Pensacola, dutifully enough, but once there immediately set himself up in an elaborate hauling business, especially lucrative just then because of the government construction going on.

Willis not only grew prosperous, but he raised a large family. Lack of business method, as he himself realized, kept him from getting rich. So when an itinerant Jew came along one day and offered to become a partner in the thriving business and to contribute business knowledge and a good bookkeeping system, Willis welcomed him.

Relations between the two partners were ideal; so much so that when the Jew expressed a liking for one of Willis' daughters, there was no parental objection. Thus one branch of the family was begun.

Later, however, the Jewish partner decided to marry a white woman; this brought about the establishment of another branch of the family.

Today both branches are living in Pensacola. Relations between them are said to be cordial. The white division of the family is engaged in a number of enterprises, all apparently prosperous. Two brothers of the colored branch have a business that is one of the largest, if not the largest, Negro enterprises in this section of the State, with a factory in addition. Willis and his partner have both long since died, as have the mules.

The influence of the Negro on Pensacola architecture is great. In the city itself many structures still stand that were built by slave labor. One striking example is Government Street, where there are many old houses that date well back to the pre-war period. Following the emancipation of the slaves, the majority of the carpenters, plasterers, and other artisans were former slaves, hence much of the construction done after the Civil War was by Negroes.

Ever since the days of Reconstruction the Pensacola Negro has played a prominent role in politics. It is to his credit that his elevation to office was the result of the esteem in which he was held by both races in the community, rather than through the efforts of carpetbaggers and scalawags.

Peter H. Davidson of Pensacola was a member of the State legislature and was seated in 1868, the session that had 19 Negroes on its roll. Davidson achieved distinction as one of the most level-headed colored members; although he was thoroughly aggressive, he sternly opposed any measures that might have brought disadvantage to his race. On the other hand he opposed any unfair laws sponsored by the carpet-bag faction, and he is thought to have been one of those instrumental in retaining the incumbency of Gov. Reed when radicals sought his impeachment.

Davidson, with Jonathan C. Gibbs, Secretary of State, fought for educational facilities for Negroes in the State. This fight finally resulted in the establishment of a uniform and progressive public educational system for both blacks and whites in Florida and to the establishment of the State normal school for Negroes, now the Florida Agricultural and Mechanical College at Tallahassee.

T. D. Tucker of Pensacola was appointed by Governor Perry, also of Pensacola, as the first president of the normal school.

George Witherspoon, who was elected to the State legislature in 1868 from Monticello, became a resident of Pensacola in 1870. He made an excellent record.

From 1868 to about the close of the century this Negro activity in politics continued. During that time more than a dozen Negroes served as policemen: outstanding among them were officers Archie Crowell, George Scilpin, Lewis Cooke, John Williams, Bob Sheppard, Robert Thomas.

Of them Cooke was perhaps the most picturesque figure. To him fell the job of carrying the city prisoners to and from their daily jobs on the streets, and overseeing their work during the day. This he did with a pair of pistols in a holster strapped around his waist and a huge double-barrelled shot gun on his shoulder. No prisoner was ever permitted a lapse of memory as to who was the guard.

Richard Gagner, a Creole, was city marshall for several years after his appointment in 1878. He was followed by John Butterfield.

George Witherspoon, who had served a term in the state legislature, was city councilman for a couple of terms. Augustus Dupont was a member of the county board of public instruction for a number of years. He served with credit and had much to do with the appointment of teachers, both white and colored. An important white figure in the system, Eliza J. Wilson, after whom a school is named, gratefully gave public credit to Dupont for her appointment.

There were many federal job holders among the Negroes. Zeb Elijah was postmaster from 1870 to 1876, and had as assistant R. H. Matthews. During the Reconstruction period there were six Negro inspectors of customs: Aaron Brown, John Hall, Joseph Raines, L. B. Crooms, F. E. Washington, and "Judge" Mitchell.

Outside of office, Pensacola Negroes wielded a considerable influence during this period. When Representative J. C. Avery, a white Pensacolan, introduced a bill into the State legislature calling for segregation on all transportation systems in the State, a committee to lobby and protest against the bill was immediately elected from the Negroes here and sent to the capitol.

It consisted of C. F. Call, editor; Robert T. Thomas, and Attorney C. H. Alston. They appeared before the legislative committee in Tallahassee and did considerable lobbying as well; the bill was temporarily defeated by a wide margin. This was in May 1903.

In 1904 a committee of Pensacola Negroes lined up with Attorney I. L. Purcell, J. Spears, and C. H. Alston when they made the first organized fight for Negroes on Florida juries. This fight was based upon a plea for abatement in a case where nine Negroes had been tried for murder by juries that were entirely white. Due perhaps to the way the motion was put, the fight was unsuccessful.

That both races in Pensacola are content with the part that Negroes play in local government is shown by the fact that this is one of the few cities in Florida where Negroes may vote at democratic primaries, despite the ruling of the United State Court that Negroes may be barred from the ticket at the will of the party.

XII

Florida Agricultural and

Mechanical College

In Florida Agricultural and Mechanical College is a co-educational institution of higher learning for Negroes, supported by the State and under the management of the State Board of Control.[79] It is classified as a "land grant college" by the federal government. The institution is accredited as a class A college by the Southern Association of Colleges and Secondary Schools. Its president, Dr. J. R. E. Lee, and his entire faculty of 99 men and women are Negroes. It has an enrollment of 1017 students. Courses are offered in the following divisions: agriculture, education and teacher training, home economics, liberal arts and science, mechanic arts, music, nurses' training and health. Extension classes are conducted during the regular school term and a summer session is held.

The campus is located near the railroad station on a site overlooking the city on what was once a slave plantation; it consists of 375 acres of beautiful rolling hill land. The altitude there is one of the highest in the State. It has on it 25 main buildings, modernly constructed, and excellently equipped with facilities for living and instruction.

The institution was established October 5, 1887 as the Colored Normal School, by the State constitutional provision and legislative enactment. It was first located on what was then called College Hill, the present site of the Florida State College for Women.

The school was placed under the supervision and direction of the State Board of Education, which sanctioned its operation for the purpose of preparing normal and manual training teachers. Professors T. D. Tucker of Pensacola and T. V. Gibbs[80] of Jacksonville were placed in charge of the work of the school, which was housed in a T-shaped building with three large rooms. There were 15 students enrolled.

During the second year the enrollment grew to 38; it continued to increase until it had outgrown its accommodations. In 1891 the school was moved to the outskirts of Tallahassee, on a hill overlooking the city. This site, a 40-acre tract, was then called Highwood, and at one time had been a slave plantation.

In 1891, the school began to offer work in four departments: normal training, manual training, agriculture, and music. It was also in this year that the school began to benefit from the passage of the Morrill Bill in the previous year. Later it was to benefit from the Smith-Hughes and the Smith-Lever Acts, since the school encompassed the ideals and aims of a land grant college.

The progress of the school is signally indicated by the fact that in 1905 it passed under the management of the State Board of Control as one of the State's institutions of higher learning. In 1900 the school received its present name. Its physical expansion has been made possible by legislative enactment and funds from the General Education Board.

From the beginning instruction included both high school and college work. This was necessary because the secondary school system of the State was regrettably retarded. As a result the high school enrollment until 1930 exceeded that of the college; since then the situation has been reversed.

Graduates of the Florida Agricultural and Mechanical College are certificated by the State Department of Public Instruction. They are filtering into the public schools of the State and a marked improvement in the quality of the work and the operation of these schools has been noticed. The worthwhileness of the school is best indicated by the increased financial support it has received from the State legislature, the General Education Board, the Julius Rosenwald Fund, and the Jeanes-Slater Fund.

The progress of the institution must be attributed to the faithful corps of workers that the four presidents of the college—T. D. Tucker, 1887–1901; N. B. Young, 1901–1922; W. H. Howard, 1922–1923; and J. R. E. Lee, 1923—assembled about them to direct the activities of the school, to the loyal alumni who have backed the institution by directing students to its halls, and to the increasing support and approbation its progress has received from the State Department of Public Instruction.

The graduates of the college can be found in all fields of endeavor, as witness the following: Prof. Daniel Rolfe, Professor of Physiology, Meharry Medical College; Dean Rufus Hawkins, Dean of LeMoyne Junior College,

Memphis, Tenn.; Prof. Arthur Floyd, Professor of Agriculture, Tuskegee, Alabama; Mr. Edward MacMillan, industrial chemist, Cleveland, Ohio; Prof. McKinley Hendricks, Dental School, Howard University, Washington D.C.; Mr. Samuel, YMCA secretary, Hartford, Conn; Mr. James Grant, musician, New York City; Attorney Lawson Thomas, Miami, Florida; Mr. Nathan B. Young, Jr., journalist, St. Louis, Missouri.

XIII

Notable Florida Negroes

Considering the short time that has elapsed since his emancipation and his still lowly economic condition, the record of the Florida Negro is creditable. The race has produced a State superintendent of education, a prominent poet, a musician of note, a woman sculptress, a novelist, and others of equal or lesser importance. Of Negroes it can be said even more truly than is often said of women: no one knows what they can do, because they are only just beginning to have a chance. They, more than any class in the population, make up the great bulk of that third of the nation that concerns our President.[81]

Augusta Savage

From a none too well-fed tot of five, roundly chastised from making "graven images" by her Methodist preacher-father, when she made a bust of him out of Green Cove Springs clay, to an internationally famed sculptress whose work is ranked with that of masters in the field, is the step that has been taken by Augusta Savage.[82]

She was born in West Palm Beach about 1896, and moved to Green Cove Springs with her parents a few years later. Her childhood playmates remember her as particularly talented; clay models of small animals, rude heads and busts of people she knew, still-life objects were fashioned by her deft fingers.

She received the limited education that the section afforded, then attended the Florida A & M College for a term. Here her rise was phenomenal. Years later, when she was about to leave for a course of study in Europe, the few friends she had made during the brief time she spent at the school outfitted her for the trip.

Mrs. Savage returned to Green Cove Springs, married, and attempted to fit herself into the life of the village after the year at school, but the attempt was not successful. In 1922 she left the town and moved to West Palm Beach, having been led to believe that there she might be able to bring her sculpture before the public.

It was during this time that she made a bust of the late railroad magnate, Henry M. Flagler. This work was exhibited at the South Florida Fair, and immediately brought forth a promise of material assistance from friends and relatives of the Flaglers, as well as encouragement to go to New York to pursue her work seriously.

This she did. She went to New York, found a job and a few months later won a scholarship that put her into the Cooper Union Art School. Her success here was even greater than it had been before; at the end of her first year's work the president of the institution awarded her a prize for some carvings, with the comment that "This year has been the best one that this school has had under my administration, and credit goes to that colored girl there."

In 1924 Mrs. Savage entered a competition with 2,000 other artists and sculptors and won a scholarship to Fountainebleu, France. The donors of the award, however, learned that she was a Negro and hastily withdrew the scholarship. A prize that she won later provided her with a scholarship to the Royal Academy of the Fine Arts in Rome, but here too she was handicapped; the winner was expected to provide her own transportation, and this she could not do.

In 1929, however, the gifted sculptress was awarded the Julius Rosenwald Fellowship for study in Paris, and spent nearly three years there, winning the same award in 1930 and 1931. In Paris her work won citations in the Salon Automne and the Salon Printemps at the Grand Palais.

Back in America, Mrs. Savage began work on a series that eventually brought her much fame. One of the series is a Negro urchin, a picture of which was later used on the cover of the magazine *Crisis*. Others were *Green Apples*, now owned by John Nail, a wealthy New York realtor; *Envy*, a carving in teakwood, showing a woman with a crooked finger at her nose, frowning on the world; busts of Major Bowes of radio fame, Dr. Walter Crump, director of the Flower Hospital in New York and others.

Many years before Mrs. Savage had expressed the desire to carve a typical group to represent Negro womanhood. After much search, she found her model in 1935, and the group was finished in December of the same year. It shows a seated woman, draped from the waist down, looking out at the world with an expression of wisdom, patience, courage, and endurance, while beside her crouches a man clinging to her with an air of furtive bewilderment and frustration. Mrs. Savage's thought was to contrast the strength of the Negro womanhood with the frequent vacillation and weakness of Negro manhood.

In 1935 Mrs. Savage opened an art studio at 321 W. 136th Street in Harlem, which soon had 100 students enrolled. The school sponsored public exhibitions of the student's work, as well as a permanent exhibit of Mrs. Savage's work, the latter at the Harlem branch of the New York Public Library. So keen is the desire of talented students to study under Mrs. Savage that early in 1936 a lad hitch-hiked from Lynchburg, Virginia to enter her class. He proved to be one of the most promising pupils.

New York has become the permanent home of the sculptress, though she spent a year recently at Philadelphia while she took charge of the Negro Art and Culture exhibition at the SesquiCentennial Exposition. She frequently visits her relatives at Green Cove Springs and West Palm Beach.

Robert Meacham

As a youth Robert Meacham taught his fellow slaves reading and writing and purchased the freedom of his mother with money he had secretly saved; in manhood he was a member of the highest lawmaking body in the State of Florida.[83]

Meacham was born in Quincy, Florida about the year 1836. He was one of his master's sons, and was educated by him. During his earlier life he carried this education to the other slaves secretly and by night, using the dim glare of a candle for light. When the slaves were emancipated Meacham was already free; he had purchased his freedom and that of his mother with money he had saved out of the gratuities given him by his master.

He became a preacher, doing much of his work in Jefferson County. He entered politics in 1867, when an appointment signed by Brevet-Major General John Pope at Atlanta made him Register of the Jefferson County District. He was later appointed a presidential elector by W.N. Gleason, president of the Convention at Tallahassee in 1868. The appointment was signed by Wm. Lee Anthony, secretary of the Convention.

In 1868 Meacham was appointed clerk of the Circuit Court for Jefferson County by Harrison Reed, then governor. The following year he was named superintendent of common schools by Reed; this appointment was for two years. After that he was appointed postmaster of Monticello by John A. J. Creswell.

Reed re-appointed Meacham to the school position for a two year term, beginning in 1871. The next governor, Ossian B Hart, re-appointed Meacham for two more years. This was also in Jefferson County.

The crowning point in Meacham's career was his election by the Florida Senate in 1876. Four years later he was made postmaster of Punta Gorda.[84] He went to Tampa in 1896, having retired from active political service because of failing health.

C. F. Call

A poet who became newspaper man, politician, teacher and finally returned to poetry, is one of the contributions that Pensacola has made to the field of Negro literature.[85]

Professor C. F. Call, who now lives among his books and his writings at 620 North F Street in Pensacola, became known to literature through the little magazine, *Happy Hours*, published in Maine for many years near the close of the last century.

Call's contributions to it covered a period of nearly a dozen years and a wide variety of material. His *Odes*, written on the death of prominent Negroes and others, were widely read, and brought him letters of appreciation from all over the world.

Later Call became a frequent and prolific contribute to the *Nation*. In his articles and stories he vividly described the ills and handicaps of Negro life in the South.

Living for a time at Monticello, Call once described the educational system under which Negroes in that section were struggling to get an education. Published in the *Nation*, the articles declared that "talk of an eight or nine month school term is useless; under present conditions it would take a Negro a hundred years to get an education."

The article resulted in a State probe of the conditions, but to Call it brought something more deadly: a visit of the dread Ku Klux, in full war regalia. They generously gave him three days to leave Monticello; he made it in two.

The brilliant young writer founded a newspaper in Pensacola, *The Exponent*, and operated it from 1898 to 1906. During these years the paper took an active part in politics, being credited with the responsibility for several sweeping reforms. So great was its influence at one election that on the following day he was ordered to appear before a body of fifteen men—all armed, of course—

and only by appearing with pistols in both coat pockets, and perhaps even more by the intervention of an influential white friend, was he able to escape with his life.

Call's contributions to *Happy Hours* began about 1890 and continued to 1900; his articles in the *Nation* were from 1894 to 1905; contributions to other publications, magazines, newspapers in northern cities covered the period from these dates until the recent past. He still writes occasionally.

Aharte Carter

The presence of two poets among Pensacola's colored folk population, both writing credible verse, is a happy surprise for this west Florida community.

Aharte Carter, student of the Tuskeegee Institute, came to public notice when his poem, *The Tuskeegee Girl*, and another composition in prose won him the school's annual award for literature in 1932. Since then his writings have appeared in the school magazine, in the *Pittsburgh Courier*, and other colored publications.

Daniel W. Roberts

Hundreds of tourists each year include in their visit to America's oldest city a trip to the little African Methodist Church. Here in St. Augustine may be seen one of the most unique monuments in the entire State: the memorial fountain to a doctor who almost single-handedly fought one of the city's worst epidemics.[86]

Dr. Daniel W. Roberts, born in Indiana one year after emancipation, was the only Negro physician among the several thousand residents of St. Augustine and vicinity when the country's worst recorded epidemics of influenza broke out in 1918.

St. Augustine suffered heavily; cases were reported by the dozen each day. The white doctors who normally cared for most of the Negro sick in St. Augustine found their hands full with other cases. The outlying areas, covering territory that stretched as far as Bayard on the north and Flagler County on the south, made heavy demands on medical service.

Into this picture of suffering and chaos, Dr. Roberts stepped. Day and night he worked, finally reaching every patient who called him. His contemporaries said of him at the time that he was visiting three times as many victims as any other physician. This, however, was not the most remarkable feature of his work. During the entire epidemic he did not lose a single patient!

Other physicians became interested in his methods. Much of the time, after the first few weeks of the epidemic, was spent assisting other doctors from Jacksonville, Daytona, and nearby cities in preparing prescriptions and remedies for their own practices. At one point the number of prescriptions written for his St. Augustine patients alone reached 60 a day.

While Roberts saved every one of his patients, he could not save himself from the natural consequences of the heroic overexertion to which he subjected himself. In February of the following year he died.

His memory did not die, however. A few years later a group of his former colleagues, white and Negro, banded together to erect a monument to him. They began a campaign to raise $1,000 for this purpose and the fund was shortly over-subscribed. Among those who quickly added their donations to the fund were several bishops in Negro churches, doctors, the president of the St. Augustine bank, and hundreds of white and colored residents. The fund was completed early in 1925.

A Jacksonville sculptor, George Leapheart, was given the commission of creating a fitting monument to Dr. Robert's memory. The result of his work was unveiled at the St. Paul's A. M. E. Church on November 8th of that year— a beautiful hand-carved, two-color marble monumental baptism fount, said to be the only one dedicated to a doctor in the country.

It is about four feet high, of white and Vermont marble. Inscribed in its base are tributes to the dead humanitarian and his work, his date of birth and death, and the names of the donors of the monument.

At the top of the fount are several insignia: one of the Knights of Pythias, a fraternal order assisted in obtaining the memorial and of which Dr. Roberts had been a member; the official medical symbol; the usual church insignia and others. The fount was placed near the altar of the church of the physician had attended during his life.

There is usually a guide for the visitors to explain about the monument. Frequent references to it are made in the church services.

Jonathan Gibbs

The highest state office ever held by a Negro in Florida was held by Jonathan Gibbs. Because of Governor Harrison Reed's dislike for secretary of state Alden it is alleged that he trumped up a charge of embezzlement and requested Alden's resignation. When it was not forthcoming, Reed declared the office vacant and appointed Gibbs. Gibbs later became superintendent of public instruction.

The most cultured member of the constitutional convention of 1868 was this same Jonathan C. Gibbs. He was a tall and slightly built Negro with a high forehead; his color indicated mixed blood. His voice was clear and ringing. In manner he was a born orator, and by nature somewhat of a sentimentalist.

Born in Philadelphia, educated at Dartmouth and Princeton Theological Seminary, Gibbs was an example of an intelligent black subjected to the influences of theological training and New England culture. He had been sent to Florida by northern philanthropists to work among the Negroes. Entering politics shortly after his arrival there, he was soon rubbing elbows with ignorance and knavery.

Governor Reed's appointment of Gibbs as secretary of state on November 1, 1868 was the signal for disturbances in various counties, resulting in open violence and bloodshed. Reed was asked to declare martial law, but instead he sent Gibbs to the center of the disturbances. Gibbs was courageous enough to criticize the carpetbaggers, a move that won commendation and support from the more intelligent element of the Negro population.

Reed's successor, Ossian B. Hart, elected in 1872, promptly made Gibbs state superintendent of public instruction. This position Gibbs held from 1872 to 1874, at a time when the school system was tottering, and the collection of funds difficult. Undaunted, Gibbs set about elevating the standards of education by travelling all over the State and making eloquent speeches, which soon made people conscious of the need for better educational facilities. In this matter the whites as well as the Negroes gave ear to Gibbs. The state legislature made appropriations for the improvement of education, and under the able guidance of Superintendent Gibbs progress continued.

When Hart died in 1874 Marcellus Stearns became governor. He wanted to ask for Gibb's resignation, but Gibbs was too popular. Stearns had promised to nominate Gibbs for Congress, but was afraid that he could not control him. He was spared the trouble of making a decision; Gibbs died before the end of the Republican rule, ostensibly from eating too heavy a dinner. It was rumored that he had been poisoned.[87]

James Weldon Johnson

James Weldon Johnson, professor of creative literature at Fisk University in Nashville, Tennessee, was born in Jacksonville June 17, 1871.[88] His early education was received at Stanton High School. He has written and published five full length books of prose and verse. His writings in Jacksonville date back to the decade immediately preceding the Spanish War.

Among the poems written at this time are: *Since You Went Away*, in 1897, the result of his desire to express in verse something of the feeling of the Negro towards the Great Emancipator; *Lift Every Voice and Sing*, the national Negro hymn. Both of these were set to music by his brother, J. Rosamond.

J. Weldon also wrote a number of poems in Negro dialect, which were published in national magazines. In the spring of 1898 he began in this city his story that was later made into the operetta Toloso, a success on the New York Stage.

His *Autobiography of an Ex-Colored Man*, a novel, begun in Jacksonville during the period preceding 1900, is so full of human interest and appeal that more than 100,000 copies of it have been sold, both in the regular $3 edition and the popular $1 form. *Along This Way*, another of his books, is also largely autobiographical. Johnson is conceded to be one of the most prolific and versatile authors in America.

J. Rosamond Johnson

J. Rosamond, brother of J. Weldon, and like him born in Jacksonville, has composed more than 300 songs, many of which have been recognized as worthy contributions to the field of classical music. He now lives in New York.

J. was born August 11, 1873. He showed unusual musical talent in his earliest years, and long before he reached manhood had begun setting to music the lyrics of his brother.

Much of Johnson's music was published in New York, but the bulk of early work was done in Jacksonville. The music for the operetta, Toloso, two musical comedies, and several tunes was written in his home, which stood near the intersection of Lee and Houston streets, razed in 1928 to make way for the Firestone Service Station.

Possibly the most well known of his compositions is the music of the national Negro hymn, first performed in Jacksonville in the Stanton High School with a chorus of 500 voices. John McCormack, Fritz Kreisler and others have recorded Johnson's music on Red Seal Victor records.[89]

W. E. Dancer

W. E. Dancer, composer of dialect and lyric poetry, was a native of Alabama, but resided in Jacksonville from 1919 until his death in 1934.[90] His writings had already made their appearance before he finished his education at Tuskeegee. In 1906 he published *Today and Yesterday*, a book of lyric and dialect poetry. In 1915 his second published work, *Fact, Fun and Fiction*, was issued at Montgomery. Both volumes drew favorable comment from critics all over the country.

Sunshine and Shadow, written in Jacksonville and published by the Sentinel Publishing Co in 1925, was largely in dialect, and followed closely the form made so popular by Paul Lawrence Dunbar in his serio-comic presentation of typical Negro situations. Many of the poems in the volume are based on observations Dancer made during his extensive travels through Florida and the southeast. One, a long and highly amusing poem written at Gainesville during a brief stay there, related humorously a very serious problem he had encountered while in attendance at a convention: bedbugs. Others were written in a more serious vein, and pathos and suffering are not missing.

Dancer died at the age of 50, but not before he had seen the fulfillment of a dream he had for years: the publication of his three books in one volume. It is obtainable in the local library.

Thomas H. B. Walker

Thomas Walker is the author of several books of prose and verse. Among these are *Crowther of Sierra Leone*, which is used as a text in the schools of Liberia; *Presidents of Liberia*, for students, containing sketches of the presidents and some of the leaders of Liberia; two novels, *Man without Blemish* and *J. Johnson, or the Unknown Man.*[91] He has re-written the book of Revelations in metrical form, and has also composed a poem, *To my Sweet Little Girl*. Some of his books have had a wide circulation: over 15,000 copies of *Man Without Blemish* and about the same number of *Presidents of Liberia* have been sold.

Dr. Walker was born in Tallahassee, received his early education there, and began preaching before he was 16 years old. He attended school in Jacksonville, Clark University, and Gammon Theological Seminary in Atlanta, Georgia. He has traveled extensively and lectured in cities as far away as Paris, France. He has pastored several prominent Methodist Episcopal churches in Florida. The title K. C. was conferred upon him by the republic of Liberia. He is the only Florida Negro minister mentioned in *Who's Who in Methodism*.

Allen Thompson Robeson

A. T. Robeson, blind musician and composer, was born of slave parents in 1859 at Madison, Florida. He lost his eyesight at the age of 14 and remained totally blind the rest of his life. He learned music by sound and could play practically every band instrument. Among his vocal and instrumental compositions are: *Just Inside the Beautiful Gate* and *Dear Old Stream Suwannee*. In 1886 he organized the Welcome Cornet Band in Jacksonville, which became nationally famous. It was then a custom to have a band precede the funeral cortege, and the Welcome Cornet Band played at hundreds such occasions. It is thought that Paul L. Dunbar's poem, *When the Colored Band Comes Marching Down the Street* was inspired by this band; the poet spent several months in Jacksonville as the guest of the Johnson brothers, previously mentioned.

The organization was disbanded in 1926. Nelson Roundtree, one of the original members, is still living.

Zora Neale Hurston

Florida's most famous Negro woman writer was born in Eatonville.[92] She was the recipient of the Guggenheim Fellowship award in 1936, and in 1937 was given an extension of the award to continue her studies of native customs in Haiti. Zora Hurston was educated at Howard University in Washington and Barnard College, Columbia University. Her books, in the order of publication are: *Jonah's Gourd Vine*; *Mules and Men*; *Their Eyes Were Watching God*; *Tell My Horse, Man of the Mountain*.

XIV

Durkeeville and Liberty City

The second low-cost housing project for Negroes in Florida was started in Jacksonville on Feb. 17, 1936. A twenty acre tract was chosen surrounded by three congested and unsanitary sections. It is located in west Jacksonville and is bounded by 6th, Payne, McGenihe streets and Myrtle Avenue. Durkeeville, named for the conveyor of the tract, was opened for occupancy June 19, 1937. It was developed by the Housing Division of the Federal Emergency Administration of Public Works and sponsored by the Municipal Housing Board. The cost was approximately a million dollars.[93]

The Houses

The attractive stucco one and two story houses occupy less than 15 per cent of the site, thus ensuring ample light, air and sunshine. $30,000 was spent for landscaping the lawns, hedges and gardens. There are no through streets and all roads are curved, so that vehicular traffic must travel slowly. Not only are children protected, but four large and two small play areas, equipped with slides, swings, basket ball courts and sandboxes are provided for their pleasure.

The 215 so-called units are arranged to accommodate families of from two to seven persons: there are 41 two-room, 101 three-room, 49 four-room, and 24 five-room apartments. These have all modern conveniences, including free

---

Although Liberty City was added to this title in the typescript by hand, no material was ultimately included. Some material is found in the general Florida guide.

electric lights, electric refrigeration and hot water; heaters are furnished in the larger apartments. Rental rates run as follows: two rooms, $2.90–3.10 a week; three rooms, $3.65–3.95; four rooms, $4.05–4.35; five rooms, $4.40–4.35.

The Tenants

Tenants were carefully selected from a long waiting list. In addition to character qualifications, their earnings had to fall within a range not less than three nor more than five times their rental.[94]

There are a number of community activities, among them a nursery school sponsored by the Mothers' Club and a Boy Scout Troop by the Dads' Club. There are vocational classes under the supervision of the State Vocational Department, and organized play groups under the Jacksonville Department of Public Recreation.

The management personnel includes a management aide, a junior management aide, and a bookkeeper-cashier. John Simms, management aide, arranged for a series of outdoor concerts last summer that proved very popular. A large platform situated in almost the middle of Durkeeville, completely surrounded by towering pine trees, furnished an ideal setting for these Sunday afternoon events; choirs and soloists from city churches furnished the music. Huge amplifiers carried the voices to every portion of the field.

It would be hard to say whether the children or the adults are the more pleased with their new surroundings. Perhaps all feel like the woman who said, "Aint but one place I like living better than this and that's heaven; an' I ain't been there yet."

XV

Religion

Nearly two hundred thousand of Florida's half a million Negroes attend some church.[95] This number, 190,893, to be exact, worship in 2,882 churches, 2,093 of them being Negro churches. There are 1,733 church edifices to house these congregations, with a total valuation of $8,452,992. Not included in this figure, however, are 22 churches from whom no report was received.

Baptists comprise more than half of the entire Negro membership in the State, with 98,194 members. The denomination has 884 churches in the State, worshipping in 775 edifices. These structures have an average valuation of $4,486; there are 44,893 Sunday school members in the denomination, approximately half of the whole State membership.

Primitive Baptists have 126 churches in the State, and 7,186 members. They have 17 church buildings. Only three of the congregations reported church schools, and these had an enrollment of 240.

Approaching closely to the Baptists in point of total membership is the African Methodist Church, with 47,541 members in 694 congregations. Six hundred eleven church edifices in the State belong to the denomination with a valuation of $2,599,135, or an average of $4,420 per church.

There is a wide gap between the memberships of these two denominations and the several next-highest. One-fourth as large as the Baptist church is the Methodist Episcopal, with its 802,130 members. This denomination has 223 churches, 143 of which are Negro and 80 partly Negro; 121 church structures house them.

The Methodist church edifices are among the higher-valued in the State, with a total valuation of $802,130, and an average valuation of $6,629, highest of the three largest denominations. The church has a comparatively small church school membership, with only 5,721 members enrolled.

The African Methodist Episcopal Zion church has 47 churches in Florida, with 13,647 members and 8,426 enrolled in its Sunday schools. The average church property valuation is high for this denomination, $10,314 per edifice. Total church property in the State is approximately one-half million dollars. The average membership per church is higher than in any other in the State, 290 persons.

The Protestant Episcopal church has a large membership among Florida Negroes. Although there are only 19 churches in the denomination in the State, they have 45,500 members. Most of them worship in the 135 churches that have only part-Negro memberships. Their church school enrollment is 1,371, and the average valuation of 18 of their 19 churches is second highest of all denominations, $15,012.

Six Negro churches and 115 part-Negro congregations have a combined Catholic membership of 1,657 among the State's colored population. Five hundred attend their church schools, and their properties are valued at a total of $95,500 for the six Negro church bodies. This gives the church an average valuation per church of $15,917.[96]

Florida has four major groups of Methodists among its Negroes: the Methodist Episcopal Zion, and the Colored Methodist Episcopal. The latter is fourth largest of the group in membership. It has 5,111 followers in the State; they worship in 68 congregations, each with its own church edifice, a privilege enjoyed by no other large Negro denomination in the State.

The average membership per church in this denomination, however, is lowest of all the major denominations, only 75 per church. The valuation of church property is high: $7,298 for the 68 churches. Sunday school membership is 3,088.

Smaller Denominations

There are 207 congregations in the State that may be thus designated, and they worship in 66 Negro churches and 141 part-Negro churches. Their combined membership is about 2,523, with 1,907 in the Sunday schools.

There are 364 other churches in the State in which the membership is either wholly or in part Negro; these comprise the Adventists, with 44 part-Negro and 9 Negro churches; the two bodies of Presbyterians, with 186 churches, 8 of them Negro; and 116 religious groups of miscellaneous classification. The

Independent Methodist Episcopal (African) church has 15 churches. The combined membership of all these groups is 1,737.

Youngest of All

Newest church to appear in the State among Negroes is the Lutheran church, of which there is one congregation in Pensacola. This church, part of the Alabama Synod, was established since the last official census of church statistics was taken. In early 1936 it was about four years old, with a membership of less than 100. It has a church building, school, and grounds valued at perhaps $3,000 and a well-rounded education and civic program.

Sanctified Churches

The churches designated as "sanctified" include a wide range of small churches, often mere store-fronts, whose membership is exceedingly fluctuating.[97] In this category are the "Church of God and Saints of Christ," the "Pillar of Truth," the "Holy Rollers" and others. They define sanctification as "to speak with unknown tongues," and the gift to heal and prophesy. It is interesting to note that these people firmly believe in devils and demons; they attribute every misfortune disease and bodily ill to the work of the devil and all sickness as the consequence of sin.

Such a sufferer is said to be possessed and rites and ceremonies are performed together with exorcisms and evocations to drive the spirit from the victim. Medical aid and attention is refused. Certain oils are used together with prayer and enchantment in ordering the demon to depart from the patient. It is reported that in some cases death has resulted because the saint obstinately refused to call in a doctor.

Services are held on Sundays and each night during the week. The nightly meetings begin late, lasting far past midnight. Every saint testifies as to his or her daily conduct and trials with and triumphs over Satan. All accidents are regarded as the snares of the devil, and there is joy in telling how he has been worsted.

Musical instruments used in the sanctified churches include the piano, the guitar, drum and tambourine. Their playing is accompanied by the beating of hands, and the beat of the drums is a rhythmic tom-tom. The noise and excitement continues until one or more of the congregation break forth into unintelligible utterance; this is called "speaking in tongues." Occasionally worshippers fall in a fit. This seems to call forth special rejoicing, and among the words of praise the word "Jesus" is frequent.

Religious Music

Next to the songs that he sings at his work and at his parties, the Florida Negro loves his religious music. This runs a wide range from the sedate hymns of the churches in the larger cities, to the semi-jazz music of the small, backwoods "sanctified" churches.

In recent years there has come an increased popularity of the swinging type of music, even in the churches. In Jacksonville there is a jazz pianist who seldom has a free night; nearly as much of his business comes from playing for sanctified church services as for parties. Standing outside the church it is difficult to determine just which kind of engagement he is filling at the moment.

Nor is the idea of the swing hymn confined entirely to the small out-of-the-way churches. Even in some of the larger churches in the city the trend is clearly noticeable. When, in Jacksonville, a series of amateur performances was staged over a long period, hardly a week passed that did not present some well known young choir-singer, singing sacred music with all the lilt and sprightliness of a jazz composition. A well-known Negro businessman in the same city, who preaches and signs in his spare time, had a special accompanist to achieve the full jazz effect in the hymns he sings.

The music in the larger churches is usually of the standard variety as to words and tunes, getting its originality through the liberties taken in presentation. In the churches of the smaller communities religious music is far less orthodox. Here many of the sacred songs are mere chants, with no words at all (and little music), in which the congregation merely hums a bit of tune for several minutes; in others the minister or some member of the congregation tells the others a line or two of some hymn, after which they sing it, then they pause and he tells them another line, and so on through all the stanzas.

The lines "told" to the congregation by the minister are not always lines of any song; sometimes they are passages from the Bible, his own personal observations or exhortations, or words that please him especially. In such a case the congregation may simply chant or moan something resembling a tune after each line by the minister.

An unusual kind of sacred music may be heard at the daily services in the Clara White Mission in Jacksonville. Here for sometimes as long as fifteen minutes the congregation chants a wordless tune that has no apparent beginning or ending to mark its stanzas. Its only punctuation is the frequent shouting of the worshippers who "get happy" or their screams when they wish to express particular emotion.[98]

At a Sanctified church in Winter Park the members sang, for about ten minutes uninterruptedly, the following words:

Sinner, you can't fool God,
Sinner, you can't fool God,
Sinner, you can't fool God,
He's got His eyes on you!

If there were any other words to the song, the congregation evidently did not know them.

Of particular liveliness is the song heard at a small Baptist church near Martin, Marion County:

I got your spirit in my heart, Lord;
I got your spirit in my heart,
And I promise you that I
Will serve you till I die—
I got your spirit in my heart.
I'm living peaceful in this world, Lord;
I'm living peaceful in this world.
And dear Lord, I promise you
I'll love my neighbors too,
I'm living peaceful in this world.

This song is apparently original with the little Marion County congregation, since it does not seem to be in use in any other church. The third and fourth lines, however, are borrowed from a Baptist revival hymn; the tune is quite original.

XVI

Spirituals

In the spiritual the Negro has made one of his most authentic contributions to American Culture. Of collections of spirituals and musical evaluations of them there is no lack, and the end, fortunately, is not in sight. It has seemed unnecessary, therefore, to attempt the inclusion of the more well-known spirituals, even though they were sung on Florida plantations. The following spirituals have never before been published, with the exception of three old spirituals. These are included that the reader may get some idea of the development of the spiritual. It would be only natural, if as the Negro's economic condition improved, there should be a shift in emphasis from other-worldliness to this-worldliness. Has this in fact happened? The reader can best judge for himself.[99]

Old Spirituals
  *Oh, Let me Come in
  *Room Enough
  Heavin goin' be my home
Modern & Modernized Spirituals
  Jesus, Lead Me
  *We Are Troubled
  *Didn't They Crucify My Lord?
  *Judgment
  *Pentecost
  I Know the Blood Will Make Me Whole
  Where the Sun Don't Never go Down

Modern & Modernized Spirituals (cont)
 *Hand Writin' on de Wall
 The Power of God is Just the Same Today
 God Sent Trouble all over the Land
 Examine Yourself
 Jesus is my Airplane
 Let me Alone
 Don't Ride that Hell-bound Train
 *Come and Jine

Afterword

Reading *The Florida Negro*

The typescript for *The Florida Negro* arrived in the mail. I responded viscerally. A manuscript had been re/discovered, having been in the archives for almost fifty years, and I wanted to tear into it—terra nova, a time capsule, a new taxonomy (the Florida "Negro" to be added to other regionalized "Negroes" in the Works Progress Administration journey through American ethnic cultures), an opportunity to add comparative material to the folk history of the African-American community in the 1930s and '40s. Here I was, an incarnation of Christopher Columbus all over again.

The initial response keyed to exploration of the contents of this remarkable manuscript got sharply derailed by chapter 1, "History," with the description of the "shouts" and "celebrations" that accompanied the arrival of the first African, already marked as a slave. I read that "to the Spanish colonist of the new Florida the slave meant food; someone to raise crops on the farms near St. Augustine" (4). What a wonderful mixture of images—cannibalism and exploitation.

The slaves' labor is literally eaten. A subversive reading to be sure. Yet the evocation of a narrator on the shores celebrating, even savoring Florida's entry into plantation agriculture, forced a more active attention to that interlocutor. Once raised, the question of authorship and point of view dogged my reading of the text. I wondered who was really telling the story, who was the "we" in the narration and to whom was the story addressed? How much should it matter to the late twentieth-century reader whether the narrator(s) stood on shore eager for those slaves, or looked out from Don Juan de Aila's ship, enslaved and fearful of the hardships that lay ahead.

The afterword is a diary of responses, intensely personal, but I hope it speaks to the burdens that this manuscript bears and to the expectations that it has to meet. This book will be of value to those of us interested in documenting the folk traditions of southern African-Americans. The collector of WPA output might well regard the book's primary importance as its having added to the compendium. But if its impact is to extend beyond the merely additive, *The Florida Negro* must be read as more than a primary source of record. It brings to the surface issues about representation and audience that were very much alive in the time when it was written and that continue to be of central concern to scholars and to the general public, of which I am primarily concerned with that of the African-American reader.

The Florida Negro, like others in the series, was a part of an overall social project that held a didactic model of the relationship between reader and text. The text was to teach and to reveal previously hidden or misunderstood racial and ethnic communities. By the very transformation from oral to written, these texts were expected also to render value and worth to the culture, folk traditions, and communities that they documented. When it came to the southern context, and to blacks in particular, these goals seemed often to have been at cross-purposes to the social relations of race and class that intervened in the production of texts, in the collection of materials, and in the interactions between interviewer and interviewee.

In the case of the regional "racial histories," as they were termed by Roscoe Lewis, African-American supervisor of the *Negro in Virginia* project, the work was to include insiders—that is researchers and writers who were themselves from the specific ethnic group. As Charles Perdue (1980) points out, however, in his commentary on the *Negro in Virginia*, the Negro writer presented a conundrum to the logic of white administrators and scholars, for whom objectivity appears to have been a white racial attribute. Thus Eudora Ramsay Richardson, for example, white state supervisor of the Virginia Writers' Project expressed anxiety about the danger of "Negro bias" and undertook the task, so she reported, of putting balance back into the text by completely rewriting it (Perdue, Barden, Phillips, xxi–xxiii). Scholars have thrown much doubt on this retelling especially in the deliberate attempt to displace authorship at the expense of the African-Americans who had actually written the manuscript. The issue that concerns us, however, remains the same for it speaks to how the black body/mind gets cued as prejudicial or "biased." Apparently, "bias" encapsulated many meanings of which two seem relevant here.

The first was that the black researchers and writers would present too negative a portrait of racial oppression and discrimination and of southern race relations. Or another way of thinking about it is that there seemed to have been a fear that once given the authority as observer and chronicler, the African-American writer would sensationalize what was meant to be scholarly, or darken an otherwise friendly, upbeat, teacherly, genre of the text. The second meaning given to "bias" seemed to hold to an obverse set of issues, that the African-American writer being too close to the materials would tend towards too laudatory an exposition of the community and its individual residents, while missing out on the underside.

Yet one person's bias could be another's social justice. The preeminent concern for the African-American writer might well have been that the forms of injustices during slavery and in the present (1930s, 1940s) be revealed and that the Negroes' struggles against the odds celebrated. In the case of the *Negro in Virginia*, the shadow of these essential divergences showed up in the preface written by Roscoe Lewis and in the introduction by Eudora Ramsay Richardson. Both attempt to shape the reading of the text and in so doing provide a condensed overview of where the fractures lay. First Mr. Lewis:

> In a real sense, the story of the Negro in Virginia is also the story of the American Negro, for the roots of more Negro families were nurtured in Virginia than in any other state. It has been our aim to tell impartially of the springs that watered those roots and of the droughts that withered them. It is, therefore, to the American Negro, and to those who seek to understand him, that this volume is offered as the written record of a people who have helped build America—a people who are perhaps the most widely discussed and the least understood, though by no means the least important in American's racial *pot-pourri* (italics in the original, v).

In his preface, then, Lewis makes the claim to impartiality and deliberately links it to question of social injustice, resistance, and to the acknowledgment of the "Negro's" contribution to the American polity. The objectivity (impartiality), as he understands it, comes through the lived experiences of being black and Virginian. The book's purpose is to serve as a testimonial spoken to other African-Americans and to those whites with a stated interest in understanding the "American Negro."

For Ramsey Richardson, the emphases lay elsewhere:

The State Supervisor of the Virginia Writer's Project (herself) is grateful for the opportunity that has come to her to understand the viewpoint of Negro leaders in Virginia, and to further an interracial cooperation that she believes has promoted good feeling between the races, and will do much toward enabling Negro citizens in Virginia to achieve a large measure of participation in the responsibilities and rewards of citizenship (v).

Where is the concern with bias in this passage and how does it put a markedly different spin on the contents of the text? Lewis would have us remember the struggles for racial parity and access. Ramsey Richardson, on the other hand, reminds us of our manners, of the importance of "making nice." In the rush to condemn the injustices, she seems to say, the Negro has to remember the costs of citizenship—"responsibility" as well as "rewards." Further, the *Negro in Virginia* functions in her mind as ambassador for greater racial rapprochement. Diplomacy, then, eschewed too critical an analysis of race relations and the politics of exclusion.

The voices of those who worked on *The Florida Negro*, and for whom questions such as these would have been vital have been muted with the passage of time between initial inception and publication. It appears, however, that questions of interpretation and balance undergird the production of these materials as well. Ex-slaves' memories of corporal punishment, meager rations, and overwork, for example, are paired with a text within a text of a slaveholder's writings on his system of benevolent slavery.

Zephaniah Kingsley's *The Patriarchal System of Society* is excerpted here as "A Slaveholder Speaks." His philosophy of practical slave-holding derives from his experience as master, slave-trader, and common-law husband of a black woman (recognized by African marital rites, we are told, although no details are given). Kinglsey's treatise fairly bristles with the expert's knowledge of the slave's psychology and mores, and of proper management—"hardly ever [having] occasion to apply other correction than shaming them" (38).

We are told that he broke the legal customary rules of Florida slave-holding: teaching his slaves to read and write, allowing them to choose their marital and sexual partners, even offering weekly festivities where he encouraged "dancing, merriment and dress" (37–38). In return his pacified slaves worked without complaint, and even, it seems, were highly valued on the open market because of their skills. A slaveholder and slavetrader, Kingsley offers a fable. Properly treated slaves fall from grace, and forfeit the rewards of paradise on earth by their own ill-will and irrational belief in religious "superstition." For the potential white reader in Florida of the 1930s and '40s, Kingsley is the idealized master, the exception that affirms the wished-for rule. All masters would be as kind, if only slaves did not take advantage.

Who was the intended audience here and who the narrator? I suspect a white interlocutor and a potentially diverse audience of which the most influential would be literate whites. Then, too, there was the need to control the ways in which Florida would have been displayed to the outside. It is apparent, however, that even if written by African-American members of the Negro unit at the state writers' program, this section of the text, and the book in its entirety likely faced the conflicting demands of appeasing/pleasing the potential white audience, while chronicling African-American history and community for African-Americans themselves. Kingsley's text brings these issues above ground in a way that acts as a sign to the late twentieth-century reader, calls one's attention to the racial politics of representation and to the relative power of writers and audience in that setting.

Within the outer frame of *The Florida Negro*, Kingsley's excerpt functions as a legitimating narrative. He writes that while the ex-slaves interviewed in *The Florida Negro* can offer only oral testimonies to their experience of slavery's brutality, the written is posed against the oral, black testimony against the white, and the former is seen as having intrinsic merit as an objective account. Indeed in the paragraph that introduces the excerpt to the reader, Kingsley's tale of slaves and slavery is characterized as being "impartial as any we can have" (37). Further, his supposed "objectivity" is reinforced through the almost mythical presence of the duly recognized "negro" wife. He is twice an insider—as a slaveholder and then as the intimate of a Negro woman, perhaps even her owner. The objectivity of the "negro" herself, on the other hand, whether Margrett Nickerson (31–34) or Mama Duck (34–37) is made implicitly questionable.

There are other instances in *The Florida Negro* when the "we" of the text distances the author from the experiences of being Negro and Floridian. These emerge for the most part in those chapters that describe the folk culture of Florida's African-American community. It is here that one feels most acutely the burden of the white? author(s) to provide explanations for those aspects of African-American culture that he/she/they deem most alien. Here the point of reference is the white reader, for whom the author(s) is the chronicler and observer of Negro traditions and communities. These instances operate by a different set of mechanisms so that the reader (the white reader) is asked first to consider the culture of the Negro as exotic, even odd, but then is made to normalize those differences through a form of analogic substitution. Take this passage, the introduction to chapter 9, "Hoodoo and Voodoo":

> We like to believe that only primitive and savage races are afflicted with this form of ignorance [superstition], but who of us is really free from superstition? Who would dare walk under a ladder, make the thirteenth at table, or rummage through Tutankamen's [sic] tomb? *It is small wonder then that the Negro, with his meager opportunity for education, should be even more credulous than we* (italics mine, 81).

Here the explanation of African-American culture is linked to the absence of the rationalizing influence of education. Voodoo is made less frightening through its similarities with white folk belief, the Negro comes to be understood or tolerated because the claim is made that he is the same as other people, or almost the same, but for the weight of history and as a consequence of his own lapses in judgment and intelligence.

Descriptions of the rites and practices of hoodoo and voodoo are told with a certain gentle humor and irony. In this chapter, they become indices not of a strong cultural tradition, but of the Negro's delayed state of assimilation to mainstream culture. Yet they are in the main, harmless. On the issue of folk medical belief, however, a different set of explanations are brought into gear, or at least these traditions render the Negro, once again, outside the sphere of civilizing influences, and indeed outside the text:

> Out of a past colored with the superstition that was his religion the Negro has developed certain practices relative to cures and beliefs that are peculiar only to himself.
> Concerted health drives and increased educational advantages have done much towards his enlightenment, but a surprising large number of Negroes still cling to those old superstitions; no doubt they have contributed to the high Negro death rate (71).

We are reminded that *The Florida Negro* was crafted by multiple authors in a situation of inherent conflict about who would be given voice and from what perspective. One could turn, then, to the part of the work whose aim seems to have been to document the gains and achievements of the African-American community and its institutions. The reins seem to have been firmly held in so that the predominant emphasis is on restraint, on the one hand, and on sacrifice on the other. This is especially the case, I would suggest in the description of the Reconstruction and post-Reconstruction eras, though the trope appears at different points in the work.

We might make a list starting with Jonathan Gibbs—"an intelligent black subjected to the influences of theological training and New England culture"— who we are told rose to prominence in the 1870s, became superintendent of education, saved the governor from a renegade impeachment, "criticized the carpetbaggers" with "support *from the more intelligent* [italics mine] element of the Negro population," and then at the point where his appointment as the Secretary of State had been solidified died of mysterious causes (103).

Or for a later period, the heroic service of Dr. Daniel W. Roberts, the sole African-American physician in St. Augustine, who in face of the epidemic devastation of an influenza outbreak in 1918 "almost single-handedly fought" to save his own patients as well of those neglected by white doctors, while at the same time offering his services to his white colleagues in preparing and dispensing drugs. Dr. Roberts pushes himself to the point of collapse, and, soon after his heroic service to both whites and blacks, he dies of "overexertion" (102). And finally, we might find the prototypic tragic hero in the evocation of John Henry in Ol' Doc. Described as "huge, muscular . . . and with long ape-like arms," (45) Ol' Doc manages to save his fellow stevedores by using his body as counterweight when the pulley hoisting a piano breaks. Bruised and bleeding, he saves the day and, to underscore his strength and heroism, he bullies the awed spectators back to work and carries on himself as if nothing had happened.

The commonalities across these individual profiles include the themes of depletion of one's own self or energies, loyalty to the status quo, and working within the racial and political system. Those who fail to do so appear as trickster heroes who, in the end, come to no good. The extended narrative of Daddy Mention (75–80) is such an example. In spite of his many successful and inspired jailbreaks and of his ability to fool hostile whites, he is finally outtricked, caught, and confined. If told by African-Americans to one another, the final fate of this familiar folk figure may well have been different.

In rediscovering a work such as this, the turn to history is perhaps the first and most useful endeavor. In his introduction, Gary McDonogh does a fine job of placing *The Florida Negro* within its historical and socio-political context. Another task of rediscovery is to wonder about the nature of the text's relationship to its late twentieth-century readers, (in this case its first public readership because it missed the initial wave of publication in the WPA series of the 1940s). As an "old" book in new clothing, so to speak, this work has to be judged by the standards of the time and place for which it was produced. Nonetheless, surely one might inquire about the nature of those standards and might even find it useful to hold the book up to the light of present-day readings of race and to the politics of representation.

Henry Louis Gates notes that the self-narrative, or autobiography, is the form that most dominates the history of African-American literary production, "denied . . . of possessing a collective history as a people, black Americans . . . published their *individual* histories . . . in a larger attempt to narrate the collective history of the 'race'" (4). In asserting the nation's interest in ethnic histories, the WPA project offered in part the support for the inclusion of a collective history of previously neglected racial and ethnic minorities. These histories, in the case of African-Americans, may be seen as an intervention by the state that allowed for the production of collective regional narratives that would, in the end, take their place alongside this strong autobiographical tradition. Yet the work of collective representation brought with it conflicts in the social relations of production: Who would write? What would be written? What was the overarching vision and goals of the text? Who was in charge? In many instances, the struggles became most intensified in the model that emerged when African-American writers and researchers reported to a state or project supervisor, who was white.

For the WPA project, the collective histories that were being produced were not solely about the specific ethnic group, but they were as intensely about the collective narrative America wanted to write about itself. Caught in this bind, the books born out of this abbreviated social project bear the marks of these struggles. In the case of *The Florida Negro*, African-Americans gained a measure of power, and were able to control the ways in which the links were made between the private realm of the individual and the social and cultural world of the "community." They were able to direct the process through which the individual self became the hyphenated Negro-Floridian-American. For the book, as a whole, however, they lost the battle to systematically control and give voice to their own histories and selves.

Notes

1. These three introductory paragraphs were omitted from later revisions which essentially eliminated a prefatory overview in favor of an introductory chronology. Some changes might also have been dealt with by the increased room for prefaces and introductions planned for later texts. Yet this chapter clearly resembles the overview chapters of other state guides.

2. It is difficult to reconstruct the secondary sources that substantiated interpretations drawn from oral history. However, among those found in the files for which I can identify complete references (especially at the Library of Congress Collection) are "Africans at Key West" (*Eufaula Express* June 1, 1860); unspecified excerpts from *Florida Historical Quarterly* (January 1929) on the legal status of the negro; Sprague (1848) on Abraham; Giddings (1858); Wilson (1875); Cutler (1923); Priestley (1929) on Spanish slaves; Corse (1931); Tenney (1934); Parks (1936, typescript); Geiger (1937); Austin (n.d.); Martineau n.d. Some of these appear in the general guide. Among sources for folklore are works by Zora Neale Hurston; collections by Elsie Clews Parsons and incidents from James W. Johnson's *Along the Way (1936)*.

3. The sources mentioned in the general guide with reference to the sixteenth-century narrative of Alvar Nuñez Cabeza de Vaca are the 1871 translation of Floridian Buckingham Smith and the 1905 edition of Fanny Bandelier. More may have been planned, since a hand-written note also refers to his "triumphal progress" to the pueblos, where Estevanico met his death. Later, Paul Diggs mentions Estevanico in his report "Forgotten Romances of Florida."

This introduction of the figure of an early black slave also establishes a competition with Virginia over the historical primacy of a black population in each state. There, Roscoe Lewis writes in his preface that "It is appropriate that the first WPA State book on the Negro be produced in Virginia; for it is here the first African natives were brought and held in enforced servitude, and here also, more than two centuries later, freedom for some 5,000,000 of their descendants was assured on the surrender grounds of Appomattox (v)."

4. From here on, the revised manuscript makes constant stylistic emendations. In order not to obstruct the text, I have only cited these when they refer to major corrections or changes in the text.

Recent work on this Fort community has been pioneered by archaeologist Kathleen Deagan (1974,1991) and historian Jane Landers (1990).

Pam Bordelon (Personal Communication, March 9, 1992) has suggested that the emphasis of these paragraphs reflects the interests of Director Corse.

5. This first mention of Roman Catholicism underscores the importance of Catholicism and the ambivalence toward it throughout the text and the Florida Negro papers, where Rachel Austin and Paul Diggs devote considerable time to the documentation of Florida black and Catholic life. This may ultimately provide more clues to the individual lives of authors, since Black Catholicism was often associated with middle-class, educated populations in cities (See McDonogh (1993) or Gannon (1964,1965) on Florida). By contrast, the attitude of various authors toward the populist Sanctified churches betrays a real distance.

6. Although Seminole-black relations were extremely important in later Florida history, the Seminoles became a Florida people only in the 18th century. This factual error was corrected in later manuscripts. Giddings (1985) was probably a major source for the material.

7. The 1938 manuscript inserts the note here "Gradually the Indian tribes in Florida became known as Seminoles, meaning *separatists*." This agrees with the Florida guide's statement that "They had broken with their old nation in the North and were now known as Seminole or 'Runaways'" (1939:41).

8. The second Spanish period refers to the period 1783–1819.

9. According to the Florida Guide, the Fort was located at Bartow in Polk County.

10. The revised manuscript of 1938 makes this the end of the chapter, relegating the longer overview that follows to a separate chapter that keeps a chronological sequence.

11. It is apparent here that the chronology of the manuscript has become confused by responding to multiple demands of an introduction, overview and summary. This section is moved to follow a chronological sequence in the revised manuscript.

12. Again, the revised manuscript follows a chronological sequence, moving this explanatory-reflective passage.

13. Information on Osceola's racial heritage and the Seminole Wars also appears in the general guide, (1939: 41–43). See also Porter (1946, 1955).

14. Taken from an interview with Henry Drummond. Amelia Island lies off the northern Atlantic coast of Florida, separated from the mainland by the St. Mary's River, Amelia River and Nassau Sound. The city of Fernandina occupies its northwestern area. James Johnson was the investigator who focussed on this area.

15. Zephaniah Kingsley lived from 1765 to 1843. All references here are to the second edition of 1829, with no publisher listed. Sections of this text—an ironic

inclusion of the master's voice—are cited in Chapter III. The revised manuscript adds more detail to this depiction, as well as mentioning provision for his dependents.

16. This plantation was located near the Georgia border (near Thomasville) and Capps, Florida. It is treated at some length in the Florida guide, (1939: 414).

17. Florida Normal later moved to Miami, although site and ruined buildings remain in West Augustine.

18. This section and those that follow draw extensively on the recollections of ex-slaves to construct a synthetic view of the world and in some cases draw on composites from repeated questionnaires. Therefore, I have generally not cross-referenced all individual interviews although I have noted at least some. More work needs to be done on this process and on other aspects of this collection, in the light of work reviewed in Yetman (1984) or suggestions by Mormino (1988). See the more extensive discussion in the introduction.

Specific readings and themes also bear more development in studies of this collection. The meaning and value of literacy, for example, was a central theme of many autobiographies by ex-slaves, especially those of Frederick Douglass and it reappears dramatically in the Margrett Nickerson interview included below. It is interesting that a hand emendation of this section might limit Kingsley's actions to the training of "*intelligent* slaves." See also Andrews (1988).

19. A biography of Meacham follows later in the text. Quincy is near Tallahassee.

20. Taken from materials of Viola Muse, Alfred Farrell and Martin Richardson, including the last's interview, "A Voluntary Slave for Seven Years."

21. Abstracts and notes in W.P.A files illuminate some sources for this and subsequent sections, including W.W. Davis (1913) and Parks (1936).

22. Yukon lies near Jacksonville. The loyalty of its slaves is also mentioned in the Florida guide (1939:350–1).

23. Many of the materials of this chapter were moved to the elaborated second chapter of the final version. Wallace (1888) is cited in the main guide as a source, as is W.W. Davis (1913).

24. Stanton was not accredited but important as school associated with such figures as James Weldon Johnson who was both pupil and principal there (Johnson 1933:125–162); it merited a special report by James Johnson. Other reports on education were prepared for individual cities by Rebecca Baker, Alfred Farrell, Viola Muse, Pearl Randolph, and Martin Richardson.

25. Later sections deal with both Jonathan Gibbs, here referred to, and Florida A & M.

26. Reports on religion in individual cities were prepared by local specialists including Austin, Baker, Farrell, Johnson, Muse, Randolph, Rice and Richardson, as well as isolated special reports. This interest continued later in the work of both Zora Neale Hurston and Paul Diggs. See author list in the appendix.

27. Gibbs merits a fuller biography later in the text.

28. This discussion of shifts in power continues at greater length in the revised

manuscript. It has also been the focus of work by later Florida historians such as David Colburn (1985) and Mohlman (1991).

29. In general this section summarizes later chapters and multiple field reports. It provides an interesting balance between reporting and critique, by which the manuscript suggests that all is not well for Florida Negroes without adopting a polemic tone which might offend white readers (or editors).

30. The incompletely edited condition of the manuscript is betrayed by simple mistakes such as the identification of John Rosamond Johnson by the name of his brother James; the spelling of Rosamond also varies in the original manuscript. The question of Zora Neale Hurston's birthplace is perhaps more serious, but was also caught at a later point in the manuscript.

31. Hurston had not arrived nor did anyone spot the misstatement of her famous home in Eatonville. See Hurston (1934, 1935, 1938).

32. Again, a longer biography of Savage is included later.

33. This ethnographic vision is very characteristic of Richardson's reports on Jacksonville, Pensacola and St. Augustine. These sections overlap to a great extent (at times, almost word for word) with reports on black life in the general guide. For example, concerning black health care, the guide writes:

> Despite the prevalence of disease and high death rate among Negroes, only seven counties (Dade, Duval, Hillsborough, Palm Beach, Pinellas, Putnam, and Volusia) have general hospitals that provide care for them; 28 other hospitals in the State, including the State Tuberculosis Hospital near Orlando, and the Florida State Hospital for the Insane at Chattahoochee, make some provision for Negroes.
>
> In recent years, two small but well-equipped hospitals for Negro tuberculosis patients have been established: one in Pensacola, with a capacity of 50 patients, a branch of Escambia County Tubercular Sanitarium; the other, the Tubercular Rest Home in Jacksonville, with 50 beds. In Miami, a white specialist conducts annual clinics for Negro physicians of Florida. At the Florida Agricultural and Mechanical College for Negroes in Tallahassee, a yearly clinic in general medicine attracts Negro practitioners from all parts of the country.
>
> Brewster Hospital, in Jacksonville, is outstanding among the dozen or more private and semi-private hospitals and training schools for nurses and interns that are operated by and for Negroes. It has been approved by the American Medical Society and the American College of Surgeons. The hospital was opened in 1931 by the Methodist Episcopal Women's Home Missionary Society.
>
> With the aid of WPA funds, the city of Tampa in 1938 completed a 60-bed hospital for Negroes at a cost of $125,000. It is equipped with laboratory and X-ray department, and employs a staff of white and Negro physicians and surgeons. The brick structure is set in a landscaped park, overlooking the Hillsborough River (1939:107–8).

Similar parallels between textual materials as well as borrowings appear in sections on folklore, literature and education. Such passages also underscore tensions within the writers' project's goals of presentation of shortcomings and an "upbeat" tone about the values and attractions of the state. Obviously, this dualism becomes more complex in a guide written by African-Americans focussed on black life in

Florida. Moreover, the passage also mentions other WPA interventions as corrections to problems, a reference which reappears in the Florida Negro discussion of Durkeeville.

34. These practices were documented in fieldwork assignments by Hurston, whose reports appear in the files.

35. The files include a long essay (43pp) on these immigrants—"The Conchs of Riviera" (FHS IV/2, Manuscripts). Another note (Box V/5) includes Hurston's "Suggestions for Songs and Ditties to be Recorded among the West Indian Conchs at Riviera Florida" (18pp).

36. This simple geography may be an exaggeration. However, the Florida Guide writes: "Miami Beach and Coral Gables are free of slums. Miami's restricted Negro district, bordering the tracks and representing 30 per cent of the city's population, virtually reaches into the heart of town, but halts abruptly at Fifth Street. A large number of residents are of West Indian stock, and many Filipinos live on the fringe of the settlement. Liberty Square, a Federal Housing project, provides modern accommodations for nearly 250 Negro families. The Booker T. Washington High School, with an average enrollment of 2,000, is the largest of the State's five accredited Negro High Schools and the St. Agnes Protestant Episcopal Church is the largest of its denomination in the South. The Negro population increases during the tourist season when resort hotels open and the unskilled-labor market reaches its peak" (1939:211). White researcher C.M. Taylor seems to have been a primary source on black life in Miami.

37. Rarely does an ironic voice come through so clearly in this text, despite criticism of state policies and local culture at other points. Again, it suggests the black experience underlying the text as well as perception of audience and editorial control.

38. Lynching does not appear in the index to the general guide, although Ocoee is mentioned. See Introduction.

39. This makes reference to the omitted chapter/visit to Raiford now included in the Appendix. Pam Bordelon (personal communication) suggests that visits to prisons were directly inspired by folklorist Lomax in the central office.

40. The tone here again opposes state neglect and federal intervention.

41. This chapter is based on slave interviews, including Samuel Simeon Andrews [Jacksonville], interviewed by Rachel Austin, October 27, 1936 (11pp); Bill Austin [Jacksonville] by Martin Richardson, n.d. (4pp); Frank Berry [Jacksonville], interviewed by Pearl Randolph, August 18, 1936 (4pp), additional information by Samuel Johnson September 11, 1937; Matilda Brooks, "A Governor's Slave" Monticello], by Alfred Farell, January 12, 1937 (4pp); Patience Campbell [Monticello], by J. M. Johnson 15 December 1936 (5pp); Florida Clayton [Pensacola], by Rachel Austin, November 20, 1936 (2pp); "Father" Charles Coates [Jacksonville] by Viola Muse, December 3, 1936 (8pp); Irene Coates [Jacksonville] by Viola Muse, December 16, 1936 (5pp); Willis Dukes [Madison] by Pearl Randolph, January 20, 1937 (5pp); Sam and Louisa Everett [Mulberry], by Pearl Randolph, October 8,1936 (5pp); Clayborn Gantling [Jacksonville] by Rachel Austin, April 16, 1937 (6pp); Harriett Gresham [Jacksonville], by Pearl Randolph December 18, 1936

(8pp); Bolden Hall [Live Oak],by Alfred Farrell, August 20 1936 (5pp); "Prophet" John Henry Kemp [Daytona Beach], by Rebecca Baker, January 11, 1937 (5pp); Edward Lycurgas [Jacksonville] by Pearl Randolph, December 5, 1936 (7pp) Henry Maxwell [Titusville] by Alfred Farrell, September 25, 1936 (7pp); Amanda McCray [Madison], by Pearl Randolph, November 13, 1936 (5pp); Christine Mitchell [St. Augustine] by Martin Richardson, November 10, 1936 (2pp); Lindsay Moore "An Ex-Slave Who Was Resourceful" [Palatka], by Martin Richardson January 13, 1937 (4pp); Mack Mullen [Jacksonville], by J. M. Johnson, September 18, 1936 (17pp); Louis Napoleon [S. Jacksonville], by J. M. Johnson, November 17, 1936 (7pp); Margaret Nickerson [Jacksonville], by Rachel Austin, December 5, 1936 (8pp); Douglas Parish [Monticello], by Rachel Austin, November 10, 1936 (5pp); Anne Scott," An Ex-Slave Who Went to Africa "[Jacksonville], by Viola Muse January 11, 1937 (7pp); William Sherman [Chaseville], J. M. Johnson, August 28, 1936 (5pp); Acie Thomas [Jacksonville] by Pearl Randolph, November 25, 1936 (9pp); Shack Thomas, Centenarian. [S. Jacksonville] by Martin Richardson, December 8, 1936 (6pp); Luke Towns, "A centenarian" [Jacksonville] by Rachel Austin, November 30, 1936 (4pp); Willis Williams. [Jacksonville], by Viola Muse, March 20, 1937 (9pp); Claude Augusta Wilson [Lake City], by J. M. Johnson, November 6, 1936 (8pp) and "A Voluntary Slave for Seven Years" interview about Cato Smith by Martin Richardson, January 27, 1937 (2pp). As noted, the connections and community fostered by black interviewers with black slaves proved an important strength of the entire project.

42. This image of feudalism was edited from the later manuscript.

43. Materials are drawn from interviews including John Henry Kemp interviewed by Rebecca Baker, January 11, 1937 and Louis Napoleon, interviewed by J. M. Johnson, November 17, 1936.

44. Details come from Rachel Austin's interview with Samuel Simeon Andrews, October 27, 1936 and the Margrett Nickerson interview included in more detail in the manuscript.

45. Details are discussed in Margrett Nickerson's reminiscences, below, and in the interview of Matilda Brooks, "A Governor's Slave," by Alfred Farell, January 12, 1937.

46. From an interview with Acie Thomas by Pearl Randolph, November 25, 1936.

47. Interview with Samuel Small by Martin Richardson, January 27, 1937.

48. "Prophet" John Henry Kemp, interviewed by Rebecca Baker, January 11, 1937.

49. Irene Coates, interviewed by Viola Muse, December 16, 1936.

50. Interview by Rachel Austin, October 27, 1936.

51. Actually, she says Georgia. See Florida Clayton, Interview with Rachel Austin, November 20, 1936.

52. Drawing on information from Douglas Parish, interviewed by Rachel Austin, November 10, 1936; Christine Mitchell, interviewed by Martin Richardson, November 10, 1936; and Sam and Louisa Everett, interviewed by Pearl Randolph, October 8, 1936.

53. See the lengthy interview of Mack Mullen by J. M. Johnson, September 18, 1936.

54. Information in this section and the next come from Amanda McCray, interviewed by Pearl Randolph, November 13, 1936.

55. Many interviews already have been used as resources without such reference to the questions of memory, selection and reliability that have challenged later readers, as discussed in the introduction and critical sources cited there. More striking here is the inclusion of the slaveowners—Kingsley's—voice without commentary. Does this create a double reading for the white or black reader—or a different kind of reading? Fraser's comments in the afterword are of interest as are modern writings on historical voice (See Young 1991).

56. Interview with Rachel Austin, Jacksonville, December 5, 1936. Some passages are omitted, dealing with punsihment of her and her sister, although the reasoning behind this emendation to the manuscript is unclear.

57. Used in story materials by white author Jules Frost. A whiter attitude seems to be detectable in the framing of this narrative and perhaps the differences in responses.

58. This is derived, as noted in the introduction, from a much more complete manuscript by Richardson. The excerpt eliminates detail on individual groups and themes of adaptation to Depression, including women's work. The longer version and its critical tone resumes with the section on the economic status of the Florida Negro. Note continual variation in population figures.

59. Again, Richardson's tone in this passage suggests an ironic more than ameliorative or saleable tone, one bordering, as elsewhere, on more acerbic social criticism.

60. Work songs were collected by several early male researchers including James Johnson, Samuel Johnson, and Martin Richardson. Johnson in particular contributed songs here from lumbermen, dockworkers and street car track work. It is striking that more of the reports on cures, conjure and voodoo were associated with female workers on the project.

61. Again, in a text concerned with the preservation of historical memory and the oral traditions which maintained history of slaves, it is striking to see the concerns which appear at several points concerning new generations, where technological changes as well as education impinge on "folk culture."

62. Prison materials use songs collected by Richardson.

63. Drawing heavily on Richardson's report on Negro Songs and Amusements, based on his observations and collections. He also mentions observations of other field workers as a source, which may refer to the similar collections of work situations and songs by James and Samuel Johnson.

64. Robert Thomas and James Johnson composed a survey of Negro Beaches in Florida. The Afro-American Insurance Company, for example, managed its own beach in the shadow of white segregated resorts.

65. This passage demands a cautious reading. On the surface, it seems blatantly stereotypic. Yet is there another edge to the limitation of this viewpoint to the

naive visitor, with an implicit contrast to those who reside in Florida and should know better?

66. Based on material on celebrations collected by Viola Muse, although heavily edited, especially with regard to Jacksonville materials.

67. The Florida Guide notes that "although Negroes make up nearly 30 per cent of Florida's population, they share little in the organized sports of the State" (1939:118). Yet this guide develops a patronizing perspective: "Fishing, which costs little and gives a return in food, is a favorite occupation among Negroes. A possum hunt likewise combines sport and the possibility of a savory dish, and the baying that announces a treed racoon is a prelude to a feast. Negro churches sponsor concerts, picnics and fish fries; social clubs provide opportunities for dancing and sometimes for games of chance such as skin (a card game), bolita and dice. Motion-picture theaters and night clubs in the city, and "jooks" in the country are operated for Negroes. At Jacksonville, a Negro club maintains a 9-hole golf course, a swimming pool, a shooting range, picnic grounds, and recreational equipment for children. The entire property, covering 36 acres, has been improved by the WPA and NYA." However discrimination, with regard to beaches especially, is also noted.

Later, Paul Diggs examined organized recreation along with other more middle-class aspects of black life in his WPA reports.

68. January 1; a widespread African-American holiday.

69. This chapter is based on work by Martin Richardson. Photographs were also made, but they are out of focus and overexposed.

70. Ybor City represents the historical Cuban, Spanish and Italian district of central Tampa. Mormino and Pozzetta (1987) also speaks extensively about *bolita*.

71. The early part of this chapter is based on materials collected in a ture death inlong report by Pearl Randolph—"Negro Customs, Cures and Beliefs" Richardson and James Johnson were also active folklore collectors. In her revision of the folklore materials, "Go 'Gator . . ." Hurston continues to make use of the Daddy Mention tales.

72. Richardson discovered the Daddy Mention stories, but, as Pam Bordelon has pointed out to me, they were used repeatedly by other project writers. These stories made their way into the general guide: the Polk County Incident (1939: 515) and the Raiford stories on (1939: 379–80).

73. Based on various reports. Note distinctive "we."

74. Dr. Abraham figures in the state guide as an attraction for Lawtey, a town between Jacksonville and Gainesville (1939: 377). Some of the dialogue survives, although the portrait is reduced.

75. The Appendix includes a variety of reports on Eatonville, both those on which this chapter could have drawn and later perspectives, including those of Hurston included in the general guide.

76. Clark figures prominently in Hurston's writings as well (1934, 1935, 1942).

77. Based primarily on work by Richardson, in various reports on the city and its culture. See McGovern (1976).

78. Rachel Austin corroborated these reports in her writings on black churches.

79. Later versions called for a much more expanded vision of this chapter on education, and ample materials were gathered on various aspects of primary and secondary education. Experts from Florida A & M were also sought for advice, corrections and revisions. An historical study of Florida A & M was published by Neyland and Riley (1960).

80. Son of Jonathan Gibbs, whose career was also cut short by an early death in 1898.

81. This chapter retains interest in both who it presents and how it presents them—drawing on neighbors and folk history as well as published sources. It also has interesting omissions, including labor organizer A. Philip Randolph, born in Crescent City, and Mary McLeod Bethune, founder of Bethune-Cookman college and a power in Roosevelt's New Deal. The files also include much longer autobiographies of James Weldon and John Rosamund Johnson. Finally, this chapter pays only scant attention to Zora Neale Hurston.

82. Based on a report by Martin Richardson of September 22, 1936, using local interviews. It disagrees in biographical particulars with the Schomburg Center's 1988 Catalogue Expedition of her work and life. Ms. Savage died in 1962.

83. It is unclear what Florida Writers' Project source was used for this, although the tone sounds as if Richardson is a possibility. A recent biographical sketch of Meacham was published by Brown (1990).

84. A shipping port on the Gulf Coast which even in 1939 had a population of only 1,833.

85. Based on interviews and report by Martin Richardson. See Appendix.

86. Based on a report by Martin Richardson, "An Unusual Monument."

87. It is illuminating to contrast this depiction of Gibbs' importance in Florida history has been recognized by sources on the Reconstruction such as Shofner (1974), Jahoda (1976) and Tebeau (1980:251). He is also cited in the general WPA guide to Florida.

His son, Thomas Van Renssalaer Gibbs, was a West Point cadet and Jacksonville lawyer as well as an active Republican. He became Vice-President of the State Normal and Industrial College, later to become Florida A & M, before his premature death in 1898.

88. A note on the manuscript suggests the omission of the two Johnson autobiographies. These presumably were to be replaced with longer biographies heavily excerpted from James Weldon Johnson's autobiography, *Along This Way* (Johnson 1933). Here, I have left the original texts.

Johnson died after a car accident on June 26, 1938; the manuscript was evidently never emended with this datum as project interest moved elsewhere although it is noted in one report on literature by James Johnson.

In addition to his published *Autobiography of an Ex-Colored Man* (first published 1912) and his own autobiography, *Along this Way* (New York 1933) Johnson has been the subject of numerous literary and historical studies including Bronz (1964); Levy (1973); Fleming (1978, 1987); Harman (1988); and Kostelanatz (1991).

Johnson's papers are found in the James Weldon Johnson Collection of Negro Arts and Letters at Yale University.

James Weldon Johnson's autobiography was well-known to project workers: James Johnson (apparently no relation) cites it in his report on Stanton high school.

Ms. Muse linked Johnson to poet Paul Dunbar, who resided for a time in Jacksonville, but was edited from her report in the chapter as a non-citizen.

89. This was taken from reports by Viola Muse on Negro Literature (as most of this chapter was) and Music. John Rosamund Johnson seems less well-documented than his literary-political brother, although he figures prominently in the former's autobiographical writings and is discussed in Levy (1973).

90. This was taken from a report by Viola Muse, Negro Literature, based on an interview with Bessie Dancer.

91. This was taken from reports by Viola Muse, Negro Literature, based on an interview with him.

92. See Hemenway (1977) and works by Hurston (1934, 1935, 1937, 1942). This biography was written before Hurston came on the project, although emendation does correct an earlier mistake that listed her birthplace as Mandarin, near Jacksonville and change the reference from "Miss Hurston" to "Zora Hurston."

93. As noted in the introduction, this kind of chapter underscores both the social conditions of the black in Florida and the efforts of the WPA to deal with them. A report on Liberty City in Miami was evidently omitted as the authors sought the right tone. In fact, the chapter starts with these paragraphs:

> A unique experiment in low-cost housing is the Negro slum clearance project started in Jacksonville in 1936. To convince Washington that the project was necessary a detailed statistical analysis was prepared, in which the following information was contained: 32 per cent of the city's major crimes came from less than 1.8 per cent of its area. Of juvenile cases 14.5 per cent of the major crimes, 17.5 per cent of the social crimes and 14 per cent of the public charges came from this same area. It is this area that is responsible for Jacksonville's very high homicide rate. Turning to diseases, 31 per cent of the syphilis cases and 27 per cent of the tuberculosis cases came from this same infinitesimal spot. It was responsible for 21 per cent of the total fire alarms and 25 per cent of the false alarms.
>
> There was no difficulty in obtaining governmental consent for the project, but practical considerations prevented its location in the area having the worst crime and disease record. However, a 20 acre tract was chosen surrounded by the three worst sections. This is located in west Jacksonville and is bounded by 6th, Payne, McGenihe streets and Myrtle Avenue. Durkeeville, named for the conveyor of the tract, was opened for occupancy June 19, 1937. It was developed by the Housing Division of the Federal Emergency Administration of Public Works.

However, an emendation and insert shorten this to the text which I have included here, possibly in concern for the image of blacks or of Jacksonville.

94. Again, the text shows an interesting emendation; the sentence "This group, it should be noted, is considerably above the lowest Negro economic group" has been scratched through.

95. This chapter draws on many texts, although again probably under the hand of Richardson. What is striking is its dealing with religion less as primitive superstition or faith than as a business. (See Gorn 1984).

96. The presence of Catholic materials among church materials of the Negro project are disproportionate to that presence, however, including lengthy essays by Rachel Austin in her supplement to Wilson Rice and several pieces by Paul Diggs as well as portions of essays by Richardson. This may reflect the historical heritage of the state and the presence of Afro-Cubans in Tampa, or raise questions about the background of authors in a state with established parochial schools for blacks.

97. Sanctified Churches seemed to exercise a continuing fascination over the fieldworkers of the Negro Unit—from Viola Muse to Zora Neale Hurston and Paul Diggs. It is interesting to contrast their vision with the white vision of Georgia's *Drums and Shadows* which caricatures excesses in the ceremonies observed.

98. The Clara White Mission was described by several FWP workers; ironically, it was also the headquarters for the segregated Negro unit.

99. This chapter remains confusing and anticlimactic. Most of the spirituals noted here were collected in Miami by the white folklorist Cora Mae Taylor (marked in text with an asterisk) whose works generally were not included in the volume. Collection with regard to modern songs also continued until the end of the project, as Stetson Kennedy has noted with regard to the work of Zora Neale Hurston (personal communication; see 1991). The lack of any texts here, or of any other conclusion, suggests the general incompleteness of the volume, and perhaps Richardson's more social and historical interests.

APPENDIXES

Appendix A

A Day in Florida's State Prison

Introduction

There were approximately 6,000 prisoners being cared for by the state of Florida at the end of 1936. Of this number, about one-third, roughly estimated, were housed in the state prison at Raiford in Union County, some forty-one miles from Jacksonville.

The remainder, according to state laws, must be sent to the 50 convict camps scattered throughout the state, there to work on the state's highways.

So much do the prisoners dread the convict camps, or 'chain gangs' as they call them, that the prisoners who remain at Raiford are thought to be the most fortunate of prisoners. Many attempts are made to use influence to remain at the prison instead of being sent with other prisoners to road camps.

Raiford does offer the prisoner certain advantages. In the state prison his hours are rigidly regulated so that he does a day's work that does not greatly exceed what he would be expected to do "outside." He can learn a trade if he wishes—may learn one if he doesn't wish—can attend literary and grammar-school classes, is subject to few of the abuses that come to the prisoner in an isolated "chain-gang" camp, has regular recreation, good meals, and a number of other benefits that he would not get "on the road."

All of this may have something to do with the explanation of the fact that of all the surprises that such a prison as the one at Raiford would give a visitor, perhaps the greatest one is that the prisoners, on the whole, seem neither to be angry at their keepers or society, but quite the reverse, are about as cheerful a bunch as would be found on the average job; certainly more jovial than the usual turpentine or sawmill crew.

Instead of finding a bunch of broken, sullen men and women, the visitor finds courteous welcome on the part of the prisoners (and apparently it is NOT the

Brother-can-you-spare-a dime variety; in an entire day not a single prisoner asked even for a cigarette). Far from hiding themselves in a morose silence, the prisoners at "Raiford" were found to be eager to tell of themselves and the causes of their incarceration; hopelessness was absent, with most of the men interviewed expressing confidence that they would soon be liberated, either because of "time off for good behavior" or because they thought someone "outside" would prevail with the Pardon Board and secure their release.

Perhaps, though, this one fact will strike the visitor to the prison more than most of the others; nearly every man and woman with whom he talks will convince him with confident frankness that once released he is going to reclaim his place in society. If the records of the prison authorities do not show that it is exactly what the prisoner DOES when he is released, that is no fault of this article. . . .

A Day in Florida's State Prison

"No suh!" It aint that-away a-tall. Whole lot of folks think that there aint nothin' but ignorant people in jail, but there's as many sort folks in here as there is anywhere else.

With this heroic defense of his 2000-odd neighbors, one of the "trusty" guides at the state prison at Raiford begins your itinerary through the penitentiary. The main men's dormitory, usually visited first by visitors, proves interesting. Most of the male inmates in the prison—who are not indigent and behave themselves—live in this building. One section houses the white prisoners; another the Negroes.

On the ground floor are large, roomy, and apparently airy cells. The walls, much to the surprise of the visitor, are elaborately covered with pictures and decorations. The pictures cover every conceivable subject; next to a late photograph of Myrna Loy may be found an almost life-size one of Mr. Armour's Star Hams. Sporting pictures seem to have almost as great an appeal as the moving picture stars.

Most of the cells on the ground floor are large, and house, according to the guide, two or more prisoners. That it is the prison's favored few, however, who "draw" these cells is broadly hinted by the guide. Being "favored," he explains, means doing "the long time," or "the whole thing" or of such conduct that the more thoughtful of the officials are eager to use the cells as a sort of merit award.

"Now you take that cell right there," the guide abruptly returns to a subject quite forgotten by his visitors. "In there we have a man who was a big Insurance official in Pensacola. Something happened with him and the company—you know how other folks' money is—and now he is one of our quietest, easiest prisoners. He don't never bother nobody, and they don't bother him. He reads a lot, though." He doesn't wish to be positive on the subject, but he thinks the man drew five or seven years for embezzlement.

"He aint here right now," he mentions as he passes another cell, "but in there we used to have a doctor from Jacksonville. I don't know what got him in, but he used to come up here every once in a while for a little spell. He aint been back lately, but he'll be here—maybe by the time y'all come back."

The furniture, too, on the ground floor appears to offer the prisoner about all the comforts one could expect in a prison. It is of wood—as contrasted with iron elsewhere—and includes tables, chairs and other 'homelike' pieces not always found even in a modest rural bedroom.

On the second floor the order of things is plainer. The cells are smaller, and house only one or two prisoners, the guide explains. Decorations are not as profuse or elaborate as they are downstairs; the conveniences of the first floor are missing. Many men are often found still lying on their cots in these cells during the usual 'work-time' in the prison; these are explained as men who are sick or otherwise unable to attend their regular duties. When not at workbench or in the field, the men must remain locked in their cells. The guide professes ignorance as to the reason that in the ground floor cells, where at least some comforts might be enjoyed while staying shut in, there are generally fewer prisoners taking "sick-leave," while in the more uncomfortable second floor cells the number is greater. "Can't tell you that, sir; you see, I only been here not quite seven years myself. But I live downstairs, though."

In another wing of the men's dormitory, the guide points out a large laundry, larger than many of the commercial laundries found in large cities. This laundry, he explains, is not the main laundry of the prison, but only one of them. Its main purpose is to take care of the bedding, linen and uniforms of the 'tenants' of the main dormitory. About two dozen men are employed at the machines.

In the hallway the guide, with the assistance of a jealously-watching prisoner, shows the visitor the elaborate system of nails and cords that is used to keep tab of a prisoner's whereabouts. He does not have an opportunity to explain the system, though; the important-looking keeper of the system does that. He points to several long rows of nails, each pegged into a hole opposite a small white card. The name of the prisoners in this wing of the building are written on these cards, he explains. "Whenever one goes out to his work or for exercise," he states, "I pulls his nail out of the hole by his name. When he comes back, I puts it back again." Then, "If his nail aint in the hole when the rest are, he better be a long way off, or he is in trouble." Asked if he ever had unintentionally gotten a prisoner "in sure trouble" by being just the least bit forgetful about a nail or two, the attendance operator grins that "Nossuh, I aint got much else to do, and I sure got plenty of time to practice."

A dignified, quiet-looking man with the vertical stripes of the 'trusty' passes (the regular convicts wear stripes horizontally woven on their uniforms; when promoted to "trusties" they are given the coveted vertical stripes). "That there is a school teacher," the guide explains. "I never did know what he did, but he was here when I come and they tell me he'll be here after I go. He teaches the other prisoners and don't never bother a soul less they bother him first."

Outside of the building and on the way to the massive kitchen that feeds Raiford's thousands the guide's attention is [detracted] a moment as he explains quietly to another prisoner who the visitors are. A neat-appearing young Negro of probably twenty-three-or-four steps up.

"Thomas Harris is my name, sir; I'm from Orlando. I hope you are having a nice time."

The cordiality of his welcome to the prison and the frank polish of his self-introduction captivate the visitor; they may explain his promotion to "trusty!" Having met all of his new "friends" he hastens to explain that "they don't like us to do much talking to folks who come in, Sir, but you know how it is when you don't see folks but just once in a while . . ." He quietly and quickly informs us that he is within a few months of parole from a ten year sentence; that he has served seven already, has learned two good trades, and is "just dying to get back to Orlando and show them that one bad step don't make a bad fellow." "I'd be very glad, Sir" he adds, "if you ever go through Orlando you'd tell anybody how well I'm doing here." With these words he leaves.

Interest in his effort to impress his "good behavior" on the folks back home prompts a question to the guide as to just what brought the youngster to the prison. "Some kind of girl trouble," the guide cryptically explains.

The kitchen is an astonishing sight to the person visiting a prison of this size for the first time. The first surprising thing is the baking department. Here are ovens so great that the tender of them looks like a dwarf; he looks still smaller as he handles the huge pans that are to hold thousands of dozens of rolls for the day's consumption. The baker is a genial, smiling little fat fellow, eager to have every visitor sample one of "the best rolls I've baked this week." The same generosity is apparent when the chef, in the adjoining room, almost forces his visitors to sample the various and numerous "dishes," or well at least smell them, that he is "cooking" in the gigantic "pots" that hold fifty gallons and more. These "pots" are hardly pots at all, but large vats around which steam is flowing. There are a dozen of them, two or more holding the "dishes" which will be used by the prisoners, others holding a variety of foods.

The kitchen is spotless, much cleaner in appearance than many restaurant kitchens. The food appears to be fresh and good; on an average day two vegetables, one starch-food, a dessert, a soup and meat were being prepared for the prisoner's noon-day meal.

The mechanical departments of the prison offer much interest. These include the shoemaking and repair department, the license-plate and tag department, the shirt and uniform department and others.

In the shoemaking department, dozens of men were found working on what was described as the latest machinery, engaged in the processes of shoemaking. Some were doing the simple task of preparing leather for others who would lay the foundations for a pair of shoes; others were operating the difficult welt machines or stitching uppers on to finished soles. Still others were rebuilding shoes that had been worn too far for further service. The shoe department was described as being one the men seek most, because of its possibilities of immediate application upon their release.

Next to the shoe department is the section where the state's license tags are made. Only Florida has about twenty-three other kinds of tags besides license tags; in some years even more than this. There are tags made on these machines for the University of Florida; tags to show that the ground you walk on is "Property of the State of Florida; Keep Off;" other tags for bicycles in those sections where they are used; so many tags, in fact, that there is an entire display case devoted to them, as well as a sample of every automobile license tag the State Prison has ever produced.

The machines in the License Tag department are of several types. There are steel molding and cutting machines, where the plates are first cut to shape; stamping machines, where the numerals are stamped onto the tags; punching machines, where holes or slots are cut into the plates, and finally the great painting machine, where the seemingly-impossible task of painting a tag in two colors at the same time is accomplished. The stamping machine is the most interesting to most visitors, the guide states. Asked for the reason for this he gives as his belief the fact that people are interested in the legend surrounding the machines that no year can pass but that some prisoner loses an arm under the gaping jaw of the steel monster. Other prisoners agree with him on the point.

The painting machine, however, is more intricate. With its long drying racks it takes a plate through differing stages of heat in such a manner that the tag that is painted freshly on one end of the machine is dry enough for a second coat when it emerges from the other end, although continuously moving all the while.

Expecting to see the women of the prison in the shirt factory, the visitor is again due for a surprise. Although there are hundreds of women at the prison, there is not a single woman at the shirt factory. (Nor in most departments of the prison's laundries). Instead, seated at the high-speed machines are skillful male convicts, white and colored, making buttonholes and putting buttons on them. There are twenty machines in one part of the shirt factory alone, and the output of them can be judged by the fact that a crew of cutters is kept busy supplying material for the sewers.

In the overall factory, however, the women are finally found. About one-third of all the Negro women in the prison, the guide explains, work either here or in one of the laundries. The women present a much more colorful lot than do the men, despite the fact that there are much fewer of them. Their ages vary greatly; one old woman—whom the guide said " has been here always since there was a prison"— appears to be every day of sixty-five; there are some who seem hardly to be in their twenties.

Here, almost for the first time, the visitor encounters a "sour" expression; most of the men have seemed tolerant of their prison life and some, like the guides, trusties and kitchen help, almost in good spirits. But some of the women are decidedly annoyed with the prison and its routine; in silence they scowl at the visitors and return their eyes to the work on their machines without having opened their lips in greetings or a smile.

Not all of them are dour, however; some of them glance at the guard apprehensively and ask hurriedly "where y'all from? Don' t you remember me? I useter live there 'fore I got in this." A few are singing at their work, others watch for an opportunity to swap some conversational tidbit with the woman across from them or next to them. The jolly loquacity of the shoe shop, laundry and license-plant, however, are missing.

Another group of women, according to the guide and an official, are to be found in the fields. The lot of these women is harder than that of any other prisoners, some of the inmates stated. They must work in the fields several hours a day, often in water above their ankles, whether they are sick or well. The prisoners estimate that there are about fifty of these women engaged in farm work.

At the death house the guide obligingly lets the visitors go first. In fact, the guide lets the visitors almost strictly alone until they have returned from the flat-roofed little stone structure in which convicted murderers and rapists pay for their crimes with their lives. The guide does not explain whether there was anything in his own dereliction that made him sensitive whenever near the death-house, but once inside of it the visitors are left at the mercy of other guides.

The death-house is the most closely-guarded of the prison's structures. A high stone wall surrounds it, with observation turrets on the wall's corners. Guards sit in all these towers at all times. Barbed wire is laid on the top of the walls, although their straight ascent for several feet into the air make climbing them all but impossible.

In the middle of the death-house enclosure is the death-house itself. It is one of the smallest buildings in the entire prison. It is square, with a narrow door leading abruptly into the death chair. Seats for a few witnesses, an operating table for the removal of the dead, and a number of electric switches comprise most of the rest of the furnishings of the dread room.

The chair is the usual chair for the purpose, with conventional metal and leather straps, sponge, etc., all of which the keeper of the death-house cheerfully offers to demonstrate with any hardy visitor as the subject of a demonstration electrocution—minus the usual voltage. Many visitors like the macabre thrill, he says, of sitting in the chair.

The women's quarters are not usually shown to visitors, although some glimpse of them may be had from outside the high wall that surrounds them. The fortunate visitors who are at the prison during the noon recess, though, may get a good glimpse of the discipline under which the women live by watching them march to their quarters from the factory, with the courtyard cleared of everyone else before a single woman begins marching, and guards are stationed every few yards to warn people not to approach the line of women.

The prison hospital is another example of the efficiency found in the penitentiary. It is clean, large and apparently has an efficient staff. Several physicians or interns are in evidence; the wards have many beds in light, airy surroundings. The prisoners in the hospital, too, duplicate the good-nature attitude found in most of the prisoners. One fellow, losing an arm and without the hope of saving it, begged for the "latest joke they're telling in town;" another began smiling when the first visitor appeared and was still smiling and saying "howdy" as the last one left. Others, asked about their ailments and progress, volunteered the information readily and cheerfully.

Visitors are given the impression all through the prison, and probably correctly, that the prisoners are given jobs that they might use to rehabilitate themselves when they return to society. The men themselves verify this. Even the prisoner who cared for business in his former life is not excluded from this effort; there are merchants in the dormitory who sell cold drinks and "snowballs" (balls of shaved ice with colored syrup poured over them) and other prisoners in the recreation yards [who] do a lucrative business on visiting days selling soda water. One old fellow does a commission business selling the wood carvings of his fellow prisoners in the carpentry and cabinet shops. Others carve leather in their cells, and sell the belts, pocketbooks and other souvenirs of their enforced vacation to visitors and officials. Picture frames with your favorite movie star already mounted, are among the useful and decorative articles available from these three artisans.

There is an excellent band of about twenty men in the prison. These musicians provide music both for the sakes of art and utility. There are concerts for prisoners and visitors, and music at morning, noon and evening by which the prisoners march to and form their cells and the dining room.

There are several forms of recreation for prisoners, including baseball, croquet and other games. Checkers and similar games, according to the guides, are played. The baseball teams are said to be good, and sometimes meet outside teams during the season.

The prisoner who wants to study may do so, the visitor is informed. There are several former teachers ("and some real professors, too" the guide proudly explains) in the prison and these have as their duties the task of lessening illiteracy among other prisoners.

Religion is not neglected. There are chaplains for both white and Negro prisoners. In fact, the Negro chaplain is said to be the only one of his race in a state institution in the country. He combines with his religious preachings a sincere love for his underprivileged flock, and often is their only advocate before prison and civil authorities. He frequently appears before Pardon Boards and similar groups on behalf of his charges, and once was credited with saving four men from the death chair. The only job he hates in the prison, he claims, is that of administering final rites to the condemned. "I don't think I'll ever have the stomach to do that and not get sick" is his way of putting it.

Despite the natural rigor and discipline of prison life, the prisoners appear to like most of their officials. Only one was described as a really vicious driver of his men; the superintendent drew the praise of every prisoner questioned. "This beats a chain-gang a mile," one prisoner said, "and if you just didn't have nowhere else to live, this wouldn't be the worst place." (1) (2) (3) (4) (5)

REFERENCES

1. Interview with Rev. A. W. Puller, Negro Chaplain of the State Prison at Raiford, Union County, Florida.

2. Statements of guides conducting Field Workers of Federal Writers' Project through prison, April, 1937.

3. Statements of prisoners interviewed.

4. Observations of Field Workers.

5. Report on Florida Prisons and Penal Institutions, Nathan Mayo, Secretary of Agriculture, Tallahassee, 1936.

Appendix B

Views of Eatonville

Eatonville, Florida, an independent, incorporated African-American community near Orlando, has become famous as the home of Zora Neale Hurston and the oft-described stage for both her fictional and folkloric work [*Jonah's Gourd Vine* (1971 (1934): 173ff); *Mules and Men* (1935); *Their Eyes Were Watching God* (1937) passim; *Dust Tracks on the Road* (1942); Hemenway (1977) and Nathiri (1991). Eatonville appears in the Richardson guide; Hurston's description of the town was eventually included in the WPA state guide. Yet various reports were submitted by Negro Project authors Pearl Randolph and James Johnson as well as later work by Paul Diggs. Together with Hurston's views, these suggest the variety of approaches and styles that the WPA writers would take. Eatonville has received a community history by Otey (1990).

All of these are transcribed from typescripts, with correction of spelling errors which may well reflect typing, in order to facilitate smoother modern reading. Punctuation varied widely among authors; the corrections on Hurston's manuscript which involved such changes (and deletion of some personal references) are noted in the fourth piece. It is striking that her final, longer contribution was severely edited for both content and style.

Pearl Randolph May 28, 1936

Eatonville, Florida has the distinction of being the only town in the state that is completely owned and governed by Negroes. It was incorporated August 8, 1889. Although only a ghost of its former self and never having had a population of more than six hundred at the peak of its existence, this small township has continued through the years to adhere to its regular routine of self-government as provided for in its original charter.

The town now has a population of three hundred, three small churches, the

Hungerford Industrial School, the public school and a general store, and a full force of city officials. It is noted for its spirited elections.

In 1889 H.W. Lawrence, a wealthy white philanthropist of Maitland, Florida donated a twenty-seven acre tract of land to a group of Negroes for a townsite. Here he erected a church which was the first structure built in the town. This was the St. Lawrence A.M.E. Church, named in honor of the donor.

At the request of Mr. Lawrence the town was christened Eatonville, in honor of a sea captain friend of his. It later developed that Mr. J.C. Eaton engaged in citrus farming and at one time employed almost the whole population of his namesake town, always giving preference to these workers.

Immediately after its incorporation the citizens of Eatonville held their first elections, choosing Joe Clark local merchant as their first mayor. The following mayors in order of their tenure in office have served since that time. C.H. Boger, Sr. (deceased) two terms; C.H. Boger Jr., (now pastor of Mt. Olive Church, Orlando, Florida) one term; Tom Pender (deceased) one term; Joe Clark (deceased) re-elected, serving two terms; John Hurston (deceased) father of Zora Neal Hurston, two terms; C.H. Boger Jr., (re-elected) two terms; B.L. Perry)now Agricultural Instructor Florida A & M College) one term. E. L. Mosley (now residing in Philadelphia) two terms; Howard Miller (present mayor) several terms; W.S. Sewell, two terms; Howard Miller re-elected and now serving.

J. M. Johnson n.d. probably 1936

Eatonville

During the days of Reconstruction in Florida, in a county then known as Mosquito County, was situated a winter resort then known as Maitland and known as such to the present day.

The climate was warm, thus making it a winter haven for those of means who sought warmer climes from the frigid blasts of Northern winters. The country abounded in citrus fruit, hence, began an exodus of Negroes to work on groves and as caretakers. Soon the Negro population dominated that of the whites. Maitland was not an incorporated town, Republicans controlled the area, and Negroes being franchised was a serious threat to officialdom of Maitland. Men walked boldly about the streets with revolvers strapped to their sides; saloons dotted the town. The whites were afraid of the Negro situation. A charter for the town of Maitland was finally granted. In the first election there a few Negroes became office-holders. Tomy Taylor, a Negro, was elected to the city council, and also Chairmen of the Board of Aldermen. Fred Lewis, a Negro, became Marshall.

Most of the Northern capital was in and around Maitland. Captain Isaiah Eaton, an English sailor, was the key man for this capital and had charge of a large estate house known as the Boyington Estate. There was a Mr. Lawrence, a New Englander, who had a large grove at Maitland and on it worked a Negro, Joe Clark a man about five feet seven inches in height, two hundred pounds, dark brown complexion and naturally intelligent, though having no academic education. This man was well liked by the majority of Negroes and had the gift of being able to dominate with ease and without offense. Captain Eaton met Clark and gave him a better position with him as foreman on the Boyington Estate. In the next election that came up in Maitland, the Negroes were talking of running Tomy Taylor for Mayor. The whites became fearful that Taylor might be elected on account of the Negro majority. Acting upon this fear Captain Eaton made a suggestion to Joe Clark about Negroes having a town of their own and completely controlled by them without any trouble from the white people. Clark liked the idea and put it up to the Negroes, who were also in accord. Thus was the beginning of Eatonville, named in honor of Captain Eaton, the first incorporated Negro town in the United States. Joe Clark bought the land from Mr. Lawrence on a purchase money mortgage, and on this land is situated Eatonville, the area of which is approximately one and one eighth of a mile, north and south, and one and one quarter mile east and west. The town is one mile from Maitland, three miles from Winter Park, and seven miles from Orlando. The first settlers were: Joe Clark, Matthew Braswell, Tomy Taylor, David Yelder, Fred Lewis, Walter Thomas, Tom Pender, C.H. Bogers, John Watson, Tim Everett, Ishmael Williams and Syke Jones.

Eatonville was incorporated as a Negro town in 1885 and a charter granted in 1886. Prior to this time there was a church, St. Lawrence A.M.E.; and an Odd Fellows Hall, St. Lawrence Lodge, given by Mr. Lawrence in 1882 and named in his honor.

In the first election held in Eatonville, August 18, 1886, there were thirty five qualified voters. Joe Clark was elected Mayor, Rev. C. H. Boger Sr. Chairman of Board of Alderman; W.T. Thomas, City Clerk; M.B. Braswell, Marshall and Tax Collector. A United States post-office was established and Joe Clark was appointed postmaster [.] He also opened a store in the town.

Negroes began coming to Eatonville and buying property from Joe Clark at a nominal sum. A jail house was built. Court was held in the local church presided over by the Mayor. A weekly newspaper was established known as the Eatonville Ledger, owned by John Starke and Company, Negroes. It was edited by Rev. Speights and Son.

In 1892, Mr. Hungerford, a Northerner noting the increase in the Negro populations suggested to Joe Clark that it was time to have a school for the colored children. A barbecue was held which was largely attended by the populace and visiting ministers. The idea of a school for Eatonville was put over. In 1898 a teacher from Tuskegee named Calhoun came to Eatonville and there met Mr. Hungerford. School problems were discussed. Mr. Hungerford donated forty acres of land for the school. Northerners contributed money toward the cause and as a result Calhoun and Booker Washington Halls were built, the first two buildings. Calhoun formed a choral class which sung before white audiences who made gratuitous contributions to the school. Mr. Clewett, a shirt manufacturer, donated another building known as Clewett Hall. At present the school has four buildings. The first principal was George Richardson, who served for fifteen years. A small tuition is charged. Students board in and some come from all sections of the country. There are at the present time over one hundred pupils who are trained through the twelfth grade.

A Negro barber of Orlando some years ago gave a five acre tract of land that he owned in Eatonville for a public school. The Negroes eager for an education went out into the raw forest and cut timber, taking it to a mill where it was converted into lumber. From this material the public school was built. The whites seeing their industriousness and anxiety for education also helped them in this undertaking. School teachers well qualified were also installed to teach the new students and in various ways they assisted in making the public school of Eatonville a permanent institution. The school gives instruction through the eighth grade.

Eatonville realized prosperity for some time, most of the inhabitants working on the surrounding groves and earning goodly sums; suddenly she began to decline. Some of the original inhabitants moved to other places. Many old houses are seen abandoned in dilapidated conditions. The jail house has been torn down, and law violators are incarcerated in the jail at Winter Park or Maitland. There was never much lawlessness among the people of Eatonville who seem to live as one big family, the source of most disturbances come from unscrupulous vandals who drift into the town "to start something."

The United States Post office was also cut out, (its headquarters was located in the store of Joe Clark) the populace receiving their mail from Maitland, the nearest post-office, via rural carrier.

Hungerford school still prospers under the capable leadership of Captain Hall, a Negro. There is running water and electricity that serve the town. Apopka Avenue is the main thoroughfare and is the only hard surfaced road in the town. The incorporation of Eatonville was enlargened in 1914 by Mayor Braswell.

The mayors of Eatonville in the order of their succession are: [list follows] The present officials of the town are Mayor, City Councilmen and chief of police. The mayor serves gratis and the chief of police receives a fee for each arrest. Elections are held annually. There are three churches, viz: Macedonia Baptist, Open Door Baptist and St. Lawrence A.M.E. Having no theaters or places of amusement, the residents for diversion go to Winter Park or Orlando. Joe Clark, the man who was a picturesque figure, being portrayed in the novel, *Their Eyes Were Watching God,* by Zora Neal Hurston, the personification of Eatonville, a strong character and a man of wealth passed on some few years ago. At his removal the town of Eatonville lost one of its strongest supporters.

With one store, one ice cream parlor, Eatonville happily goes on boasting of its Negro municipality [and a population of 185]. [Source listed, H.B. Lester, Mayor of Eatonville].

Paul Diggs, Lakeland, September 22, 1938

To the House by the Lake

When you turn off the main highway No. 17, you enter a road that is full of winding curves, and flanked on each side by foliage and large oaks which are laden with moss. On and on, passing beautiful winter homes of the tourists and orange groves until you enter the village of *Eatonville*, Florida. This village has the distinction of being the only incorporated colored townsite in Florida. Through the village to the extreme west about one-half mile beyond "Claude Mann's Filling Station" will be found on the right about one-quarter mile from the hard road the house which is the home of America's noted colored writer, *"Zora Neale Hurston."* Miss Hurston is the author of "Jonah's Gourd Vine", "Mules and Men", "Their Eyes were Watching God", and she is now completing her latest book, "Tell My Horse", a story of life in Haiti.

The house in which Miss Hurston occupies is located close to Lake Buck. It is a weather-boarded house, very spacious, and comfortably arranged in the interior. Around the house will be found games for recreational amusements, such as: Badminton, croquet, and holes for golf putting. Which makes its physical setting ideal for a country lodge.

About fifty feet from the edge of the shore of Lake Buck, there is projecting out into the water a dilapidated dock, where one may use for diving off into deep water, or for fishing. This dock serves aside from enjoyment other purposes that necessitates household managements. Occasionally a boat ride is enjoyed from the dock on this beautiful lake whose shores are bedecked with foliage, large oaks, and cypress trees.

While standing on the dock, occasionally one may see a turtle gently swimming in the water, [or] suddenly a fish will jump out of the water sending the sprays high with a splash. The stillness on a calm day spell peace, but when the wind is high the ripples play tag with each other.

One writer says: "I live in the house by the side of the road and is friend to man." I would say, " I have visited the house by the side of the lake, and it is a friend to nature."

Zora Neale Hurston, no date

(This is the copy that is included with some minor editorial changes in *Florida: A Guide to the Southernmost State* (1939): 362.)

Eatonville When You Look At It

Maitland is Maitland until it gets to Hurst's corner, and then it is Eatonville. Right in front of Willie Sewell's yellow-painted house the hard road quits being the hard road for a generous mile and becomes the heart of Eatonville. Or from a stranger's point of view, you could say that the road just bursts through on its way from Highway #17 to #441 [*US 17 to US 441*], scattering Eatonville right and left.

On the right after you leave the Sewell place you don't meet a thing that people live in until you come to the Green Lantern on the main corner. That corner has always been the main corner, because that is where Joe Clarke, the founder and first mayor of Eatonville, built his store when he started the town nearly sixty years ago, so that people have gotten used to gathering there and talking. Only Joe Clarke sold groceries and general merchandise, while Lee Glenn sells drinks of all kinds and whatever goes with transient rooms. St. Lawrence Methodist church and the parsonage are on the same side of the road between Sewell's and "the shop" and perhaps claim the soul of the place, but the shop is the heart of it. After the shop you come to Widow Dash's orange grove, her screened porch, "double hips," and her new husband. Way down on the end of the road to the right is Claude Mann's filling station and beyond that is the last house in Eatonville, the big barn on the lake [that is lived in by Zora Neale Hurston; this ending is omitted in the Guide].

Take the left side road and except for Macedonia Baptist church, people just live along that side and play croquet in Armetta Jones' backyard behind the huge camphor tree. After the people quit living along that side of the road, the [Robert; omitted in published guide] Hungerford Industrial school begins and runs along the road for some distance as far as the land goes. The inadequate buildings stop short in the cleared land on the fringe of Eatonville proper. And west of it all, villages and schools, everybody knows that the sun makes his nest in some lonesome lake in the woods back there and gets his night's rest.

But all of Eatonville is not on the hard road that becomes Apopka Avenue as it passes through town. There are back streets on both sides of the road. The two back streets on the right side are full of little houses squatting under hovering oaks. These houses are old and were made out of the town's first dreams. There is loved Lake Sabelia, with its small colony of very modern houses lived in by successful villagers [like Kelly Baldwin and the Williams; omitted in published guide]. Away in the woody rises beyond Sabelia is Eatonville's Dogtown that looks as if it belonged on the African veldt. Off the road on the left is the brown-with-white trim modern public school with its well kept yards and playgrounds that [Guide—which] Howard Miller always looks after though he can scarcely read and write. They call this part of town Mars Hill, as against Bones Valley to the right of the hard road. They call the tree-shaded lane that runs past the schoolhouse West street and it goes past several minor groves until it passes Jim Steele's fine orange grove and dips itself into Lake Belle, which is the home of Eatonville's most celebrated resident, the world's largest alligator.

NOTE: The published guide also includes an explanation of the alligator:

> This legendary alligator, it is said, is no other than an ex-slave who escaped from a Georgia plantation and joined the Indians during the Seminole wars. When the Indians retreated he did not follow but made instead made "big medicine" on the lake shore. He transformed himself into an alligator, the god of his tribe and slipped into the water. Now and then he resumes human form, so people say, and roams the country about Eatonville. At such times all the alligators in the surrounding lakes bellow loudly all night long. "The big one has gone back home," whisper the villagers.

This story is drawn from a second typescript attributed to Hurston, printed below, but alters its tone and cadence to produce a more familiar European tale instead of the rhythms and details of Hurston's usual folklore. The introductory

paragraph in the guide also condenses information from the first paragraphs in this
alternate report, omitting the story of how Eatonville became a separate community.

Eatonville
(WPA Guide text attributed to Hurston)

Eatonville, Florida began on a steamer bound from Brazil to New York. Four
men, all veterans of the Civil War were returning from a trip to South America
which had been planned while they were comrades in arms. They had been very
young men who joined the Union forces in the last year of the struggle. On the
way back to American from Brazil, they had drifted into talking of what they
would do with their lives and finally decided to pioneer into the wilds of South
Florida. In the year 1880, the state was a wilderness below Palatka . The names of
the adventurous young men were Vanderpool, Boynton, Kedney and one Captain
Eaton under whom the others had served in the war.

Back in the states, they got in touch with two other bosom friends, Louis F.
Lawrence and E.C. Hungerford. This party made its way down into Orange
County (which was then known as Mosquito county) and took up homesteads of
160 acres each. Most of these men were from New York state, but the rest were
from the mid-west.

Soon these settlers had induced a few others to join them and began to modify
their surroundings to their tastes and needs. They were all educated men and
stamped their taste and breeding on the community from the very beginning. By
1884 they had advanced to the place where they wished to incorporate their town
of Maitland, Florida. But the laws of the state required thirty registered voters and
they had not that number as yet. So the Negroes who had been attracted to the
new settlement to work were pressed into duty as citizens, enough voters were
secured and the founding fathers went up to Gainesville and got the charter for the
town of Maitland.

This arrangement proved a boomerang, however, since the Negro voters soon
outnumbered the whites. They all lived around what is known now as Lake Lily,
but what was then called St. John's Hole. They could be seen all day washing
clothes in primitive fashion on the shores of the lake which did not suit the white
citizens either. So Mr. Louis Lawrence took the initiative in suggesting to the
Negro leaders that they start a town of their own and offered forty acres as a town
site at a very attractive price. A very aggressive Negro named Joe Clark bought the
land and later sold it to lots of other Negroes. Everything went off in good will and
in good faith. The Negroes moved over to their new site which was one mile west
of Maitland and went to work on their new site with enthusiasm establishing their
town. Mr. Lawrence asked that the new town be named for his friend Cap. Eaton
and this was done. (Capt. Josiah Eaton was his full name)

Eatonville received its charter of incorporation March 15, 1886 and thus became
the first Negro settlement in Florida, and the first incorporated Negro town in the
United States. The first election was held in August 18,1886. Joe E. Clark was the
first man elected to the office of mayor.

The first Negro publication in the state was *The Eatonville Ledger* edited and owned by a Rev. Speight. The press on which the paper was printed was owned by the Negro stockholders.

The city ordinances of Eatonville were formulated and issued under the administration of Mayor John Hurston during his first term of office 1897–98. Joe E. Clark, President of the Council; Walter T. Thomas,Clerk.

Through the efforts of Russel C. Calhoun, himself a graduate of Tuskegee Institute, the Robert Hungerford Normal and Industrial Institute was founded in 1901. The money was donated by Mr. E. C. Hungerford, one of the original settlers of Maitland, but the school was named for and dedicated to the memory of his nephew, Robert Hungerford. He had been a brilliant young physician who had sacrificed his own life while treating a Negro patient during a contagious epidemic. During the lifetime of Russel Calhoun the school prospered and became the most important Negro school in South-Central Florida. Since his death in 1917 it has steadily declined until it is of no importance.

There is a legend that has grown up about the huge alligator which inhabits Lake Belle at Eatonville. He is said to be an ex-slave who escaped from a Georgia plantation during the Indian wars in Florida. On his escape he made his way down into Florida and joined the fighting forces of the Indians under Osceola and Billy-Bowlegs. When they were defeated and scattered, this Negro made great African medicine on his own on the shores of what is now known as Lake Belle and at the finish he transformed himself into the American counterpart of his clan god, the crocodile, and slid into the waters to wait a friendly time. He had said time and time again to his comrades that he would never die by the hand of the white man nor be re-enslaved.

It had been a sad period for the Indian forces that ended with the alligator incarnation of the former African priest. Osceola had been tricked into captivity, Billy Bowlegs had been slain, their ragged forces had been driven south and east before the conquering arms of the white man at last. Some had been removed to Oklahoma and the more relentless had been forced to seek refuge in the trackless wilds of the everglades. The African priest saw no hope for himself in following further the fortunes of war. He announced his intentions to his brothers in arms, made his nine-days preparation before the day of the big medicine, stood before his sacred fire with his supplications and entered the lake to wait the coming of his kind as he predicted. Now and then he assumes human form and lives in the village and about. There is a tremendous all night bellowing of alligators in the lake when he returns. Then the village says, "The Bog One has gone back home."

Hiram B. Lester is the present mayor, August 18-. It has come to be for the past several years that Mayor Lester or his brother-in-law, Howard Miller are always in office. They hold office in alternate terms, one year Mayor Miller, the next year Mayor Lester.

Present population, 315.

Occupations: Most of the men pick fruit or are otherwise employed in the orange groves of the fruit growers. Average earnings for the fruit-pickers are $25–40 per week in season. Average pay in the groves in summer is $1.50 per day. Most of the grown women work too as domestics in the wealthy white families of Maitland and Winter Park. Practically no one works in summer because the wealthy people are gone north and the summer pay is not attractive. The majority of the citizens prefer to go fishing and swimming whether they have any money saved up or not.

There is a public school with three rooms and three teachers that cares for pupils through the ninth grade. It is well-kept and clean.[1]

NOTE

1. All these reports celebrate Eatonville's independence in a tradition that Hurston herself had stressed, as in her introduction of the community in *Jonah's Gourd Vine*:

"You mean uh whole town uh nothin' but colored folks? Who bosses it, den?"

"Dey bosses deyself."

"You mean dey runnin' de town 'thout de white folks?"

"Sho is. Eben got uh mayor and corporation."

"Ah sho wants tuh see dat sight." (p.173).

Yet all fail to underscore, much less criticize, the era of Jim Crow restriction and segregation as an alternative to white elective domination by blacks that had excised Eatonville from Maitland. In the introduction, I noted similar reticence with regard to the case of Ocoee, while the black community of Rosewood, burnt out in the 1920s, appears nowhere in the guide.

Appendix C

Contributors to *The Florida Negro*

This working list is based on the manuscripts filed in the Florida Historical Society (FHS), the Library of Congress Manuscript Division (LC) and the P.K. Yonge Library (PKY), University of Florida (locations are designated by Box and File for FHS; by file for LC and by volume for PKY). If a location is not cited, the report is not readily available at that source, although some confusion may arise from partial or retitled files. Since the ex-slave interviews are widely available, only a basic FHS source is given. If multiple copies exist at the same source they are not cited, unless there is some special interest in them (e.g. works that appear in both the Folklore files and Negro Studies Project (NSP) of the WPA Manuscripts at the Library of Congress.

This list includes all people who appear as authors unless the papers represent extracts derived from other published works, the range of dates of manuscripts and any other suggested indications about them, including location or status. Race is mentioned where known. Since some people, like Cora Taylor and Paul Diggs, submitted collections of numerous 1–2 page articles; in these cases a summary of themes is provided rather than a complete bibliography. Authors who appear only once or twice are marked with an asterisk to indicate that they may not have been core project members.

Materials appear alphabetically to facilitate cross-reference. Materials reproduced in appendices are underlined. If these materials contributed to the Florida Negro manuscript, this is also noted here as well as in annotations.

Above all, this list should be a tool; I hope that it will be augmented and clarified by further research.

LOTT ALLEN (editor or supervisor; 1936, white)*
Lucius Lamar Douglas [Orlando] no interviewer, Lott Allen Editor. 8pp. May 18, 1936. FHS Box 7/file 1.

RACHEL A. AUSTIN (secretary, then fieldworker; Jacksonville, 1936, black)
SLAVE INTERVIEWS: Samuel Simeon Andrews [Jacksonville]October 27, 1936
11p. FHS Box IV/4.
Interview with Florida Clayton 2pp. November 20, 1936 (Used in FN manu-
script, Chapter II) FHS Box II/3
Clayborn Gantling [Jacksonville] April 16, 1927. 6pp. FHS: Box IV/5
Margrett Nickerson [Jacksonville] December 5, 1936. 8pp. FHS Box IV/4. (Used
in Entirety in The Florida Negro Chapter III).
Douglas Parish [Monticello] November 10, 1936 5pp. FHS Box IV/4
A centenarian [Luke Towns] [Jacksonville] November 30, 1936 4pp.FHS Box-
IV/4
OTHER MATERIALS: Supplement to Negro Churches, St. Augustine (Wilson
W. Rice April 27, 1936 6pp) 12 pp. LC A878, Florida/Contemporary Cul-
ture/Religious Organizations. PKY Negro Churches.
Young Winston Davis [Jacksonville] 9pp. FHS Box IV/6

L. REBECCA BAKER (Daytona Beach, 1936–7, black)
SLAVE INTERVIEW:"'Prophet'" John Henry Kemp [Daytona Beach] January
11, 1937 5pp. FHS Box IV/5.
OTHER MATERIALS: Negro Art (Daytona Beach) May 22, 1936 2pp. Supple-
ment September 25, 1936. 3pp. LC A878 Florida Cultural Life/Lifestyle.
Negro Churches (Daytona Beach) July 10, 1936, 12pp. LC A878 Contemporary
Culture/Religious Organizations. PKY: Negro Churches.
Negro Education (Daytona Beach) September 21, 1936. 8pp. LC A877 (NSP)
Contemporary Culture/Education; PKY: Negro Education.
Negro Ethnography (Daytona Beach) May 22, 1936. 4pp. LC A879 NSP Florida
Historical Material. PKY: Negro History
Negro Music (Daytona Beach) July 28, 1936. 7pp. FHS Box V/4

RUTH BARR (editor and interviewer, white)
———— and Modeste Hargis "The Voluntary Exile Among the Free Negroes of
Pensacola" *Florida Historical Quarterly* July 1938. FHS Box II/3; LC A879 Florida
Historical Material (1860–1936).

LINDSAY M. BRYAN (white)
Barnyard Talk n.d. 2pp. LC A591 Florida Folklore.
Florida's 'John Henry' Lindsay M. Bryan. March 2, 1938. 8pp FHS Box VIII/5.
Stories of Florida (for schools)

RUTH BOLTON (Jacksonville? 1939–40? Black?)
Afro-American Insurance Company n.d. 2pp. LC A877 NSP Contemporary
Culture/Economic Conditions (in Appendix)
Beds for Negro Tuberculosis Patients n.d. 1 p. LC A878 NSP Florida Contempo-
rary Culture/Social Organization and Benevolent Organization.
Clara White Mission June 9, 1939. 5pp. LC A878 NSP Florida Contemporary
Culture/Social Organization and Benevolent Organization.

Jacksonville Negro Welfare League. June 13, 1939. 3pp. FHS Box II/7
Lincoln Golf and Country Club n.d. 2pp. LC A878 NSP Florida Contemporary
Culture/Social Organization and Benevolent Organization.

B. F. BORCHARDT (Supervisor) White *
Steven Harvell. [Tampa] B.F. Borchardt. local supervisor May 17, 1937. FHS Box
VII/3

F. HILTON CROWE (St. Augustine; transcription of notes only) *

BARBARA BERRY DARSEY (1940; white) *
Interview with Emmett William Sebring. 2000 words. Miami. n.d. FHS Box
VIII/2.
Negro Songs of Labor and Religion. Bradley Eberhardt interviewed by . . . 2/29
and 3/4 1940. 28pp.

PAUL DIGGS (Lakeland, 1938–9, black) A Paul Diggs Appears in the Lakeland
City Directory, 1945 as the manager of Lake Ridge Homes married to Louise,
principal of the Washington Park School (c). According to S. Kennedy, he was
black although working out of the Tampa Office (1938–9)
  SLAVE INTERVIEWS (Late): Life Story of William Stone [St. Petersburg] July
14, 1938 5pp. FHS Box IV/6.
  Grandma Effie Knowles [Lakeland] July 28, 1938. 7pp.FHS Box IV/6
  Interview with an ex-slave who is reputed to have the power to remove pains
with her hands" [Georgia Love, Lakeland] n.d. 4p. FHS Box I/6.
  OTHER MATERIALS: African Songs, Superstition and Voodoo. August 18,1938
3pp. FHS Box II/1; LC A879 (NSP) Florida Folklore/Superstitions and Super-
natural.
  Hon. Henry Wilkins Chandler, A.B., A.M. [Lakeland, d.1937] November 25,
1938. 3pp. FHS Box 1/4.
  Characteristic Traits in Regard to Negro Funerals. November 18, 1938. 1p. FHS
Box II/1. LC A878 NSP Florida Folklore and Customs.
  Circus Jargon October 7, 1938 FHS Box II/11.
  Colloquial and Vernacular Unsed among Colored People in South Florida.
November 10, 1938. 1p.November 10, 1938. FHS Box II/11; LC A878 (NSP) Florida
Folklore/Dialects and Jargons
  A Colored Picnic [Lakeland] September 9, 1938. 5pp. FHS Box I/7. LC A878
(NSP) Contemporary Culture/Lifestyle.
  Colored City Auditorium -Lakeland. October 7, 1938. 1p. FHS Box I/14 LC
A878 (NSP) Contemporary culture/Lifestyle.
  Early History and First Organized Efforts of Catholicism for Negroes August
12, 1938. 9pp. FHS Box VI/4 7pp. LC A879 NSP Fl Historical Material (1860–
1936).
  Fish Not Biting Today. November 4, 1938. 3pp. FHS Box II/1.
  The Florida Negro in Music. October 14, 1938. 4pp. FHS Box V/4.
  The Florida Negro and Cubans living in the Same Community in Tampa,
Florida. August 26, 1938. 5pp. FHS I/6.

Florida Negro Non-Accredited HS July 29, 1938 5pp. LC A877 (NSP) Contemporary Culture/Education.

"Follow Me Through Florida" November 10, 1938 10pp. FHS Box II/5. LC A878 (NSP) Contemporary Culture/Lifestyle.

Forgotten Romances of Negro History Sept 30, 1938. FHS Box VIII/4; LC A879 NSP Florida Historical Material (1939–1939).

Clara Frye Memorial Hospital Tampa Nov 25, 1938 2pp. LC A878 NSp Contemporary Culture/ Social Organizations and Benevolent Organizations.

"Georgia Sleeping" Drawing FHS I/6.

"John Gilbert Still Believes in His Herbs" December 2, 1938. 3pp. FHS Box II/1. LC A879 (NSP) Florida Folklore/Superstitions and Supernatural.

"Going in from de Cotton Fields" September 9, 1938 1p. FHS V/4.

The Health of the American Negro July 22, 1938 6pp. LC A878 (NSP) Contemporary Culture/Lifestyle.

Herbs and Plants Used by Negroes in Fl Nov 4, 1938. 7pp cont Nov 10. FHS Box VIII/5; LC A879 (NSP) Florida Folklore/Superstitions and Supernatural.

How the Negro Boy Plays Golf. July 8, 1938 3pp. LC A878 (NSP) Contemporary Culture/Lifestyle.

Interviews with Negroes in Service in Lakeland, Fl October 21, 1938 3pp. & Nov 4, 1938 3pp FHS Box VI/2 LC A877 Contemporary Culture/ Economic Conditions. Jeanes Teachers in Florida (Colored) August 26, 1938. 2pp LC A877 (NSP) Contemporary Culture/Education.

Lakeland Public Library [For Negroes at Washington Park H.S.] November 18, 1938. 2pp. FHS Box I/14; LC A878 (NSP) Contemporary Culture/Lifestyle.

"Little Angel of Ashly Street—Miss Eartha M.M. White. October 14, 1938. 1p. Box I/6.

Music Jargon November 4, 1938 1p. FHS Box II/11.

A Negro Community and Business Section- Bartow March 24, 1939. 9pp. FHS Box VI/2; LC A878 (NSP) Contemporary Culture/Lifestyle.

A Negro Community—Pierce, Fl December 2, 1938 4pp. FHS Box VIII/6; LC A878 (NSP) Contemporary Culture/Lifestyle.

Negro Education in Florida. November 18, 1938. 3pp. FHS Box I/ 13; LC A877 (NSP) Contemporary Culture/Education.

Negro Education: Mary McLeod Bethune July 8, 1938 3pp. LC A877 NSP Florida-Biographical.

Negro Educators (Con't) Prof William A Rochelle July 15, 1938 7pp LC A877 NSP Florida-Biographical.

Negro Educator J R E Lee July 28, 1938 1p.LC A877 NSP orida-Biographical.

Negro Educators Charles Sumner Long PD July 28, 1938 1p.

LC A877 NSP Florida-Biographical.

Negro Farmer and 4-H Clubs in Hillsborough County, Fl July 8, 1938 4pp. LC A878 NSp Contemporary Culture/ Social Organizations and Benevolent Organizations.

Negro in Business (Sept 2) 4pp Negro Business (Sept 30), 1938 6pp; Oct 7, 1938

4pp; Negro Businesses (October 14, 1938) 3pp; The Negro in Business (October 28, 1938) 3 pp. LC A877 Contemporary Culture/Economic Conditions.

Negro Newspapers FHS Box VI/1; LC A879 NSP Florida Historical Material (1936–1939):

(1) The Tampa Bulletin 9–22–38. 2pp
(2) Rev M.D. Potter ed TampaBulletin August 19, 1938 2pp.
(3) The Orlando Sun 3pp 9–22–1938
(4) The St. Petersburg Public Informer 10–21–1938
(5) Orlando Fl Sentinel 10–28–1938 2pp
(6) Negro Newspapers Influence on Public 10–28–1938 2pp.
(7) The Christian Advocate/C Recorder 9–23–1938
(8) List of Newspapers August 18, 1938
(9) FHS negro Newspapers in Florida October 7, 1938 6pp.

Negro Spiritual December 2, 1938 FHS Box V/4

Negroes in the Profession Oct 7, 1938 3pp. FHS Box VI/1; LC A877 Contemporary Culture/Economic Conditions.

Negroes Fraternity in Florida: Phi Beta Sigma. November 10, 1938. 3pp. FHS Box I/ 13; LC A878 NSP Contemporary Culture/ Social Organizations and Benevolent Organizations.

Newspapers and Periodicals in the US. Oct 28, 1938 4pp. FHS Box VI/1; LC A878 (NSP) Contemporary Culture/Lifestyle.

The New Maid (play): a. Letter from Diggs to Corse, November 4, 1938 b. Play, The New Maid. 5pp. FHS: Box Iv/3

Notable Negroes FHS Box I/4 Biography

(1) [Rev H.W. Bartley, Bartow] October 7, 1938
(2) Samuel Decatur McGill [lawyer, Jacksonville] December 9, 1938 1.p
(3) Dr. J.R.E. Lee, President Florida A & M. December 2, 1938 1p.
(4) "Florida's Only Negro Sheriff [Charles F. Dupont,Monroe] n.d. From *Tampa Tribune* October 2, 1938 1.p. Also LC A877 Contemporary Culture/ Economic Conditions. (All these are also at LC A877 NSP Florida-Biographical, which adds #4, #5, and #7 and these additional biographies):
(5) Dr. L.A. Howell Tampa Dec 9, 1938. 2pp
(6) Cyrus T. Green July 22, 1938. 3pp.

An Old Colored Settler who Still Maintains his Home in A White Neighborhood. [H.C. Menefield, Lakeland] October 7, 1938. 2pp. FHS Box I/4.

Polk County Ushers Union Nov 25, 1938 1p. FHS Box VI/4; LC A878 NSP Florida/Contemporary Culture/Religious Organizations.

Recreations : The Supervision of Recreation and its relation to Crime Prevention July 23, 1938. 8pp. LC A878 NSp Contemporary Culture/ Social Organizations and Benevolent Organizations.

St. Paul AME Tampa August 12, 1938 4pp. FHS Box VI/4 LC A878 NSP Contemporary Culture/Religious Organizations.

St. Peter Claver Church and School for Negroes and Cubans, Tampa. August 12,

1938 7pp. FHS Box VI/4; LC A878 NSP Contemporary Culture/Religious Organizations.

Sanctified Church September 2, 1938 8pp. FHS Box VI/4 LC A878 NSP Contemporary Culture/Religious Organizations.

Schools: Florida Normal and Industrial Aug 3, 1938 6pp LC A877 (NSP) Contemporary Culture/Education.

Scouting Among Florida Negro -Boy Scouts of America. November 10, 1938. 2pp. FHS Box II/5. LC A878 NSP Contemporary Culture/ Social Organizations and Benevolent Organizations.

Sports in Negro Colleges. December 9, 1938. 5 pp. FHS Box I/ 13; LC A877 Contemporary Culture/Education.

Superstitions. August 18, 1938. 2pp. LC A879 (NSP) Florida Folklore/Superstitions and Supernatural.

To the House by the Lake (Eatonville) September 22, 1938. 2p. FHS Box I/4. A Tough Yarn About And Old Colored Man. August 31, 1938. 2pp. FHS Box II/1. LC A878 NSP Florida Folklore/Stories.

Rudolph Von Charlton, Pianist March 24, 1938 LC A878 (NSP) Contemporary Culture/Lifestyle.

Witchcraft AF 498/3 Septemebr 29, 1936. LC A879 (NSP) Florida Folklore/Superstitions and Supernatural.

ALFRED FARRELL (North Florida—Tallahassee, Live Oak—, 1936–7, black). Pam Bordelon has confirmed Farrell as a *Magna cum laude* from Lincoln University.
SLAVE INTERVIEWS: A Governor's Slave [Matilda Brooks, Monticello] January 12, 1937. 4pp. FHS: Box IV/5

Bolden Hall [Live Oak] 5pp. August 20, 1936. FHS Box IV/4 Slave Interview. Dell Bess Hilyard [Miami] n.d. 4pp. FHS VIII/2

Negro Art (Tallahassee) 1217/6 May 29, 1936. LC A 878 NSP, Florida Contemporary Culture/Lifestyle.

Negro Churches (Tallahassee) 1062/6 June 10, 1936. FHS Box VI/4. LC A878 NSP Florida/Contemporary Culture/Religious Organizations.

Negro Education (Jacksonville) April 7, 193612 pp. FHS Box I/13. LC 877 Contemporary Culture/ Education. PKY: Negro Education.

Negro Education (Live Oak) May 12, 1936 329wds/ 2 LC 877 Contemporary Culture/ Education. PKY: Negro Education.

Negro Education (Tallahassee) 1,303 words 7pp April 26, 1936. ; LC 877 Contemporary Culture/ Education. PKY: Negro Education.

Negro Ethnography (Live Oak) Sept 27, 1936 3pp. LCA878/Florida Contemporary Culture/General. PKY:Negro History

Negro Ethnography (Tallahassee) June 16, 1936 2pp. LC A878 Florida contemporary Culture/General. PKY: Negro History.

Negro History (Tallahassee) AF 13 pp June 16, 1936. LC A879 Florida Historical Material (1936–1939). PKY: Negro History.

Negro Music (Tallhassee) 5pp 772wds June 12, 1936. LC 877 Contemporary Culture/ Education

Negro Religion (Live Oak) Sept 29, 1936. FHS Box VI/4; LC A878 NSP Florida/Contemporary Culture/Religious Organizations. UF: Negro Churches.

Witchcraft 498 words, 3pp. September 29, 1936. FHS VIII/4; LC A879 (NSP) Florida Folklore/Superstitions and Supernatural.

FROST, JULES [Abner] (Tampa Unit. Also wrote WPA History of Ybor City report; COLUMNETTES (poems) published The Ogg Press, Tampa 1936. Newspaperman, white)

Samson Forrester September 12, 1938. 8pp. FHS Box VII/3

Ha'ints October 20, 1937 7pp. FHS Box VII/3

"Steven Harville, Ex-Slave" 4pp. Tampa July 9, 1937. FHS Box VII/3.

"Mama Duck" Stories of Florida. Prepared for Use in Public Schools. May 19, 1937. Tampa 4pp. FHS Box VII/3

"A Marine in Ebony" Uncle Dave July 9, 1937 18pp. FHS Box VII/3

MAY F. GARDNER*

"Some Different Negro Work Songs" [St. Augustine] October 25, 1939. 3pp. FHS Box V/4.

RUBYE K. GOEBEL*

SLAVE INTERVIEW: Laura Saunders June 13, 1937. Rubye K. Goebel and Mary K. Roberts. 8pp. FHS Box II/6 or 7.

MODESTE HARGIS (Pensacola, White, 1937) SEE RUTH BARR.

Richard Lindsay. July 6, 1937. 2pp. FHS Box II/7.

Nellie McCann August 6, 1937 FHS Box VII/2

Thomas Moreno. June 1, 1937. 8pp.Interviews with Colored People Who Live in West Florida. FHS Box II/6

Alex Thompson June 4, 1937 4pp. FHS Box II/7

A True Story (statewide) 2pp. LC A878 Florida Folklore/Customs.

Joe Youder. May 27, 1937 3pp. FHS Box II/7.

ZORA NEALE HURSTON (Eatonville, Writer and Folklorist, 1938–9, black).

Art n Such

Eatonville 2pp. FHS Box VIII/6.

Eatonville Alligator Legend 1p. (Guide text). A591 Folklore Project/Traditional Lore: Negro Lore.

Eatonville When You Look at It Oct 1, 1938 2pp. FHS Box VIII/6. LC A878 NSP Florida Contemporary Culture/Lifestyle.

The Fire Dance, An African Grotesque 5pp. LC A6r Negroes

Florida Folklore/Miscellaneous Material LC A878 contains material collected by Hurston as well as some merely edited by her in drafts for a folklore chapter. Her collection is evident in the First Version of Folklore (13pp.) and perhaps Daddy Mention 10pp.

Florida Folklore FHS Box II/1.

(1) Negro folk Tales [Roy Tyle, Maitland Garage] No Date. A591 Folklore Project/Traditional Lore: Negro Lore.
(2) Negro Mythical Places 5pp. A591 Folklore Project/Traditional Lore: Negro Lore.
(3) Uncle Monday. 1p LC A878 Florida Folklore/Lifestyle.
Folklore 1st Version of rough Copy 11pp FHS II/1
"Go 'Gator and Muddy the Water" July 14, 1939 28pp. LC A62 Negroes. FHS Box V/1
Goldsborough n.d. 1p FHS Box VIII/6.
Negro Legends (alligator Lake Belle)/West Hell 7pp. LC A591 Folklore Project/Traditional Lore: Negro Lore.
New Children's Games no date 9pp. FHS 2/4
The Sanctified Church 8pp. FHS Box VI/4; LC A878 Florida/ Contemporary Culture/Religious Organizations.
Stories 46pp. ??ZNH?? LC A591 Folklore Project/Traditional Lore: Negro Lore.

J. M. JOHNSON (Fernandina Office on Education. 1937–8, black)
SLAVE INTERVIEWS: Patience Campbell [Monticello] December 15, 1936. FHS Box IV/4.
Mack Mullen [Jacksonville] September 18, 1936. 17pp. FHSBOX IV/4.
Louis Napoleon [S Jacksonville] November 17, 36 7pp. FHS Box IV/4.
William Sherman [Chaseville] August 28, 1936. FHS BOX IV/4.
Claude Augusta Wilson [Lake City] November 6,36 8pp. FHS Box IV/4.
OTHER MATERIALS: Abstract of A. Park's *The Negro in the Reconstruction of Florida*. 4pp. FHS VI/3.
"Black Soldiers in Civil War in Florida" transcribed from W.W. Davis (hand). FHS Box I/10.
Creative Negro Literature in Florida. LC A 879 NSP Florida Historical Material (1936–1939).
Eatonville n.d. 5pp. FHS Box VIII/6.
An Evening at Mt. Pleasant 5pp n.d. (Mother Reed) LC A878 NSP Florida/Contemporary Culture/Religious Organizations and A591 Folklore Project/Traditional Lore, Negro Lore (1).
Florida Beaches for Negroes Robert T. Thomas and ———. Feb 5, 1937. 12pp. LC A878 Florida Contemporary Culture/Lifestyle.
Gamblers Songs (Stagger Lee) n.d. 2pp LC A878 Florida Folklore/Stories.
James Weldon Johnson and Stanton High School n.d. 6pp. (From *Along this Way*). LC A877 NSP Florida-Biographical.
Life of a Ship Loader. n.d. 4pp LC A878 Florida Folklore/ Songs, Ballads and Rhymes.
Negro Education (Fernandina) May 22, 1936. 2pp LC 877 Contemporary Culture/ Education; PKY: Negro Education.
Negro Education. [Union Academy, Gainesville] April 28, 1936. 2pp. FHS Box II/13. PKY: Negro Education.
Negro History (Fernandina) with M.Richardson 12pp. PKY: Negro History.

Negro History (Jacksonville) April 20, 1936 31pp. PKY:Negro History.

Negro History (Ocala) May 4, 1936. 5pp. LC A879 Florida Historical Material (1936–1939)

Negro Religion in Florida. n.d. 6pp. FHS Box VI/4

Negro Songs and Amusements n.d. 14 pp. LC A878 NSP Florida Folklore/ Miscellaneous.

"The Treasure Seekers Night of Terror" n.d. 5pp. FHS Box VIII/5

Work Songs n.d. 6pp. LC A878 Florida Folklore/Songs, Ballads and Rhymes.

SAMUEL JOHNSON (Jacksonville, 1937–8, Black).

SLAVE INTERVIEW: Additional Information Frank Berry [Jacksonville] Samuel Johnson September 11, 1937. FHS: Box IV/5.

OTHER MATERIALS: Boylan-Haven School July 2, 1938. 3pp. LC 877 Contemporary Culture/ Education.

Church of God and Saints of Christ. June 15, 1938. 11pp. FHS Box VI/4.

Edward Waters College. July 2, 1938 4pp. LC 877 Contemporary Culture/ Education.

Negro Workaday Songs October 8, 1937 5pp. FHS Box V/4; LC A878 Florida Folklore/Songs, Ballads and Rhymes.

Workaday Songs September 24, 1937 3pp. FHS Box V/4; LC A591 Folklore Project/Traditional Lore. Songs of lumber and Stevedores in FN ms.

VIOLA MUSE (Tampa, 1936–7, Black)

SLAVE INTERVIEWS: "Father" Charles Coates [Jacksonville] 8pp. December 3, 1936. FHS Box IV/4.

Irene Coates [Jacksonville] December 16, 1936 5pp. FHSBox IV/4.

Willis Dukes [Madison] PR 5pp. January 20, 1937 FHS Box IV/5

Randall Lee [Palatka] 12pp. n.d. FHS Box IV/6

An Ex-Slave who Went to Africa [Anne Scott, Jacksonville] January 11, 1937. 7pp. FHS Box IV/5.

Willis Williams. [Jacksonville] 9ppMarch 20, 1937

OTHER MATERIALS: Black Angel Statues [Jacksonville] September 24, 1936. 3pp FHS VI/4.

Celebrations and Amusements Among Negroes of Florida. 20pp. January 19, 1937. FHS Box I/7 (p. 13 onwards used in text). PKY: Negro in Cities.

Negro Art. 8pg. April 10, 1936. FHS Box I/2

Negro Churches (Tampa) June 6, 1936 1073 wds /6p. LC A878Florida/ Contemporary Culture/Religious Organizations. PKY:Negro Churches.

Negro Education (Tampa) 4pp. April 27, 1936. PKY: Negro Education.

Negro Folklore and Customs. George Petty. [Palatka] 15pp. November 9, 1936. FHS Box II/1.

Negro History (Tampa) 3777wds /19pp. June 2, 1936.LC A879 Florida Historical Material (1936–1939). PKY: Negro in Cities.

Negro Literature. April 16, 1936. 8pp. FHS Box II/12.

Sanctified Church 1033/8pp July 30, 1936. LC A878 NSP Florida/Contemporary

Culture/Religious Organizations.
An Unusual Exhuming [Jacksonville] January 13, 1937. 3pp. ch

PEARL RANDOLPH (Orlando, 1936–7, Black)
SLAVE INTERVIEWS: Frank Berry [Jacksonville] August 18, 1936. 4pp. FHS Box IV/4
Sam and Louisa Everett [Mulberry] October 8, 1936. FHS Box IV/4
Harriett Gresham [Jacksonville] 8pp. December 18, 1936 FHS Box IV/4.
Edward Lycurgas [Jacksonville] December 5, 1936 7pp. FHS Box IV/4
Amanda McCray [Madison] November 13, 1936 5pp. FHS Box IV/4
Acie Thomas [Jacksonville] November 25 1936 9pp. FHS Box IV/4.
OTHER MATERIALS: Eatonville May 28, 1936 2pp. FHS Box VIII/6; PKY: Negro History.
Negro Art (Orlando) 488wds 3pp. May 20, 1936. LC A878, NSp Florida Contemporary Culture/Lifestyle.
Negro Churches (Orlando) April 28, 1936 803/5 LC A878 NSP Florida/Contemporary Culture/Religious Organizations. UF: Negro Churches.
Negro Customs, Cures and Beliefs (Jacksonville) 26pp. March 16, 1936. FHS: Box VIII/5. Also edited version, used in Florida Negro.
Negro Education Public Schools [Lake City] 3pp. September 18, 1936.FHS 1/13. PKY: Negro Education. LC 877 Contemporary Culture/ Education
Negro Education (Orlando) 659wds 4 pp. May 27, 1936 LC 877 Contemporary Culture/ Education. PKY: Negro Education.
Orlando July 15, 1936. 3pp. PKY:Negro History.
A Queer Garden:Aunt Aggie's Bone Yard October 4, 1936 273wds. 3 pp. FHS: Box V/3. LC 878 Florida Folklore/Local Lore.
Unusual Character [Steve Reynolds, Jacksonville] January 14, 1937. 5p. FHS Box I/4.

WILSON R. RICE (NWU 1936, Black)
Negro Churches (Jacksonville) March 16, 1936 17pp. FHS Box VI/3 . PKY: Negro Churches.
Negro Churches (St. Augustine) April 27, 1936 6pp.; Supplement by R. Austin LC A878 Contemporary Culture/Religious Organizations. PKY: Negro Churches.
Negro Folk Customs and Folklore (Miami) 2pp, May 6, 1936 NWU. LC A879 (NSP) Florida Folklore/Superstitions and Supernatural.
Negro Literature May 4, 1936. 2pp. LC 877 NSP Florida-Biographical.

MARTIN RICHARDSON (Jacksonville, 1936–7, Black, Primary author for the manuscript).
SLAVE INTERVIEWS: Bill Austin [Jacksonville] 4pp. n.d. FHS Box IV/5
Neil Coker [Jacksonville] 5pp. Grandin. n.d. FHS Box IV/6
Ambrose Douglas [Brooksville] n.d. 4pp. FHS Box IV/6
Arnold Gragston [Eatonville] n.d. 4pp. FHS Box IV/6.
Christine Mitchell [St. Augustine] 2pp. November 10, 1936). FHS Box IV/4

"An Ex-Slave Who Was Resourceful" [Lindsay Moore, Palatka] 4pp January 13, 1937 FHS Box IV/5

Shack Thomas, Centenarian. [S. Jacksonville] December 8, 1936 6pp. FHS Box IV/4.

A Voluntary Slave for Seven Years January 27, 1937 2pp. FHS:Box IV/5.

OTHER MATERIALS: *A Day in Florida's State Prison MR 13 pp. 3,581 wds n.d. LC A878 Florida Contemporary Culture/General.*

Fernandina 541/4 May 26, 1936. LC A878 Florida Folklore/Local Lore.

Jacksonville Religion 2pp. PKY: Negro Churches

Miscellaneous Superstitions [Duval] January 13, 1937. 4pp.FHS Box VIII/4

Negro Art (Pensacola) 1030/6pp May 8, 1936. LC A878 NSP Florida Contemporary Culture/Lifestyle. PKY: Negro in Cities.

Negro Churches (Pensacola) April 28, 1936 9 pp. PKY:Negro Churches/Negro in cities (notes).

Negro Education (Pensacola) 6pp. PKY: Negro in Cities.

Negro Ethnography (Jacksonville) March 20, 1936. 13 pp. PKY: Negro History.

Negro Ethnography (Pensacola) 8pp April 26, 1936. LC A878 Florida Contemporary Culture/Lifestyle. PKY: Negro History.

Negro Ethnography St. Augustine, May 12, 1936. 9pp. LC A879 NSP, Florida Historical Materials (1860–1938). PKY: Negro History?

Negro Folklore and Customs. Bolita. August 17, 1936. 21pp. FHS Box II/8.

Negro Folk Customs and Folk Lore:Emancipation Day in Pensacola 2pp. April 28, 1936. 2pp. LC A878 Florida Folklore/Customs and Celebrations.

Negro History (Fernandina) with J. Johnson. 12pp. PKY: Negro History

Negro History (Pensacola) 15 pp. April 24, 1936. 15pp. LC A879 Florida Historical Material (1936–1939). PKY: Negro in Cities.

Negro Literature (Professor C.F. Call) Pensacola May 4, 1936. 4pp. LC A877 NSP Florida-Bigraphical. PKY: Negro in Cities.

Negro Music (Pensacola) May 6, 1936 5pp. LC A877 Florida contemporary Culture/General. PKY: Negro in Cities.

Negro Songs and Amusements May 18, 1937. 15pp. FHS Box V/4; LC A878 Florida Folklore; A878/Songs, Ballads, and Rhymes.

Rustic Decoration, Jackson County March 31, 1937. 4pp. LC A878 NSP Florida Folklore/Lifestyle.

Augusta Savage—Sculptress. September 22, 1936. 5pg. FHS Box I/2 Art. LC A878 NSP Florida Contemporary Culture/Lifestyle

Slave Days in Florida 21pp. April 3, 1937. Corresponds to Ch. II of the Florida Negro ms. FHS: Box IV/d; Box IV/7 PKY: Negro history.

Song of the 'Blue Jay' and Prison Songs , n.d. FHS: Box V/4 5pp. LC A878 Florida Folklore A878/Songs, Ballads, and Rhymes. 7pp.

"An Unusual Graveyard" [Hornesville] March 18, 1937. 3p. FHS Box I/8.

An Unusual Hobby. [Interlachen] n.d. 6pp. FHS Box V/3. LC A878 Florida

Folklore/Local Lore
An Unusual Monument. April 16, 1937. 4pp. (to Roberts, black doctor of influenza epidemic in St. Augustine). LC A877 Florida-Biographical.
Unusual Settlements in Florida July 15, 1937. 2pp. PKY: Negro History
What the Florida Negro Does n.d. 51 pp. (finished by 1938). LC A877 Contemporary Culture/Economic Conditions. PKY: Negro Occupations
　(Excerpted in text).

MARY K. ROBERTS* (1937 ??)
Laura Saunders June 13, 1937. Rubye K. Goebel and Mary K. Roberts. 8pp. FHS VIII/2.
Sarah Rhodes [New Smyrna] August 3, 1937. Mary K. Roberts and Zelia Sweet. 7pp. FHS Box VIII/2.

ROSE SHEPHERD* (1938–9, White)
Personal Interview M.N. McCullough. [Jacksonville] December 13, 1938 6pp. FHS VI/7; LC A879 Florida Narrative Stories.
Voice Recording. August 30, 1939. 5pp. FHS Box V/5.
Voice Record Eartha M. White. October 19, 1939. FHS: Box V/5.

ZELIA SWEET*
Sarah Rhodes [New Smyrna] August 3, 1937. Mary K. Roberts and Zelia Sweet. 7pp. FHS Box VIII/2

ELLEN TARRY* (1938; perhaps New York contributer who contributed to Ottley and Weatherby 1967?)
Mary McLeod Bethune January 6, 1938. 5pp. and Factual Material on MMB ET 6pp plus sources January 6, 1938. LC A591 Folklore Project/Traditional Folklore. Negro Lore (4)

CORA M. TAYLOR (Miami, White).
SLAVE INTERVIEWS: Victoria Harris. [New Smyrna] Zelia Sweet. 9pp. August 17, 1937. Box VII/11.
Interview with Susie Moss [Sweetenton] May 4, 1937. FHS Box VIII/2.
OTHER MATERIALS: Bibliography of the Negro. 8p. n.d. FHS Box I/CH
Clipping from the Remnant. Priscilla Mitchell. n.d. 1p. FHS Box II/7; LC.
Folk Lore February 10, 1936, February 19, 1936 2pp, "Modernized Spiritual as sung by Elder C.H. Butler, Evangelist. "Don't Ride that Hell-Bound Train." FHS Box V/1.
Folk Song and Game composed by CMT Hoppity Hip 2pp. February 19, 1936; May 13, 1936. FHS Box II/4.
Interview and Poem with Rev. Jonathan Moxcie (Miami) January 15, 1936. 7pp. PKY:Negro Churches.
Interview with white informant, Ellen N. Allen May 12, 1937. FHS Box II/7. LC A879 Florida Slavery material (1)
　Music and Spirituals:
　　Old Time Plantation Songs and Spirituals February 10, 1936; February 19, 1936 "The Angels Beckon Me to Come" 1p. "Ober Yonder" 1p.

Modern Spirituals. February 19, 1936; March 25, 1936 "Come and Jine" Parody to come and DIne. 2pp. "Talk On" 1p. "Pentecost" 12pp.

Words for Negro Songs May 4, 1936. 7p? Jesus, Lead Me.

Old Time Plantation Songs/Modern Negro Spirituals. 10pp. "Oh, Let Me Come In," "Hark From the Tombs,""Greeting Song," "The New Jerusalem," "Let Me Alone", "Didn't they Crucify My Lord?" "We are Troubled" (Music)

Old Time Plantation Song March 10, 1936. "He's The Lily of the Valley," "Shine, Shine", "Judgment"(M), I'm Goin' Home t' Live With God," "The Good Lord's been Here", "Room Enough", "Please Don't Drive Me Away," "Sick and Afflicted," "Lord, I feel Like I'm on My Journey Home (April 27, 1936)," I Aint Afraid o' Dying,'

Folk Lore: Plantation Songs March 18, 1936 "Running Up the Shining Way," "The Lord Will Povide," "Glad was My Heart," "Sabbath Home." 5pp.

Old-Time Plantation Songs April 15, 1936. "Goin T' Join de Ban'," "In de Morning" "I Want t' Go Walk," Modern "This Little Light O' Mine"

Old-Time Negro Spirituals May 14, 1936 5pp. "I'M in Your Hands" "Trinidad Folk-Song" ("Russio-japanes War Song" Interview Helen Sifontes, ed. matter.

Songs March 27, 1936 "Heaven Goin' t'be my Home"; Don't You Feel the Fire a-Burnin'; "I Know it Was the Blood," "Come On," "The Last Day," "Mary Had a Little Lamb," "Don't You Grieve," "Ring Jerusalem," "Hand Writin' On De Wall" "Hold My Hand" All FHS Box V/4. FHS:BOX V/4. Many cited by Title in Florida Negro Text.

Three Score and Ten Club 3pp May 11, 1936.LC A878 NSP Florida Contemporary Culture/Social Organization and Benevolent Organization.

To a Remnant 5pp. LC A878 Florida Folklore/Songs, Ballads and Rhymes.

A Visit To Booker T. Washington High School, Miami, Fl. December 12, 1935; December 24, 1935. IIIB. Ethnography #270. 6pp. FHS Box I/13,14.

Religious Fervor January 15, 1936 7pp. FHS VI/4

Religious Fervor of the Negro February 28, 1936. PKY:Negro Churches.

"Who's Who in Colored Town, Miami Florida:

    (1) "Alonzo P. Holly, M.D. title page for *God and the Negro or the Bible Record of the Race of Ham.*

    (2) card of FAITH HOME RESCUE MISSION/ Rev. N.E.Taylor 1p.

    (3) Anniversary card of Rev. James Emanuel Coleman, Pastor FIRST ZION Baptist Church, Deerfield.

    Bibliography. Who's Who in Colored Town. January 2, 1936; February 5, 1936. 1p.

Mr. and Mrs. J.E. Coleman. n.d. 3pp.

Rev. J.W. Drake. 1 p.

Rev. James Royal Evans, A.M. CMT 2p. n.d.

Major A.C. Goggins. 6pp.n.d.

Mrs. Mamie Hamilton. n.d..1p Investigator Juvenile Court

Alonzo P.B. Holly. 4p.

Paul Davidson Moss 4p. n.d. 1p.

The Rev. Johns S. Simmons. April 20, 1936. 6pp.

Rev. N.Emma Taylor. n.d. 2 p.

[Miscellaneous short biographies: Rev. James Royal Evans, A.M.; Mamie R. hamilton; Rev J.E.Coleman; Alonzo P. Holly; other leaders, Colored Churches in Miami. 4pp. n.d.

All From FHS Box I/5. PKY: Negro in Florida Cities.

ROBERT T. THOMAS* (1937)

Florida Beaches for Negroes. By ——— and James Johnson 12 pp. Feb 5, 1937. LC A878 Florida Contemporary Culture/Lifestyle.

GRACE THOMPSON* (1936)

Negro Music (Jacksonville) March 26, 1936 13pp. FHS Box V/4.

PORTIA THORINGTON (secretary, 1936 black)

A Voo-doo Doctor. 11pp. August 12, 1936. 11pp. FHS Box VIII/5. LC A879 (NSP) Florida Folklore/Superstitions and Supernatural.

WHITE, EARTHA* (Jacksonville; Eartha White Mission)

Some sayings of my mother, Eartha White on Clara White June 30, 1938 4pp. A591 Folklore Project/Traditional Lore: Negro Lore.

Works Cited

The text refers to a range of publications by the Federal Writers' Project (and, after 1939, by the successor Writers'Program) which may have various authorial designations including state project names. These have been included therefore in a separate section by title. Other secondary references follow.

WPA Publications

Almanac for Thirty-Niners. Palo Alto: J.L. Delkin. 1938.

Birds in Florida . Tallahassee: Florida Department of Agriculture 1942?.

Boats Across New England: The Story of the Farmington Canal. Compiled by the Writers Program of the Works Project Administration of the State of Connecticut. Hartford: State Board of Education. 1941

Cavalcade of the American Negro. Illinois Writers' Project. Chicago: Diamond Jubilee Authority. 1940.

Copper Camp: Stories of the World's Greatest Mining Town. New York: Hastings House. 1940.

Drums and Shadows: Survival Studies among Georgia Coastal Negroes. Athens: University of Georgia Press. 1940. New York: Hastings House. Reprinted with an Introduction by Charles Joyner. Athens: University of Georgia Press. 1986.

Florida, a Guide to the Southernmost State, Compiled and Written by the Federal Writer's Project of the Work Projects Administration for the State of Florida. New York: Oxford University Press (Sponsored by the State of Florida Department of Public Instruction). 1939.

The Floods of Johnstown. Johnstown: Mayor's Committee. 1939.

Georgia: A Guide to its Towns and Countryside. Athens: The University of Georgia Press. 1940.

A Guide to Key West. New York: Hastings House. 1941.

Gumbo Ya-Ya: A Collection of Louisiana Folk Tales. Compiled by Lyle Saxon, Edward Dreyer and Robert Tallant. Boston: Houghton Mifflin. 1945.

The Italians of New York: A Survey Prepared by Workers of the Federal Writers' Project, Works Progress Administration in the City of New York with 24 Plates by the WPA Federal Art Project of the City of New York. New York: Random House. 1938. Translated as *Gli Italiani di New York.* New York: Labor Press. 1939.

Jewish Families and Family Circles in New York 1939.

The Jewish Landsmanschaften of New York. NY: I.L. Peretz Yiddish Writer's Union. 1938.

Libraries and Lotteries: A History of the Louisville Free Public Library Cynthiana, KY: Hobson Book Press. 1944.

A Maritime History of New York. Garden City: Doubleday. 1940. *Maryland: A Guide to the Old Line State.* New York: Oxford University Press. 1940.

Mississippi: A Guide to the Magnolia State. New York: Viking Press. 1937.

Nebraska Folklore Pamphlets #23. Lincoln: Nebraska Writers' Project April. 1940.

The Negroes in Nebraska. Lincoln: Woodruff Printing Co. 1940.

The Negro in Virginia. New York: Hastings House. 1940.

New Jersey: A Guide to its Past and Present. New York: The Viking Press. 1939.

New York Panorama, A Comprehensive View of the Metropolis, Presented in a Series of Articles Prepared by the Federal Writers' Project of the Works Progress Administration in New York City. New York: Random House. 1938.

Pennsylvania: A Guide to the Keystone State. New York: Oxford University Press.1940.

Planning Your Vacation in Florida: Miami and Dade County. Northport, NY: Percy & Daggett. 1941.

Puerto Rico: A Guide to the Island of Boriquén, Compiled and Written by the Puerto Rico Reconstruction Administration in Co-Operation with the Writers' Program of the Work Projects Administration. New York: The University Society (Sponsored by the Puerto Rico Department of Education. 1939.

Rhode Island: A Guide to the Smallest State. Boston: Houghton Mifflin. 1937.

Seeing Fernandina: A Guide to the City and Its Industries. Fernandina. 1940.

Seeing St. Augustine. St. Augustine: Record Co. 1937.

Seminole Indians of Florida. Tallahassee: Florida Department of Agriculture. 1941.

The Spanish Missions of Florida. St. Augustine. 1940.

The Story of Cement, Compiled by Workers of the Writers' Program of the Work Projects Administration in the Commonwealth of Pennsylvania. Chicago: Albert Whitman & Co. 33rd in an Elementary Science Series. 1943.

These Are Our Lives: As told by the people and written by members of the Federal Writer's Project of the Works Progress Administration in North Carolina, Tennessee and Georgia. 1939. Chapel Hill, NC: University of North Carolina. 1939.

U.S. One: Maine to Florida. New York: Modern Age. 1938.

Washington: City and Capital Washington: Government Printing House. 1937. Reprinted Hastings House. 1942.

Who's Who in the Zoo. New York: Halcyon. 1937.

Other References

Alsberg, Henry G. *The American Guide.* New York: Hastings House. 1949.

Andrews, William. *To Tell A Free Story.* Urbana: University of Illinois Press. 1986.

Austin, Willey. *Anti-Slavery History, State and Nation.* MS in WPA files, Library of Congress. n.d.

Bailey, D. T. A Divided Prism: Two Sources on Black Testimony on Slavery. *Journal of Southern History* 46:381–404. 1980.

Bandelier, Fanny. *The Journey of Alvar Nuñez Cabeza de Vaca and His Companions from Florida to the Pacific, 1528–1536*. New York: A.S. Barnes & Co. 1905.

Blassingame, John, *The Slave Community: Plantation Life in the Antebellum South*. New York: Oxford. 1972.

—— ed. *Slave Testimony: Two Centuries of Letters, SPeeches, Interviews and Autobiographies*. Baton Rouge: Louisiana State. 1977.

Botkin, B. A. *Lay My Burden Down: A Folk History of Slavery*. Chicago: University of Chicago Press. 1945.

Bronz, Stephen W. *Roots of Negro Racial Consciousness in the 1920s*. New York: Libra. 1964.

Brown, Jr., Carter."Where are Now the Hopes I Cherished?" The Life and Times of Robert Meacham," *Florida Historical Quarterly* LXIX July (1): 1–36. 1990.

Butterfield, Stephen. *Black Autobiography in America*. Amherst: University of Massachusetts Press. 1974.

Cayton, Horace R. and St. Clair Drake. *Black Metropolis: A Study of Negro Life in a Northern City*. New York: Harcourt Brace and Company. 1945.

Coker, William S. "Tom Moreno: A Pensacola Creole" *Florida Historical Quarterly* LXVII (3) January: 329–339. 1989.

Colburn, David. *Racial Change and Community Crisis: St. Augustine, Fl, 1877–1980* New York: Columbia University. 1985.

Corse, C. D. *The Key to the Golden Islands*. Chapel Hill: University of North Carolina. 1931.

Cutler, Henry G. *History of Florida*. Chicago: Lewis. 1923.

Davidson, James West and Mark Hamilton Lytle. The View From the Bottom Rail. In *After the Fact: The Art of Historical Detection*. New York: McGraw Hill. Volume I:177–212. 1986.

Davis, Charles T. and Henry L. Gates, eds. *The Slave's Narrative*. New York: Oxford University Press. 1985.

Davis, W. W. The Civil War and Reconstruction in Florida. Ph.D. Dissertation. 1913.

Deagan, Kathleen. *Sex, Status and Role in the Mestizaje of Spanish Colonial Florida*. Gainesville: University Presses of Florida. 1974.

—— (editor) *America's Ancient City: Spanish Saint Augustine, 1565–1763*. New York: Garland.

Escott, Paul. *Slavery Remembered: A Record of Twentieth Century Slave Narratives*. Chapel Hill: University of North Carolina. 1979.

Felker, Christopher. Adaptation of the Source: Ethnocentricity and 'The Florida Negro.' In *Zora in Florida*. Steve Glassman and Kathryn Lee Seidel, eds. Orlando: University of Central Florida Press. 146–158.

Fleming, Robert E. *James Weldon Johnson and Arna Wendell Bontemps: A Reference Guide*. Boston: G.K. Hall. 1978.

——*James Weldon Johnson*. Boston: Twayne. 1987.

Foster, Frances S. *Witnessing Slavery*. Westport, Conn: Greenwood Press. 1979.

Gates, Henry L.ed., *Bearing Witness: Selections from African-American Autobiography in the Twentieth Century*. New York: Pantheon.

Geiger, Maynard. *The Franciscan Conquest of Florida*. Washington: Catholic University of America. 1937.

Giddings, Joshua. *The Exiles of Florida or the Crimes Committed by Our Government Against the Maroons*. Columbus, Oh: Follett, Foster. 1858.

Gannon, Michael. *The Cross in the Sand*. Gainesville: University of Florida. 1965.

—— *Rebel Bishop: The Life of Augustine Verot*. Milwaukee: Bruce Publishing. 1964.

Gorn, Elliott. Black Spirits: The Ghostlore of Afro-American Slaves. *American Quarterly* 36 (4):549–566. 1984.

Harman, Judith E. James Weldon Johnson, a New Negro: A Study of his Early Life and Literary Career, 1871–1916. Ph.D. Dissertation, Emory University. 1988

Hemenway, Robert. *Zora Neale Hurston: A Literary Biography*. Urbana: University of Illinois Press. 1977.

Hurston, Zora Neale. *Jonah's Gourd Vine*. Philadelphia: J.B. Lippincott. 1934.

—— *Mules and Men*. Philadelphia: J.B. Lippincott. 1935.

—— *Their Eyes Were Watching God*. Philadelphia: J.B. Lippincott. 1937.

—— *Tell My Horse*. Philadelphia: J.B. Lippincott. 1938.

—— *Moses, Man of the Mountain*. Philadelphia: J.B. Lippincott. 1939.

—— *Dust Tracks In the Road*. Philadelphia: J.B. Lippincott. 1942.

—— *Spunk: The Selected Short Stories of* . . . Berkeley: Turtle Island Foundation. 1985.

Jahoda, Gloria. *Florida: A Bicentennial History*. New York: Norton.

Johnson, James Weldon. *Along this Way*. New York: MacMillan. 1933.

—— *Negro Americans, What Now?* New York: Viking. 1934.

Kennedy, Stetson. *Palmetto Country* by Stetson Kennedy. 1942. Reprinted by University of Florida Presses with a new afterword by the author. 1989.

—— *Southern Exposure*. Garden City, NY: Doubleday & Co. 1946.

—— Working With Zora In Grant, A. ed. *All About Zora*. 1991 Winter Park: 4-G. 1991. 61–68.

Killion, R. and Charles Waller. *Slavery Time when I was Chillun down on Marster's Plantation*. Savannah: The Beehive Press. 1973.

Kingsley, Zephaniah. *A Treatise on the Patriarchal, or Co-operative System of Society as it Exists in Some Governments, and Colonies in America and in the United States, Under the Name of Slavery, With its Necessities and Advantages*. By an Inhabitant of Florida. n.p. 1829.

Kostelanetz, Richard. *Politics in the Afro-American Novel*. New York: Greenwood Press. 1991.

Landers, Jane. Gracia Real de Santa Teresa de Mose: A Free Black Community in Spanish Colonial Florida. *American Historical Review*, 95 (1) February:9–30. 1990

Levy, Eugene. *James Weldon Johnson: Black Leader, Black Voice*. Chicago: University of Chicago Press. 1973.

Mangione, Jerre. *The Dream and the Deal: The Federal Writer's Project, 1935–1943*. Boston: Little, Brown and Company. 1972. Reprinted Philadelphia: The University of Pennsylvania Press. 1983.

Martineau, Harriet. *Society in America* London: Sanders and Ottley. Vol 2. 1837.

McDonogh, Gary. *Black and Catholic in Savannah, Georgia* Knoxville: University of Tennessee Press. 1993.

McGovern, J. *The Emergence of a City in the Modern South: Pensacola 1900–1945*. DeLeon, Fl: E.O. Painter. 1976.

McKay, Claude. *Harlem: Negro Metropolis*. New York: E. P. Dutton. 1940.

Melosh, Barbara. *Engendering Culture: Manhood and Womanhood in New Deal Public Art and Theater*. Washington DC: Smithsonian Institution. 1991.

Mohlman, Geoffrey. "Lincolnville: A History of Black St. Augustine." New College B.A. Thesis. 1991.

Mormino, Gary. "Florida Slave Narratives" *Florida Historical Quarterly* LXVI (4) April 1988: 399–422.

Mormino, Gary and Pozzetta, George. *The Immigrant World of Ybor City*. Urbana: University of Illinois. 1987.

Nathiri, N. ed. *Zora: Zora Neale Hurston, A Woman and Her Community*. Orlando: Sentinel. 1991.

Neyland, Leedell W. and John W. Riley. *The History of Florida Agricultural and Mechanical College*. Gainesville: University of Florida Press.1960.

Olney, James. "'I Was Born'": The Slave Narratives, Their Status Autobiography and Literature. *Callaloo*, 20 (Winter):46–73. 1984.

Osofsky , Gilbert. *Harlem: The Making of a Ghetto*. New York: Harper & Row. 1965.

Otey, Frank. *Eatonville*. Winter Park, Fl: 4-G Publishers. 1989.

Ottley, Roi. *New World a-Comin': Inside Black America*. Cleveland: World Publishers. 1943.

Ottley, Roi, and William Weatherby eds. *The Negro in New York: an Informal Social History*. New York: New York Public Library. 1967. Preface by James Baldwin, xv-xix.

Parks, A. S. 1936. The Negro in the Reconstruction of Florida. In *The Quarterly Journal* (Florida A & M) October V (4): 35–61. 1936.

Penkower, Monty Noam. *The Federal Writer's Project: A Study in Government Patronage of the Arts* Urbana: University of Illinois. 1977.

Perdue, Jr., Charles, Thomas E. Barden and Robert K. Phillips, eds. *Weevils in the Wheat: Interviews with Virginia Ex-Slaves* Bloomington: Indiana University Press. 1980.

Porter, K., The Negro Abraham. *Florida Historical Quarterly* XXV(1):1–43. 1946.

——— Osceola and the Negroes. *Florida Historical Quarterly* XXXIII (3–4):235–239. 1955.

Priestley, Herbert. *The Coming of the White Man, 1492–1848*. New York: MacMillan. 1929.

Rawick, G. ed. *The American Slave: A Composite Autobiography*. Westport, Cn: Greenwood Press. 19 vol. 1972.

Schomburg Center. *Augusta Savage and the Harlem Schools of Art*. NY: Schomburg Center. 1988.

Shofner, Jerrell. *Nor is it Over Yet: Florida in the Era of Reconstruction, 1863–1877*. Gainesville: University of Florida Press. 1974.

Smith, Sidonie Ann. *Where I'm Bound: Patterns of Slavery and Freedom in Black American Autobiography*. Westport, Conn; Greenwood Press. 1974.

Smith, Buckingham. *Relation that Alvar Nuñez Cabeza de Vaca Gave of What Befel the Armament in the Indies Whither Panfilo de Narvaez Went for Governor*. San Francisco: Grabborn Press. 1891. Reprinted 1929.

Soapes, Thomas. The Federal Writer's Project Slave Interviews: Useful Data or Misleading Source? *Oral History Review* 2:33–38. 1977.

Sprague, John T. *The Florida War*. New York: Appleton Company. 1848.

Starling, Marion W. *The Slave Narrative: Its Place in American History.* Boston: G.K. Hall. 1981.

Tebeau, Charlton. *A History of Florida.* Coral Gables: University of Miami Press. 1980.

Tenney, J. F. *Slavery, Secessiona and Success: The Memoirs of a Florida Pioneer.* San Antonio: Southern Literary Institute. 1934.

Tyler, Ronnie C. and Lawrence Murphy. *Slave Narratives of Texas.* Austin: Encino Press. 1974.

Wallace, John *Carpetbag Rule in Florida. The Inside Workings of the Reconstruction of Civil Government in Florida After the Civil War.* Jacksonville: Da Costa Print. and Publishing House. 1888.

Wilson, Henry. *The Rise and Fall of Slave Power in America* Boston: James R. Osgood and Co. 1875.

Yetman, Norman R. *"Life Under the Peculiar Institution": Selections from the Slave Narrative Collection* New York: Holt, Rinehart and Winston. 1970.

―――― Ex-Slave Interviews and the Historiography of Slavery. *American Quarterly* 36 (2):181–210. 1984.

Young, Robert. *White Mythologies: Writing History and the West.* London: Routledge.

Index